Finance and Industrial Policy

Finance and Industrial Policy

Beyond Financial Regulation in Europe

Edited by
Giovanni Cozzi, Susan Newman,
and Jan Toporowski

OXFORD
UNIVERSITY PRESS

OXFORD
UNIVERSITY PRESS

Great Clarendon Street, Oxford, OX2 6DP,
United Kingdom

Oxford University Press is a department of the University of Oxford.
It furthers the University's objective of excellence in research, scholarship,
and education by publishing worldwide. Oxford is a registered trade mark of
Oxford University Press in the UK and in certain other countries

Published in the United States of America by Oxford University Press
198 Madison Avenue, New York, NY 10016, United States of America

British Library Cataloguing in Publication Data
Data available

Library of Congress Control Number: 2015951302

ISBN 978-0-19-874450-4

Printed in Great Britain by
Clays Ltd, St Ives plc

Foreword

Massimo D'Alema

Industrial policies are back on the European political agenda. Six years into the deepest economic crisis and recession in the European Union since its inception, it has now become evident that only through a significant increase in public and private investment towards innovative and cutting-edge technologies will Europe succeed in creating more jobs and stimulating growth.

Indeed, as highlighted in this groundbreaking edited volume, future growth will require Europe to become more innovative and to embark on a serious and effective government-led industrial strategy. To this end, Jan Toporowski, in his chapter 'Towards Financially Sustainable Prosperity', clearly emphasizes that the current and almost exclusive focus on the need for more expansionary fiscal policies to spearhead aggregate demand in Europe is clearly not enough. To reignite and sustain economic recovery we need to complement progressive fiscal policies with industrial policies that go well beyond the provision of residual incomes and infrastructure through public works.

Therefore, European governments and European institutions have a central role to play that goes beyond cutting red tape and fixing market failures. Instead, we need strong European states and institutions to invest in areas where the private sector cannot or is not willing to be active. A very good example is given by Mariana Mazzucato who reminds us, in her contribution, 'The Myth of the "Meddling" State', that the US has spent the last few decades using active interventionist policies to drive private sector innovation in the pursuit of broad public policy goals, such as, for example, financing and supporting the development of the algorithm at the heart of the Google search engine! On the other hand, the state in Europe has been put on the back seat of industrial and innovation strategies, thus severely undermining growth potential even before the crisis.

We need Europe to put innovation and industrial development at the core of progressive economic policies. At the same time, we need to call for a different kind of innovation. As highlighted by Riccardo Bellofiore and Francesco Garibaldo in Chapter 2, innovation in Europe should be based on societal needs and demands, be socially responsible, and based on an open cooperation between different actors, cross-cutting sectors and technological domains.

Several contributions in this book also highlight how in recent decades the financial system has been deeply procyclical; it has not sufficiently funded working capital and long-term investment, which is crucial for innovation. Daniela Gabor, for instance (Chapter 6), points out how the European financial system has undergone important changes in size, scope, and complexity during the last thirty years. Their business model has moved away from supporting investment in innovation and technological transformation and has become more reliant on leverage creation and trading of risk funded in wholesale markets. This has had detrimental consequences for growth and has significantly undermined industrial and innovation strategies. Thus, it is crucial, as highlighted by Kollatz-Ahnen, Griffith-Jones, and Bullmann, to fully reconsider the role that the financial system plays in supporting productive investment and within this a clear assessment of the role played by both public development banks, such as the European Investment Bank (EIB), and private banks, in promoting sustainable economic growth.

The current economic crisis and recession have presented us with an opportunity: to bring Europe on a new developmental trajectory where sustainable and equitable growth, innovation, and employment take centre stage. It is, however, essential for progressives to realize that abandoning the excessive and almost exclusive focus on monetary criteria and of balancing budgets is a necessary but not sufficient condition for economic recovery. Instead, we need to make sure that more progressive fiscal and monetary policies are also accompanied by a reconsideration of the role that the state plays in supporting industrial development and innovation. At the same time, we need to make sure that the financial system does not generate excessive risk and that it serves the real economy. The pressure is on and the opportunity has arisen for a responsible, equitable, and sustainable economic strategy. The question remains: do we have the political will to embark on a new economic path?

Acknowledgements

This edited volume is formed out of a joint project of the Foundation for European Progressive Studies (FEPS) and the International Institute for Social Studies (ISS), Erasmus University Rotterdam, entitled 'Beyond Financial Regulation, European Industrial Policies in the Wake of the Global Financial Crisis'. The editors are grateful for the support of ISS and FEPS. In particular we would like to thank Peter van Bergeijk of ISS and Ernst Stetter, Secretary General of FEPS, for their encouragement and support.

We would also like to extend our appreciation to Fundació Rafael Campalans whom, together with FEPS, organized the workshop 'Beyond financial regulation: European industrial policies in the wake of the global financial crisis' in Barcelona, Spain, 22 and 23 November 2013, at which a number of contributors to this book presented. We are particularly grateful to Esther Niubó, Director of Fundació Rafael Campalans and Cristina Gonzalez for organizing an excellent workshop.

We would also like to thank Ischi Graus for her exceptional support in the coordination of the project. We extend our gratitude to Aimee Wright of Oxford University Press for her patience and assistance in preparing the volume for publication.

Last but not least we thank all the contributing authors of this volume whose chapters reflect their vast experience and research expertise.

Contents

Contents

List of Figures

List of Tables

List of Contributors

Michel Aglietta is Professor of Economics at the University of Paris X Ouest Nanterre; Economic Adviser to the Centre d'Études Prospectives et d'Informations Internationales; and, since 2013, a member of the French Senates Haut Conseil des Finances Publiques.

Nicolas Balas is Assistant Professor in Management Studies at the Montpellier University School of Management. His primary research interests centre on issues of resistance to corporate restructuring, controversy and discursive analysis of strategic decision-making, in particular within technology-intensive industries.

Joachim Becker is an Associate Professor at the Institute for International Economics and Development at Vienna University of Economics and Business. His research focus is on issues of development and crises, particularly in the European peripheries and Latin America.

Riccardo Bellofiore is Professor of Political Economy at the 'Hyman P. Minsky' Department of Economics at the Università di Bergamo, Italy. Member of the Scientific Committee of the Italian edition of the 'Opere Complete di Marx ed Engels'; Member of the International Symposium on Marxian Theory.

Udo Bullmann is Member of the European Parliament, Group of the Progressive Alliance of Socialists and Democrats in the European Parliament; until being elected to the European Parliament in 1999, he was university lecturer and Jean-Monnet Professor for Studies on European Integration at the Justus-Liebig University of Giessen, Germany.

Predrag Ćetković is researcher and lecturer at the Vienna University of Economics and Business. His research includes macroeconomics, Post Keynesian Economics, Marxian Economics, industrial development and financial markets.

Giovanni Cozzi is Senior Lecturer in Economics at the University of Greenwich (London, UK) and member of the Greenwich Political Economy Research Centre (GPERC). He was Senior Economist at the Foundation for European Progressive Studies (FEPS), Brussels, Belgium and Research Fellow at the Centre for Development Policy and Research (CDPR) at the School of Oriental and African Studies where he collaborated on a three-year European Commission FP7 funded project assessing the Challenges for Europe in the World of 2030 (AUGUR).

Massimo D'Alema is President of the Foundation for European Progressive Studies (FEPS), Brussels, Belgium; President of the Italian political foundation called

Fondazione di Cultura Politica Italianieuropei. Former Prime Minister and former Foreign Minister of Italy.

Marc Fovargue-Davies is a Research Associate in the London Centre for Corporate Governance and Ethics (LCCGE).

Daniela Gabor is Associate Professor at the Bristol Business School, University of the West of England, United Kingdom.

Francesco Garibaldo is Director of Instituto per Lavoro (IPL), Bologna, Italy; Member of the International Association for Industrial Relations; Member of the Italian Association of Sociology and of the International Advisory Board of Concepts and Transformation—International Journal of Action Research and Organizational Renewal; former Member of the Consiglio Nazionale dell'Economia e del Lavoro (CNEL: National Council of Economy and Work).

Stephany Griffith-Jones is Financial Markets Director at the Initiative for Policy Dialogue (IPD) at Columbia University; Member of the Foundation of European Progressive Studies (FEPS) Scientific Council; Member of the Warwick Commission on Financial Regulation; and was Professorial Fellow at the Institute of Development Studies.

Matthias Kollatz-Ahnen is Member of the Federal Senate in Berlin (Germany) and former member of the European Investment Bank (EIB) board of governors.

Sue Konzelmann is a Reader in Management at Birkbeck, University of London, Director of the London Centre for Corporate Governance and Ethics (LCCGE) and Research Associate of the Centre for Business Research, University of Cambridge.

Michele Mastroeni a Senior Research Associate at the Conference Board of Canada. Prior to his current position, he worked as a Senior Analyst at RAND Europe, and held an Innogen Research Fellowship at the University of Edinburgh. Before moving to the UK, Mastroeni was a senior policy advisor for the Ministry of Research and Innovation in Ontario, Canada. His expertise includes national, regional, and sector based innovation systems.

Mariana Mazzucato holds the RM Philips Chair in the Economics of Innovation at SPRU in the University of Sussex. Previously she has held academic positions at the University of Denver, London Business School, Open University, and Bocconi University. Professor Mazzucato is winner of the New Statesman SPERI Prize in Political Economy and in 2013 the New Republic called her one of the '3 most important thinkers about innovation'. She advises the UK government and the EC on innovation led growth.

Susan Newman Senior Lecturer in Economics at the University of the West of England and a Senior Research Associate in the Faculty of Economic and Financial Sciences at the University of Johannesburg.

Florence Palpacuer is Professor of Management Science at the University of Montpellier 1.

Alessandro Rosiello is a Senior Lecturer in Entrepreneurship and Innovation at the University of Edinburgh. He combines innovation theories, Schumpeterian economics and direct experience of product commercialization to study innovation processes in a variety of industrial settings; entrepreneurship and small business finance; commercialization of new technologies; and the processes of industrial clustering at regional level.

Jan Toporowski is Professor of Economics and Finance in the School of Oriental and African Studies, University of London; and Visiting Professor of Economics in the University of Bergamo, Italy.

Rudy Weissenbacher is researcher and lecturer at the Vienna University of Economics and Business, Institute for International Economics and Development. His research focuses on regional development in European peripheries.

1

Introduction

Susan Newman, Giovanni Cozzi, and Jan Toporowski

Since 2008 the North Atlantic Financial crisis has revealed major structural weaknesses in the architecture and operations of (global) finance as it has evolved in the decades since the collapse of the Bretton Woods system. The wave of capital account liberalization, financial deregulation and rapid technological progress that promoted financial innovation and fostered growing interconnectedness across financial markets and banking sectors resulted in a highly fragile global financial system that promoted speculative behaviour and harboured high risks of contagion. Such pathologies of the pre-crisis global financial systems have been prevalent across the spectrum of academic literature and informed a policy debate focused upon curbing the excesses of finance that emerged out of deregulation through re-regulation and re-orientation towards macroprudential regulatory and supervisory frameworks reflected in Basel III, the Dodd-Frank regulatory reform in the US. Thus, the immediate policy responses to the crisis of 2008 focused on banking and finance, beginning with the bank bailouts and followed by regulatory reform aimed at fostering a more stable and less speculative global and European financial architecture.

As the crisis evolved from one of banking into crises of sovereign debt and unemployment in a number of European economies, policy focus turned also to austerity. In the name of fiscal responsibility, highly indebted European countries were urged by the, so-called, Troika (European Commission, European Central Bank, and International Monetary Fund (IMF)) to reduce government spending significantly. According to conventional wisdom, increased economic activity would be brought about by a combination of appropriately paced fiscal consolidation and improved conditions for businesses to create new job opportunities and growth that amounted to greater labour market flexibility (see, for example, Buti and Padoan 2012; European Commission 2012).

However, austerity policies have not had the desired effect. Rather they have had a negative impact on both public and private investment, welfare and employment and it is ultimately setting the conditions for long-term stagnation in Europe. Since 2007, private investment has declined significantly in many European countries and aggregate demand has slowed down. In the South Eurozone (which comprises Italy, Spain, Portugal, and Greece), for instance, investment decreased from 21.7 per cent of gross domestic product (GDP) in 2007 to around 14 per cent in 2014. At the same time investment in the North Eurozone (which comprises Germany, France, Belgium, the Netherlands, Luxembourg, Austria, and Finland) declined from 17.7 per cent to 16 per cent of GDP. Unemployment still remains high in many Eurozone countries. According to International Labour Organization (ILO) forecasts, the unemployment rate will remain, at best, between 8 and 9 per cent over the period 2014–2016, compared with 6.7 per cent in the early 2000s. European Economic growth in the near future is expected to be modest. Recent IMF estimates predict an average annual growth rate of 1.3 per cent for the Eurozone as a whole between 2014 and 2018. This is much lower than the pre-crisis period where GDP growth averaged 2.2 per cent per annum in the period 2002–2006. Even where employment has stabilized, much of this is in low wage, low productivity activities.

In view of the protracted recession in southern countries of the EU, and the less than spectacular recovery of Western European economies, industrial and investment policies are very much back in vogue in EU policy discourse. Industrial policy no longer carries the status of being 'a dirty word' as it did during the heyday of the Washington Consensus when the debate was organized around the legitimacy of the state to intervene in the economy where the role of the state was contrasted with its complete absence, as in the strictest/ most extreme reading of neoliberalism. However, despite this welcome opening towards the role of industrial policies in fostering growth and jobs, the dominant political discourse at European level has been confined on the role that public and private investment can play in improving infrastructure such as broadband and energy networks, as well as transport infrastructure and industrial centres, education, research and innovation, and renewable energy and energy efficiency and on the need for further harmonization (see, for example, European Commission 2014b). Indeed, the 'Integrated Industrial Policy for the Globalisation Era Report' of the European Commission (2010) emphasizes how a new innovative industrial strategy for Europe has to be based on better access to finance for business (in particular for Small and Medium Enterprises (SMEs)), better harmonization of the European legal framework, increased protection of property rights, and better coordination of education, research and development and greater coherence in science, technology and innovation cooperation with the rest of the world (European Commission 2010).

Proclamations of the return of industrial policy are also evident in the literature, notably in the 2011 special issue of Policy Studies (Bailey, Lenihan, and Arauzo-Carod 2011), the 2009 debate between Ha Joon Chang and Justin Lin (Lin and Chang 2009), and the extensive review by Naudé (2010), and more recently by Warwick (2013). What these historical surveys have revealed is that industrial policy never really went away. Warwick (2013) presents numerous examples of industrial policy from OECD (the Organisation for Economic Co-operation and Development) countries throughout the 1990s and 2000s. Rather, industrial policies over the last three decades or so have taken varied, disparate, ad hoc, isolated and unconnected forms that are in stark contrast to the highly integrated 'vertical' industrial strategies that were typical of post-Second World War industrial development. While industrial policy is increasingly viewed as necessary for industrial upgrading, differences of opinion on both the means and ends of industrial policy persist (see, for example, Lin and Chang 2009). The re-emergence of industrial policy since the crisis reflects the reconceptualization of industrial policy itself from one which saw manufacturing as causally significant in economic growth—as in theories of cumulative causation—to its redefinition, via the (neo-Listian) Developmental State Paradigm, as universal or indiscriminate state support of the private sector. The 'new industrial policy' reflects neoclassical micro economic thinking in that, aside from considerations of factor productivity, all economic sectors look alike and contribute in the same way, albeit not in equal magnitude), to GDP and GDP growth (Tregenna 2011; Fine and van Waeyenberge 2013). This perceived insignificance of manufacturing as an analytical category or strategic sector is evident in the title of Warwick's exposition of the new industrial policy as 'Beyond Industrial Policy'.

The re-orientation of industrial policy reflects both the continued prominence of neoliberal ideology in policy formulation and radical changes over the last three decades in the way in which production is organized from highly vertically integrated structures under Fordism to post-Fordist organization characterized by flexible specialization, vertical disintegration, and geographical dispersion. In this way, industrial policy in the context of advanced industrial economies have been recast so as to focus on innovation as necessary under the heightened imperative to improve competitiveness that has resulted from the globalization of production (Milberg, Jiang, and Gereffi 2014). This thinking is evident in the motion for a European Parliament Resolution on an 'Industrial Policy for the Globalised Era', adopted on 27 January 2011 (European Parliament 2011). It is worth noting that 'finance' appears just five times in the fifty-five-page European Parliament report 'Industrial Policy for the Globalised Era'. Mention of finance was in relation to specialized finance for research and development (R&D) and innovation and sources of long- and short-term finance for SMEs.

Another concern in the current European policy debate is that financial sector regulation and industrial policy have tended to be discussed separately, except in relation to the financing of industrial investment. Whilst the issue of predictable and suitable finance for industry is critical for successful industrial policy that brings about sustained economic growth, and indeed stressed in the contributions from Konzelmann and Fovargue-Davies and Mastroeni and Rosiello in this volume, discussion has largely failed to take account of how finance has intervened in the restructuring of industry over the past three decades. It is our contention that, in order to be successful, European investment, industrial and financial policy formulation needs to be cognizant of the heterogeneous economic structures and growth trajectories of European economies, and the interconnectedness and interdependencies of growth paths that present specific challenges to policy as well as highlight the need for cooperation across the region.

There now exists a large body of literature that invalidates the notion of the financial sector as unproblematic intermediary between savers and firms ranging from methodological individualist approaches that reject the efficient market hypothesis on account of pervasive market imperfections (as in the New Keynesian approach) or the tendency for actors to deviate from 'rationality' owing to the nature of human psychology (as in behavioural economics) at one end of the spectrum and more systemic accounts of unprecedented changes in the structural relations between financial markets, households and firms, and the increasing complexity of these relations, over the last three decades (Froud, Johal, and Williams 2002).

What has also received less attention in mainstream policy and academic discourse has been the structural weaknesses that have appeared out of specific economic development models namely, the precise macroeconomic framework and policy approach and relations with the region and the wider global economy that characterized the growth trajectories of national economies in the lead up to the crisis. Almost a decade on from the watershed moment, the wider economic, political, and social repercussions of the crisis continue to unfurl with little indication of sustained rapid recovery. This is decidedly evident in Europe as austerity ravages countries across the EU with particular voracity in Southern European states, polarizing societies and politics.

In view of the discussion above, the contributions to this volume build upon, and complement, recent contributions to the literature on post-crisis industrial policy, notably the edited volumes by Bianchi and Labory (2011) and Bailey, Cowling, and Tomlinson (2015), and debates around the notion of an appropriate financial architecture that serves the real economy in a number of ways:

1. by assessing the nature of the global financial crisis and its relation with the process of global and industrial restructuring;

2. by assessing the business practices of banks and discussing the potential role of development banks to foster and finance innovation and industrial dynamism;

3. by analysing the broad evolution of the 'European model' of economic development in the decades leading up to the crisis with particular attention to the relationship between finance and industry and how this is played out at regional and sector levels; and

4. by discussing the need for integrated and mutually supportive financial, investment and industrial policies at national, the regional (sub- and supranational), and at EU levels as well as sector specific interventions.

Thus, the chapters in this book together aim to contribute to policy debate and formulation in three ways. First, by intervening in, and bring together, current discussions of banking policy, regulation and reform to reassert the need for financial institutions that will back up and finance an industrial policy to revive the European economy. Second, by reviewing the role of industrial and investment policies in supporting innovation, creating jobs and generating sustainable economic growth. Third, by advancing alternative policy proposals aimed at generating sustainable economic growth and employment in Europe.

The chapters in Part I, 'Finance, Economic, and Industrial Restructuring' provide analyses of the nature of growth and industrial and economic restructuring in relation to finance in the lead up to the crisis. While they differ in terms of theoretical underpinnings, the analyses presented in Part I all reveal the path dependent nature of finance and industrial restructuring as pre-existing institutional structures interact with changing political configurations, policies, and practice.

Financialization and economic restructuring are analysed at the Regional (European) level by Bellofiore and Garibaldo in relation to broader global processes in Chapter 2. The chapter discusses the European crisis and examines the specific form of industrial and economic restructuring that took place in the lead up to the crisis in relation to both internal and external dynamics. Bellofiore and Garibaldo analyse the causes and forms of corporate restructuring, changes in industrial organization and capital–labour relations in the years preceding the crisis. In doing so, the authors characterize the recent growth model of the European economy as based on a neo-mercantilist model of competition. The authors argue that rather than home-grown, the shift towards neo-mercantilist competition reflects a more general global phenomenon of corporate strategies. Bellofiore and Garibaldo propose an alternative model for recovery that emphasizes effective demand management on the one hand and cognizant of the dynamics of supply on the other, and the tendency towards oversupply that characterizes neo-mercantilist competition.

Chapter 3 by Aglietta picks up on the discussion of competition discussed in the chapter by Bellofiore and Garibaldo. Aglietta's contribution theorizes competition in relation to finance at the level of the firm and their implications for corporate strategies and investment decisions. In doing so, he reveals heterogeneity across Eurozone countries in terms of the character of industrial competition that prevails. Aglietta sketches the transformation of corporate governance in France in line with the shareholder value movement that typifies financialized corporate strategies that result in increasing short-termism of investment decision making. By contrast, corporate governance in Germany has been motivated by the maximization of 'stakeholder value' and the co-determination of investment and distribution between labour and capital. Aglietta argues that stake holder value promotion in Germany has fostered long-termism and investment in innovation amongst German firms and consequently allowed for the development of globally competitive industrial champions in contrast to France's waning industrial competitiveness. These ideas are strongly reflected in Chapter 5, where Balas and Palpacuer deploy the concept of financialization, understood as a the shift in corporate governance and strategy outlined by Aglietta in Chapter 3, in their analysis of the intersections of industrial policy and changes in the nature of global competition for the case of the Grenoble microelectronics.

Chapter 4 by Becker, Ćetlović, and Weissenbacher, titled 'Financialization, Dependent Export Industrialization and Deindustrialization in Eastern Europe', provides an analysis of the development trajectory of Eastern European economies over the last three decades that is informed by Latin American Dependency theory. The authors' central thesis is that financial direction of global capital accumulation has produced new types of dependent relations between national economies. In the case of Eastern Europe, this has taken the form of increased dependence on capital inflows that have, in turn, reshaped the financial sector and processes of industrialization in ways that have been contingent upon, and interacted with, prevailing industrial structures, historical processes and uneven economic trajectories, accumulation strategies of domestic and foreign capital, and domestic policy responses in the respective economies. Their Analysis reveals that countries of Eastern Europe have followed one of two growth trajectories: i) export industrialization with financialization which characterize economic development in and ii) financial dominated growth model.

In tracing their economic trajectories from early transformation to present day, Becker, Ćetlović, and Weissenbacher reveal differences in the experience of early transformation of Eastern European economics that are, in the first instance, rooted in their uneven industrial development both with respect to each other and in relation to Western Europe that were shaped varying dependent relationships historically and, latterly, result from policy choices and prevailing economic model that came out of the precise balance of political and economic forces in each context and their relationship with Western European capital. The authors show how development trajectories since the late 1990s have taken the form of new dependent relationships with Western Europe, bifurcating between the Visegrád states, Romania, and Slovenia receiving the bulk of Western Europe foreign direct investment (FDI) in manufacturing, as they have become closely integrated with the German export sector, on the one hand, and the Baltic and South Eastern European countries receiving FDI in financial intermediation, real estate, and business activities, on the other. The authors thus show how interdependencies between the growth models of national economies arise out of, as well as reinforce, the stratification of the European economy.

In the final part of the chapter, the authors show how the patterns of FDI in manufacturing show divergent patterns of subordinate integration into the European Economy and result in structural dependence on foreign capital being translated into concrete political processes. Their analysis informs both the types of industrial policy that would redress different forms of dependence in order to boost domestic industries which include de-euroization (both in exchange rate policy and the reduction of euro denominated foreign debt) and other measures that would allow states to regain room for manoeuvre towards more active exchange rate and industrial policies, and the challenge of such a radical policy reorientation that would necessitate a change in the balance of forces.

Chapter 5 investigates economic restructuring in the era of financialization at the level of an industrial cluster. Whilst uneven across economies and sectors in Europe, state intervention in industry has been evident throughout the Washington Consensus period. Balas and Palpacuer analyse the case of the microelectronics industry located in Grenoble, in the Southeast of France, where 'cooperation between the scientific, industrial and political communities' date back to the early 1960s. In particular, Balas and Palpacuer focus upon the experience and eventual breakdown of the CROLLES 2 ALLIANCE (C2A) between 2002 and 2007. The experience of C2A tells a story of how the forces of global competition and financial balance sheet management have altered the scope for cooperation between technology firms and the negative affect that financialized corporate strategies have had on innovation and employment in Grenoble.

Balas and Palpacuer challenge the 'deterministic approaches of innovation embedded both in cluster theory and its ramifications under the industrial upgrading paradigm of global value chain analysis (GVC)' in theory and practice. The microelectronics cluster in Grenoble was developed in line with the 'idealized image of local development provided by Porterian "clusters"'. The *French Silicon Valley* 'emerged under the strong influence of the

State in financing the growth of the industry in the 1960s and 1970s'. Since then, Balas and Palacuers' analysis reveals, the local innovation network has taken three distinct forms: i) a technical, state-driven development to ii) a market-oriented approach in the wake of the 1990s technology bubble, and iii) a more recent phase of financialization where innovation become strongly globalized and the advantages of proximity were somehow reproduced in distant networks, thanks to a strong standardization of the innovation process itself.

The form that financialization took in the microelectronics industry since the 2000s promoted specialization of firms along the value chain together with an externalization of production activities by large semiconductor corporations aiming to become *fab-less* as a way to increase shareholder returns. C2A was launched in this context with a logic and organizational structure (*lab-fab* model) that at once was inadequate in dealing with the market conditions of the time and at odds with financial model of capital accumulation in the microelectronics industry that had begun to dominate. It was precisely because of these tensions that led to NXP (Next Experience, one of the three partners of the consortium) to announce its withdrawal from C2A in December 2006. By analysing the process in reaching a policy plan in light of the imminent break up of C2A, Balas and Palpacuer analysis reveals 'the strongly political nature of locational decisions for innovation activities in GVCs, and the unstable, at times conflictual, ways in which compromises are built, challenged or sustained among local and global actors on these questions'.

Chapter 6, the final chapter in Part I, focuses on the evolution of the banking sector in Europe in the run-up to the crisis. Gabor offers fresh, and little discussed, insights into the causes of the financial crisis as they originate in the financial sector, banking in particular. She shows how the crisis revealed that European banks had undergone a transformation that involved increasing size, scope, and complexity in contrast to the dominant view in the pre-crisis period that saw European Banks as operating along the lines of traditional relational banking models. Gabor concludes that the European crisis was a crisis of financial connections. She explains the motivations for increasing bank interconnectedness (the attractiveness of repos), as arising from the broader shift from 'relational banking' to market based banking models, originate and distribute with the trade and management of risk as key source of profit. Increasingly interconnected banks increased financial fragility rather than fostering a better distribution of risk and potential for interbank cooperation in times of market/financial stress as earlier theories of bank interconnectedness predicted.

Gabor's chapter further explores how post-crisis regulatory initiatives at both European and global (the Bank for International Settlements (BIS),

Financial Stability Board (FSB)) level have proposed to govern such fragile relationships, and draws implications for the emergence of a more stable European banking. She argues that the European Financial Transactions Tax may (could have) provide(d) the most transformative path to complex business models of large European banks business reliant on cross border funding, trading and market making activity.

Taken together, the analyses presented in part one present a multidimensional picture of the nature of growth paths within the European economy highlighting their differences, similarities, interdependencies and interconnectedness. This highlights both the necessity of alternative strategies aimed at shared prosperity based on collaboration between nation states and across industries, as well as throwing up key challenges for industrial and financial policies. Some of these policy possibilities and challenges are investigated in the remaining chapters that focus upon the roles that the state and the financial sector play in promoting innovation, technological development and investment in Europe.

Chapter 7 by Toporowski argues that the key credit process in a prospering economy is the transformation of credit into incomes (rather than the transformation of credit into asset values), principally through business investment but also, as a substitute in crisis, through fiscal means. The chapter then proceeds by showing how the process of transforming credit into incomes has been impaired since 2008 by a financial crisis of industry, followed by the building up of unproductive liquid assets in large corporations, with the counterpart of those assets in the growing indebtedness of small and medium sized enterprises. These financial difficulties have been 'accommodated' by the drastic fall in business investment that has driven economies into recession. The dilemma for industrial policy is therefore how to revive business investment and support it fiscally at a level that will be sustainable not just in terms of government indebtedness, but also in terms of business finances.

The question of innovation policy is discussed by Mazzucato in Chapter 8, 'The Myth of the "meddling" State'. By drawing upon historical examples of heavy state intervention in bringing about dramatic progress in innovation across the world economy, Mazzucato dispels the often held polarized view of dynamic entrepreneurs driving innovation in contrast to the overly bureaucratic sluggish policy apparatus of the 'meddling' state. Mazzucato shows that in numerous cases of successful development in innovation industries in the US, it was the state that led the way in financing risky investments in both the basic and applied research and, in some cases went as far downstream as to provide early stage risk finance to companies themselves that were deemed too risky for private finance. It was only once returns were in clear sight that private business investments flowed in.

Mazzucato presents evidence from across the world of state led innovation strategies from which she draws several lessons that could inform innovation and industrial policy in post crisis Europe. She argues that the problems of funding for innovation have been misdiagnosed as reluctant capital when the key problem is lack of state funding that can encourage investment of private risk capital. Further, the state itself needs to be reimaged as lead risk taker and entrepreneur to rebalance the tendency for risk to be socialized while profits are concentrated in private hands. In this light, there is much greater scope for direct state involvement in innovation and technological transformation.

Mazzucato argues for the important role that the state plays in promoting innovation and the need to have more direct mechanisms such as innovation funds that can be used to finance the next round of innovation and technological transformation. Her policy advice stresses coherence and emphasis within macro growth policy, reinstatement of the role of the state as key partner in innovation processes rather than corrector of market failures, and correction of the skewed distribution of competitiveness across Europe through greater cooperation.

Mazzucato's chapter sets the parameters of the debate on industrial and innovation policy that are picked up in greater detail in the subsequent contributions by Mastroeni and Rossiello in relation to the issue of risk finance, and Konzelmann and Fovargue-Davies on the context specificities of policy formulation.

In Chapter 9, Mastroeni and Rossiello drill deeper into the role of innovation and industrial policy for regional industrial development by critically reviewing recent debates and policy in order to improve theoretical coherence and implementation of policies that can be used to unleash the economic potential in both developed and catching-up regions, by taking into consideration the technological, institutional, social, and financial factors of growth.

Mastroeni and Rosiello recognize the growing interest in regional industrial development (namely the promotion of regional systems of innovation) as a shift away from both old structuralist and neoclassical approaches to industrial policy and focus upon questions of conceptual strength and practical implementation in recent approaches to industrial development. In particular, they analyse and assess the potential efficacy of the so-called 'smart specialization' (SmSp) strategy that has become prominent in post 2008 regional innovation policy.

They identify venture capital as 'a (key) component' of the regional system of innovation (RSI) in light of the difficulties that (small) tech firms face in accessing traditional bank finance or fund raising on stock markets on the one hand, and the market expertise and networks that venture capital investors can provide, on the other. They highlight the challenge presented by the highly cyclical nature of this type of investment and suggest characteristics of both investment opportunities and investment finance that would lead to adequate financing in Regional Innovation Systems. The varying and complex relationships between venture capital and specific RSIs and their outcomes are illustrated by four cases where various attempts by government to strengthen systems of innovation were made: i) venture capital policy in Israel in the 1990s; ii) the Scottish biotech sector since the 2000s; iii) the Irish indigenous software sector in the period after the dot.com bubble burst; and Sweden's IT and life sciences sectors in the period from 2003 to 2010.

What Mastroeni and Rosiello comparative analysis reveals is the uniqueness, unevenness, complexity, and dynamism of institutional structures and internal and external networks that make up innovation systems and the challenges that this poses for policy formulation. The authors conclude that effective frameworks for regional innovation policy need to: reflect the unique evolutionary path of an innovation system; have interconnected institutional structures in relation to the innovation system; take a dynamic approach to development and policy framework to deal with the constantly evolving nature of the institutional structures as new practices are established; and learn from the experiences of past policies. In contrast to the limited success of innovation and investment policy in Scotland and Ireland, Sweden's success can be attributed to 'the interconnected nature of the institutional structures related to the innovation system'.

The issue of contextual complexity and institutional specificity of policy implementation is also pursued by Konzelmann and Fovargue-Davies in Chapter 10, titled 'Public Policy Working: Catalyst for Olympic Success'. The authors explore the possible role of the state in addressing challenges faced by British industry. They do this by analysing the experience of state involvement in building international competitiveness in elite sport in the run up to the 2012 London Olympic Games. Their analysis reveals that a clear vision for the future and an institutional structure that coordinates the process of competitive improvement is as critical to policy success as predictable financing.

In common with Mastroeni and Rosiello, Konzelmann and Fovargue-Davies take a systems approach to their analysis of elite sport. Each system has its own culture and institutional structure and starting point which means that industrial policy will have limited effectiveness if simply transplanted from one system to another. While the precise institutional structure, dynamics, and relations will differ, there are certain common components of an innovation/ industry system that are critical for success. In the case of elite sport as successful development system involved the establishment of UK Sport, with arm's length relations from Government that shielded it from short-term political goals, and the National Sport Governing Bodies which together share responsibility for creating and maintaining a system supportive of international competitiveness. According to Konzelmann and Fovargue-Davies, what made the UK elite sport system work was a clearly articulated, expert-driven, vision together with effective communication and corporation between the various institutions. Moreover, and echoing Mastroeni and Rosiello, sustained success will be conditioned upon systems that learn and develop.

Chapter 11 by Cozzi reviews some of the core constraints that have developed in the Eurozone in relation to investment and growth as a result of the shift towards economic liberalism and advances some alternative policies for promoting growth and investment. In particular, the author argues that financial liberalization, coupled with a dominant fiscal policy stance that sees fiscal policies as a tool to encourage fiscal profligacy and unsustainable public debt, has brought the Eurozone into a low investment low growth scenario.

The chapter reviews the impact of financial sector liberalization and fiscal policies on investment and growth in the Eurozone since the late 1980s. Cozzi then advances some alternative policy proposals to bring the Eurozone into a more sustainable growth path. In particular, the author argues for the need to fiscal policies as having the fundamental function of ensuring high levels of aggregate demand and of supporting economic growth. In turn, this implies that until investment has strongly recovered from its long-term decline and households are able to spend without incurring high levels of debt, expansionary fiscal policies, both at EU and national level, are a necessary tool to stimulate growth and investment.

Further, Cozzi's chapter highlights the need to reconsider the role that the financial system plays in promoting investment, industrial development and innovation. He argues that since the onset of the North Atlantic financial crisis, economic policy proposals have been either reactive or preventive, rather than building the foundations of a more sustainable economic system. In particular, in the financial sector policy reforms have focused on strengthening financial regulation but have not necessarily strengthen the role that the financial sector should play in financing and supporting productive investment in feasible and innovative projects in the real economy.

Chapter 12 by Kollatz-Ahnen, Griffith-Jones, and Bullmann highlights how during the past decades the overall trend on investment has been negative and has declined significantly, in particular since the onset of the North Atlantic financial crisis. This had negative repercussion for European industries and has set in motion a process of de-industrialization across Europe.

Kollatz-Ahnen, Griffith-Jones, and Bullmann argue that it is essential to slow down this process of de-industrialization though the right industrial and investment policies. In particular, the authors highlight the need to increase industrial production and capacity by at least 40 per cent until 2020 in order to reverse the trend to further de-industrialization. However, in order to boost industrial production it is important to significantly increase overall investment, which is currently too low in many European countries. This boost cannot be achieved under a 'business as usual scenario' of continued austerity coupled with a mild increase in investment, as proposed by European Commission President Juncker in his 315 billion Investment Plan for Europe.

Instead, the authors argue for a more progressive industrial and investment strategy. In particular, they highlight that an industrial policy for a new path of higher and sustainable growth has to be (i) additional, cannot be achieved with reframing existing rather small budgets, it needs to be (ii) an appropriate size, where the euro 315 billion (if really additional) could bring a significant push in the right direction, but where at least the double is closer to the real needs for a new higher growth path.

The authors identify three main tools at EU level to raise sufficient funds for investment: a) A shock absorbing capacity for asymmetric shocks (e.g., an Unemployment Benefit Scheme) and/or a budget capacity for the Eurozone serving the purpose to act against asymmetric shocks, where neither one nor the other finds for the time being sufficient support; b) a push for investment in competitiveness, where the European Investment Bank (EIB) can play a role in financing projects for competitiveness in companies through Europe; and c) A push for investment in infrastructure, where the budget has to play a major role as most of infrastructure does not create sufficient revenue (if any) to pay for investment, operation and maintenance; only the rather small segment of viable (i.e., profitable) infrastructure, for example toll roads, can be driven by private actors.

The contributions to this volume draw attention to the importance of an integrated approach to financial sector regulation and reform, macro policy, investment, and industrial policies to redress the structural relations between finance and industry brought about via the various processes of financialization. In doing so, this book has been able to highlight a number of alternative configurations for finance and industrial policy; our coverage is, however, far from exhaustive. One such omission is the role of mutual financial vehicles in diversifying the financial sector in such a way as to address the structural constraints addressed in the chapters of this volume (Michie and Llewellyn 2010; Michie 2011). The focus of mutual and co-operative banking on retail customers suggests that this may be a way forward for the banking of the future. However, research still needs to verify the ability of mutual banking to provide long-term finance on the scale required by capital-intensive industry (Toporowski 2002). Similarly, it has been beyond the scope of this book to present a comprehensive survey of industrial policy approaches or specific strategies. While there is no dedicated study on the role of Green Investment Banks and industrial policy as a medium for developing environmentally sustainable industries, it is our view that these will play a critical role in industrial policy. The studies in this book present a number of structural challenges to successful industrial and innovation policies that stem from the specific relationship between finance and industry in the twenty-first century. A green industrial strategy will need to contend with these challenges.

An alternative strategy would involve the ability to reassess the role of the state as an economic actor able to promote policies aimed at growth, innovation, and industrial reconversion. And it may require that these policies increasingly take place within a European framework of coordination, collaboration and with a common strategy for the revival of industry and its competitiveness that allow for national and sector specific variation, benefit all member states and promote equality and economic evenness across Europe.

The European Commission has recently highlighted the need to move away from an exclusive focus on austerity and to identify a set of economic policies that can strengthen the link between investment, structural reforms and fiscal responsibility (European Commission 2014a). In particular, on investment, the European Commission, proposed to boost investment by implementing a 315-billion-Euro Investment Plan for the period 2015–2017. This plan institutes a European Fund for Strategic Investment (EFSI), which will support investment in infrastructure, such as broadband and energy networks, as well as transport infrastructure, particularly in industrial centres, education, research and innovation, and renewable energy (European Commission 2014b). In parallel, the European Commission proposes the institution of a Capital Markets Union (CMU) with the scope to reduce fragmentation in the EU's financial markets. In particular the proposed objective of the CMU is to bring about a more diverse supply of finance to SMEs and long-term projects by complementing bank financing with deeper and more developed capital markets (European Commission 2014b).

Although these policies are presented as the right foundations for more sound and sustainable growth in the future of Europe, it is evident that they are not sufficient for changing the direction from the existing economic paradigm and to bring Europe towards a new developmental trajectory. Fiscal consolidation and labour market flexibility are still seen as two of the key elements for creating stability and establishing a more productive economic system. However, such policies are reinforcing the deflation of the European economy rather than complementing and supporting the Commission's stated aim of economic growth. Further, there is a clear lack of coordination between economic policies, and these often have conflicting aims and objectives. In addition, proposals such as the Investment Plan for Europe are significantly impaired by the requirements imposed by the Stability and Growth Pact, which prescribe balanced budgets, or small surpluses set at an arbitrary 3 per cent of GDP, over the business cycle. After five years of economic recession and decline, it is time for a new approach based on sustainable industrial policies.

References

Bailey, D., Lenihan, H., and Arauzo-Carod, J. M. 2011. 'Industrial Policy after the Crisis'. *Guest Eds of Policy Studies*, 32(4): 303–478.

Bailey, D., Cowling, K., and Tomlinson, P. (eds) 2015. *New Perspectives on Industrial Policy for a Modern Britain*. Oxford: OUP.

Bianchi, P. and Labory, S. (eds) 2011. *Industrial Policy after the Crisis: Seizing the Future*. Northampton, MA: Edward Elgar Publishing.

Buti, M. and Padoan, P.C. 2012. 'From a Vicious to a Virtuous Cycle in the Eurozone—the Time is Ripe'. Vox Research-based policy analysis and commentary from leading economists. Available at: <http://www.voxeu.org/article/vicious-virtuous-circle-eurozone> (last accessed 20 February 2015).

European Commission. 2010. 'An Integrated Industrial Policy for the Globalisation Era. Putting Competitiveness and Sustainability at Centre Stage'. Communication from the Commission to the European Parliament, the Council, the European Central Bank, the European Economic and Social Committee, the Committee of the Regions and the European Investment Bank, COM(2010) 614.

European Commission. 2012. 'Labour Market Developments in Europe in 2012'. *European Economy 5/2012*, Directorate General of Economic and Financial Affairs.

European Commission. 2014a. 'Annual Growth Survey 2015'. Communication from the Commission to the European Parliament, The Council, the European Central Bank, The European Economic and Social Committee, the Committee of the Regions and the European Investment Bank, COM(2014) 902 Final.

European Commission. 2014b. 'An Investment Plan for Europe.' Communication from the Commission to the European Parliament, the Council, the European Central Bank, the European Economic and Social Committee, the Committee of the Regions and the European Investment Bank, COM(2014) 903 Final.

European Parliament. 2011. 'Industrial Policy for the Globalised Era'. *European Parliament resolution*, 9(March). Available at: <http://www.europarl.europa.eu/sides/getDoc.do?pubRef=-//EP//TEXT+TA+P7-TA-2011-0093+0+DOC+XML+V0//EN> (last accessed 10 September 2015).

Fine, B. and Van Waeyenberge, E. 2013. 'A Paradigm Shift That Never Was: Justin Lin's New Structural Economics'. *Competition and Change*, 17(4): 355–71.

Froud, J., Johal, S., and Williams, K. 2002. 'Financialisation and the Coupon Pool'. *Capital and Class*, 26(3): 119–51.

Lin, J. and Chang, H. J. 2009. 'Should Industrial Policy in Developing Countries Conform to Comparative Advantage or Defy it?' *DPR Debate, Development Policy Review*, 27(5): 483–502.

Michie, J. 2011. 'Promoting Corporate Diversity in the Financial Services Sector'. *Policy Studies*, 32(4): 309–23.

Michie, J. and Llewellyn, D. T. 2010. 'Converting Failed Financial Institutions into Mutual Organisations'. *Journal of Social Entrepreneurship*, 1(1): 146–70.

Milberg, W., Jiang, X., and Gereffi, G. 2014. 'Industrial Policy in the Era of Vertically Specialized Industrialization'. In *Transforming Economies: Making Industrial Policy*

Work for Growth, Jobs and Development, ed. Salazar-Xirinachs, J. M., Nübler, I., and Kozul-Wright, R. Geneva: International Labour Organization, 151–80.

Naudé, W. 2010. 'Industrial Policy: Old and New Issues'. Working Paper No. 2010/106, United Nations University, World Institute for Development Economics Research.

Toporowski, J. 2002. 'La banque mutuelle: de l'utopie au marché des capitaux. Le cas britannique' (The mutual bank from utopia to the capital market). *Révue d'Économie Financière*, 67(3): 45–55.

Tregenna, F. 2011. 'Manufacturing Productivity, Deindustrialization, and Reindustrialization'. UNU-WIDER Working Paper No. 2011/57, September.

Warwick, K. 2013. 'Beyond Industrial Policy: Emerging Issues and New Trends'. OECD Science, Technology and Industry Policy Papers, No. 2.

Part I
Finance, Economic, and Industrial Restructuring

2

Beyond Keynesianism

Recovery *and* Reform in a European New Deal

Riccardo Bellofiore and Francesco Garibaldo

Our contribution deals with three interrelated topics: the nature of the global financial crisis and its relation to the process of global industrial and economic restructuring; the nature of the European crisis and of its internal disequilibria; hints on the policies required for European growth.

2.1 The Global Crisis: Managing the Effective Demand

There are many narratives on the global financial crisis; most of them insulate the world of finance, as the main culprit, from the real economy activities, supposed to be the victims. Our theoretical framework is that the traditional view of a conflict between industrial and financial capital is no longer held. On one side, the process of financialization of the new capitalism (a money manager capitalism) regards capitalism as a whole, from the process of circulation to the process of accumulation; the macroeconomic level as well as the corporate governance (value for shareholders and short-termism), the new productive structures, based on the centralization without concentration (distributed global supply chains and the de-structuration of old corporate model). On the other side, starting from the nineties, managing the effective demand became an objective that was increasingly difficult to achieve.

2.2 How Did the Crisis Reach the EU?

In the US, the country with the highest level of imbalance of the current account of the balance of payments, the demand was managed through a growth based on private debts to sustain the required levels of consumption, a politically active regime which has been labelled as a privatized Keynesianism. The three characters in the drama of the 'new' capitalism can epitomize this attempt: traumatized workers, manic depressive savers, and indebted consumers—all performed by the same actor. Workers, due to the deregulation policies affecting the labour market and the new patterns of social regulations of work, were living in a situation of increased insecurity with diminishing possibilities of saving and not only allowed to but forced to consume, unrelatedly to their earned incomes. This model collapsed on itself, starting with the housing bubble in the US in 2007.

Europe was involved in this collapse primarily because the position of net exporter of Germany and its satellites, with a current account surplus, was the other side of the coin of US growth, based on private debts beyond the actual earned income; so the collapse of one side triggers dire consequences in the other. The transmission mechanism was the new financial integrated system between the US and the Eurozone. The rescue operation based on shifting debts from the private to the public economic sphere ignited the crisis in Europe.

We are, therefore, convinced that the Eurozone crisis was not endogenous, but came from outside.

The EU was involved in this crisis in a very specific situation; to identify the main features of this situation the development of the EU since the Maastricht Treaty should be analysed. In Europe after the Maastricht Treaty and the Delors Plan, a process of heightened 'destructive' competition can be highlighted, which culminated in record levels of mergers and acquisitions in the two years immediately before the start of the current crisis, 2006–2007 (UNCTAD 2013). Greater centralization was dictated by the oligopolistic strategy of controlling larger market shares. Yet the merger movement jeopardized the existing oligopolistic structure in many industrial branches, so that, increasingly, some of the big players were themselves at risk. The opening up of Eastern Europe to Western European capital after the fall of the Berlin Wall in 1989 accelerated the industrial restructuring which had begun in the late 1970s, while an additional powerful stimulus came from China's entrance into the global manufactures market.

European corporations, in the EU-15 area, started two interlinked processes of restructuring the existing industrial facilities in Europe and structuring new ones mainly in China, but also in other Asian countries and in Brazil and Russia, due to the existing legal restrains in those countries; the overall result of these investments was adding new global and European industrial capacity.

In Europe the new plants were built in the Eastern countries, with the final result of an eastward shift of the industrial barycentre, roughly around a point in between Vienna, Bratislava, and Budapest. These new industrial facilities are organized as a network of plants to produce parts (supply chains) for the EU-15 final producers (original equipment manufacturers (OEMs)) and of final assembly of cars, white goods, shoes and clothes, and so on. The overall restructuring process was therefore based on parallel choices of outsourcing and/or of offshoring large chunks of previously centralized activities;[1] it implies a huge transformation of the nature and structure of corporations. Product activities can be organized through 'heterogeneous cycles, with parallel tasks, associated by addition' (Georgescu-Roegen 1971: 237–8). This is a fundamental point as it implies that there can be parallel cycles, functionally connected through a small temporal displacement with the result of reducing enormously all the production times—both the lead times, that is the operative time in the manufacturing part of the process, and the overall time to market, that is from the design to the commercialization of the products. For economic reasons, rather complex to explain theoretically, in order to fully deploy its advantages this process must require a mutual utilization of the equipment or/and the resources needed. When the prime reason for setting up the productive network is not merely cost cutting, it leads towards forms of strategic integration between the sub-suppliers and the contractor companies.

2.3 The Neo-Mercantilist Approach and the Consequences on the European Industrial Structure

The outsourcing and offshoring strategies allow the possibility of achieving various different objectives (Bardi 2002):

1. Offloading a part of the investment and warehousing costs onto others;

2. Offloading some of the responsibilities of the employment levels onto others;

3. Differentiating the hourly cost, on a par with other factors, between inside and outside, thus taking hold of a higher proportion of the value creation or, in the case of a negative situation, reducing the losses;

4. Offloading the *just in time* costs onto others: in practice, the sub-supplier must be equipped, through specific models of work organization, to

---

[1] (International) Outsourcing means that domestic firms give up parts of their intermediate production chains and buy instead parts from foreign suppliers. As such, this can be seen, as a form of 'international production sharing'. Offshoring on the other hand means that domestic firms set up new factories abroad to produce the intermediary products themselves. This is an intra-firm relationship, where the mother company keeps ownership control over its supplier (Galgóczi, Keune, and Watt 2008).

absorb all the 'variations' that the contractor experiences both in terms of the volumes and principally in terms of the speed of the response in changing the mix—in some cases less than an hour, generally speaking within 4–5 hours;

5. Optimizing the investments and the working process both for the contractor and for the sub-supplier that specialize in concentrating on well-defined activities.

In the case of the European OEMs there is a clear distinction regarding the reason for relocating capacity abroad. In the case of relocating within the EU boundaries the main reasons are the points from 1 to 4, with no particularly stress on the wage differentials but a strong emphasis on the labour protection levels, as the rush to invest in new facilities in Spain demonstrates (Barber 2013).

Germany utilized these new strategies in a very effective way, from the point of view of corporate efficiency and profitability in the framework of an export led, or mercantilist, model of growth.

The political economy of the European Union has evolved on the premise that net export balances could be achieved. However, not every country is in a position to attain that goal: the core six countries of the former Common Market with Austria and the three EU's Scandinavian countries do see export growth as being more significant than the expansion of domestic demand. Within the export oriented countries there is a definite hierarchy among the big three who happen to be also in the Eurozone. The first in the hierarchy is Germany whose export dynamics did not and do not depend on nominal exchange rates with the other main currencies. Rather, German exports are tied to technological innovations and to the widespread array of capital goods sectors. The price competitiveness element comes from what, for all practical purposes, is wage deflation. Indeed, Germany extended that policy to the whole of the Eurozone upon the formation of the euro. The second in line is Italy because her export orientation is exactly the opposite of Germany's. It was based on a weak currency, on competitive devaluations. But with the euro the weak currency approach has vanished and Italy needs wage deflation even more than Germany. Third in line is France. Paradoxically, France has a net export objective but only occasionally achieves it. Yet the policy posture of France is to combine financial conservatism with wage deflation and neo-mercantilist goals, though the latter are seldom attained. Neo-mercantilism to where? The European Union's extra trade absorbs a substantial part of total EU exports. But the bulk of the surpluses of net exporters are realized within the EU itself. In relation to China, Japan and Korea the EU countries have a growing deficit, determined by the trade with China. Yet in this case we have significant differences, depending on the nature of the deficits: active vs passive deficits.[2] For whom should Europe (the EU) work? For Germany the European Union is the main area of profitable effective demand. It is the area where the Federal Republic's economy realizes most of its external surpluses. These in turn represent the financial means with which German corporations internationalize their activities in the rest of the world. The net balances are mostly obtained in European markets.

According to some authors (e.g., Danninger and Joutz 2007), the German export boom has since the 1990s been based on big productivity gains. They analyse four hypotheses:

1. Improved cost competitiveness through moderate collective wage agreements since the mid-1990s;
2. Ties to fast growing trading partners as a result of a desirable product mix or long standing trade relationships;
3. Increased export demand for capital goods as a response to a global rise in investment activity;
4. Regionalized production patterns through offshoring of production to lower cost countries, partly as a result of European economic integration.

These authors stress the importance of the second and fourth factors. The productivity gains were implemented without a spin off for employees' general conditions (wages, social provisions, and working conditions). To the contrary, there has been wage moderation and a reduction of social provisions with the shrinking of the domestic market. The offshoring of production to lower cost countries, also within the EU-27 area, to implement a very aggressive export strategy, has compounded this situation.

Employers' strategy for overcoming the limits of the traditional relative high wage situation of post-war Germany changed dramatically in the 1990s. There was a huge shift from the automation strategy of the 1970s to the offshoring of upstream activities mainly to Eastern Europe and partly, as it is also the case for Northern Italy, to the old EU-15. There has been a contemporaneous huge shift of investments to Eastern Europe, on such a scale that Sinn (2006) can write that 'German firms are currently engaged in an investment strike to use the Marxian term.'

According to Sinn, this shift has been so huge that the depth of German industry in terms of share of own value added in manufacturing output went down from 36 per cent to 33 per cent. The rationale of this strategy is that high tech investments can grant Germany a gap with the new competitors such as India and China, making the medium-high sector of these mass markets available for its exports, ahead of a never ending catch-up attempt by India

[2] See Bellofiore and Garibaldo (2011) for a full analysis of the EU situation.

and China. These markets have such a dimension that even if only the richest parts of these emerging economies become available they are enough to guarantee adequate returns on investments, as happened to Volkswagen in China.

In this context the present crisis, which initially hit German exports hard, was a major challenge for German capitalism as a whole.

Which general consequences for the EU stemmed from this German strategy? The overall effect of this strategy, according to Simonazzi, Ginzburg, and Nocella (2013), was 'the impoverishment of the productive matrix of peripheral countries and the quality composition of trade flows'. They have clearly explained the importance of the different composition of the productive matrix within the Eurozone. They have also highlighted that the competitive advantage of Germany, in comparison with the other Eurozone countries, is only partially related to the differences in price competition, but on the quality of the products and the coherence of the productive matrix with the external trade demand, namely from China and other countries, with a new emerging middle class. Based on their analysis the strategic relevance is more evident, for the German model, of the industrial reorganization we have described before, namely of a European networks of suppliers and of the relocation abroad of parts production, namely in eastern countries of the EU. The impoverishment of the productive matrix they describe is of paramount importance because as a consequence 'an expansion of the German internal demand, albeit necessary, would not suffice to provide a viable response to the long-term sustainability of the euro area' (Simonazzi, Ginzburg, and Nocella 2013: 671). As a matter of fact, each increase in demand will be transmitted primarily to the German production transnational value chain system.

The European neo-mercantilist model was put under severe stress due to the shrinking of USA and Southern European export markets. The fallacies in the design of the euro came to the fore. Firstly, the institutional setting of the Eurozone and the German self-defeating obsession for fiscal austerity, vis-à-vis the financial crisis, pushed the Eurozone into a double dip recession. Secondly, the idea that what was viable for Germany, that is, an export driven growth, could be viable for the Eurozone as a whole, suffers from a 'fallacy of composition'. There are, indeed, clear imbalances of the current account balances among the Eurozone countries. Namely, for us, the imbalances are the symptoms of and underlying cause: the nature of the economic model shortly sketched before, intertwined with the underlying power relations among nations both in terms of market and political power. Simonazzi, Ginzburg, and Nocella quote Felipe and Kumar arguing that 'the lack of competitiveness of peripheral countries'—the cause of the imbalances—'is not due to the fact that they are expansive or the labour productivity has not increased. The problem is that they are stuck at middle levels of technology and they are caught in a trap. Reducing wages would not solve the problem' (Simonazzi, Ginzburg, and Nocella 2013: 666).

Another root of the process of change in Europe, before the crisis, is the capital—labour *relation*. The European situation represents the actual implementation of the Kalecki scheme (Kalecki 1943) of a capital strike due to an actual reduction of the profit's levels, as a result of the success of the labour movement success in the late 1960s and the first half of the 1970s. The rollback strategy initiated in the mid-1970s, largely achieved in the 1980s, and accelerated and sharpened after the 'fall of the wall' (1989), led to the fragmentation of the working class, also achieved through new productive networks, and to the progressive weakening of the national trade unions in the EU countries. This was instrumental in setting up a highly fragmented labour market. The progressive freedom of circulation of capitals and not of workers in the eastern countries was the way to realize what Sinn (2006) nicknamed as the German Bazaar economy.

The centralization process through acquisitions and mergers did not lead to concentration in the classical manner of vertically integrated firms. Instead, productive networks, or *filières*, based on the outsourcing of upstream production activities, and made up of many small and medium enterprises, have been set up by the OEMs.

Summing up, two main closely interrelated and reinforcing processes have profoundly changed European and global 'industrial capital': centralization without concentration, and a model of competition based, in a neo-mercantilist framework, on the endless pursuit of a never-ending expansion of all kind of consumption, engendering the necessity to seek new markets. This struggle has been fought by adding new productive facilities, when the existing ones already carried significant unused capacity. We are therefore convinced that this is also a crisis driven by oversupply in key sectors, because the productive capacity of the new plants competed with that of the same firms in the Euro-15 countries, leading to a state of endemic overproduction, by an excess of investments, in key industries such as automobile and 'white goods'.

In a capitalistic regime the excess of supply over demand—a paradox in itself, because of the unbelievable amount of existing and unfulfilled individual and social demands—is of course always relative. It depends on the impossibility to sell commodities, goods and services, with a profit; to be more precise, with an acceptable profit. To be 'acceptable' is a social and not an absolute measure. Overcapacity and income stagnation, when not outright deflation, for the working class urged countries, to find outlets for their outputs. This, in turn, has led to an enormous space for manoeuvre for financial capital. The leading role of financial capital pushed up the crossbar of profit acceptability, in some cases to totally unrealistic limits for any sound industrial activity, in a vicious circle.

This situation was compounded by huge investments, facilitated due to the liberalization of capital market, in the new potential markets (such as China), with the consequence of building up new excess capacity. The perspective of these 'green prairies' for European producers led, therefore, to a run for creating industrial bridgeheads in these new potential markets. For Europe the neo-mercantilist approach, together with a process of industrial restructuring, was the way in managing the effective demand through a current account surplus of the balance of payments. The surplus was not evenly distributed within the EU and the Eurozone, with a clear advantage for Germany and its satellites. The profits resulting from this position of advantage were invested abroad along two different paths: directly, from each country into US 'toxic' finance; within Europe, to finance the trade deficits of the Southern countries of Europe, reinforcing the internal current account surplus, mainly of Germany. For European (especially French and German) banks and finance the Treasury bonds of the European periphery played a role similar to subprime loans in the US.

2.4 An Alternative Model of Recovery

This analytical framework goes beyond a pure Keynesian approach. The issue is not only of managing (and nowadays increasing) effective demand, although this is of course necessary, but at the same time in understanding the supply side of the story, and then of planning a course of action accordingly. An exit from the actual depression, therefore, requires not only reflationary policies but also industrial policies and structural reforms; a type of structural reform far from orthodox proposals.

We don't rule out the importance of the reflationary part, namely the suggestions of debts mutualization, of a project of European investments (Varoufakis, Holland, and Galbraith 2013), and of industrial policies, pointing towards an improvement of the productive matrix of the peripheral countries, that is, a production upgrading through a process of diversification cum specialization (Simonazzi, Ginzburg, and Nocella 2013), in order to realize a European re-equilibrium. While we agree upon the analytical framework of Simonazzi, Ginzburg, and Nocella, and on a large part on the proposals on industrial policies, we are not convinced about the objective of a 'high road' of competitiveness strategy in the European experience. That strategy also suffers from a 'fallacy of composition'; it is functionally dependent upon the distribution, through the supply chain, of a 'low road' to other parts of the system, and namely on a dual labour market structure and very low levels in working conditions. We are also not convinced about a path to recovery based principally on a high investment, high technology, high profit model, as we will argue in our concluding remarks.

We would like to focus on the more controversial part of the argument, also for heterodox economists and social scientists: the need for structural reform. The overproduction, expressed by an excess of investments in productive capacity, is not a consequence of the crisis and of a sharp reduction in mass consumption, but one of the reasons for the crisis, because of a 'destructive competition' between global players, compounded by the financialization of their corporate governance. We are also convinced that the destructive competition race originates from the overall economic model. What we mean is that the problem also concerns the model of consumption, that is, of the quality of the demand. In the actual framework of the European industrial production it seems more and more difficult to foresee from where an effective demand will come, and it is questionable from where it is more desirable that it will come. In other words, yes, we should innovate the European production system, but what type of innovation are we talking about? In order to provide an answer to what is needed we need to start an inquiry about what, why, how much, for whom, and how we should innovate.

What is innovation about? A new innovation concept is needed. Of course, if macroeconomic as well as social aspects are taken into consideration, it becomes necessary to pose a series of questions.

Regarding social aspects:

a. Innovate what? The products, the processes, or both? Today an efficient process and high level of technical quality are prerequisites.

b. Innovate to achieve what? To generically satisfy a client/consumer irrespective of the nature and the quality of the demand? Or, by contrast, to establish the hierarchies of the objectives? A set of priorities decided in a democratic process, that is, in a process where the elected and democratic bodies have the power to set the economic agenda.

c. Why innovate? As a condition to be competitive in general? Or more selectively, for setting up a different match of supply and demand?

d. Who is responsible for the unexpected social consequences (side effects) of how the innovative processes are managed? How should risks be managed? It means that innovation must take into account not only technological cleverness, but also social, cultural and philosophical dimensions, and how to design complex governance systems and to reform the EU institutional setup. It must embody in its guidelines a gender and nature-friendly orientation in the design, composition, and technological structuration.

From this perspective, the problem is the overall quality of the products/ services. In a macroeconomic perspective, focusing the driver of innovation on the capacity to establish a new kind of demand leads to a new concept of innovation. It is based on a public and private domestic demand, both individual and collective, thus converging with the conclusion on the social side.

The nature of the demand to satisfy is not idiosyncratically European but global; therefore it can lead to a new global supply of products/services. Furthermore, there is another important innovation possibility deriving from the collaboration between different economic sectors; for example, in the case of supplying sustainable mobility, cooperation can be devised between the automobile and urban planning sectors or between government systems and governance systems on a meso-territorial scale. Indeed, the concept of a mobility platform implies a task to be fulfilled not only for mobility, but also for the architecture of the urban areas, and on a synergy specifically designed between the two action strands.

Besides, innovation is not necessarily high tech; from the open innovation perspective, innovation can also be the original combination of existing technologies.

A different kind of innovation, eventually, should be:

a. Based on societal needs and demands;

b. Socially responsible as regards risks;

c. Based on forms of international division of labour, agreed upon through international multilateral agreements;

d. Technologically 'conservative', that is oriented to utilize all combinations of technology, beyond the Frascati Manual's distinction of high and low technologies (Bender et al. 2005);

e. Based on an open cooperation between different actors, crosscutting sectors and technological domains, namely the divide between industrial production and services.

This kind of innovation requires a huge diffusion of innovation capabilities all along the value chain, not only as a requisite for OEM. It is a shift from a technocratic to a democratic innovation concept.

An export led model of growth for the Economic and Monetary Union (EMU) zone and the EU area as a whole is flawed for two interconnected reasons. Firstly, because of the changing nature of international competition, and secondly, because the idea that what is good for Germany and/or Italy can be good for Europe as a whole suffers from the fallacy of composition, as already illustrated.

As to the changing nature of international competition, Germany is a case in point of the neo-mercantilist countries, the idea that the high export model generates and delivers more wealth to the exporting country because of the substitution of low or unskilled jobs with medium or high skilled jobs looks more and more like wishful thinking. According to Sinn (2006: 14), 'Thus total German employment calculated in fulltime equivalents fell by 1.36 million people during the past ten years.' There is not a purely market-driven way to spread innovation capabilities across the labour force as a whole.

Besides, the neo-mercantilist approach has made Germany more exposed to the effects of the crisis; it is not by chance that Germany registered the highest peak of production downturn among the EU-15 countries.

This is the reason why the shift to societal needs and demands as the driver of growth in a newly cooperative international division of labour, along with a broad social responsibility in preventing ecological and social risks, is needed. It should be remembered that the 'beggar thy neighbour' policy, as Joan Robinson nicknamed the neo-mercantilist policy, leads to export devaluation and unemployment in other countries; the opposite should have been part of a broad scheme of international cooperation.

Therefore a new kind of innovation as the driver of a new social and macroeconomic framework is required in Germany and in Europe to support a sustainable recovery. Thus the recovery for Germany and Europe should be based on a new investment on people's ingenuity and capabilities, and on a societal environment supporting it.

What is required is a new kind of innovation whose driving power is a new type of autonomous demand, both public and private. It has to be domestic on the European scale (i.e., not externally driven), both for individual and collective goods and services; an intervention targeted to not yet or not fully satisfied needs. This task cannot be accomplished through the workings of the spontaneous (anarchic) function of the market of this new capitalism. What is needed is what Minsky defined as the socialization of finance, investments, and employment.

2.5 Conclusions

Minsky commenting on the reception of Keynes' notion of the socialization of investment in the post war period was very critical on the path which was taken to reach full employment. To avoid the socialization of the ownership of industry, the choice was in favour of 'a large government sector, in part financed by deficits' (Minsky 2008a: 156), because it is possible to achieve 'an approximation to full employment . . . as long as government, through its budget, is big enough' (Minsky 2008a: 156). The overall consequences were that 'as the gap between consumption at full employment, even allowing for transfer schemes, and full employment output must be filled with either government spending that uses resources or private investment if full employment is to be sustained, measures to induce investments by increasing profitability have been insinuated into the tax and spending systems. Thus a high profit, high investment economy has been created in which tax and government spending policies are evaluated on the basis of their impact upon private investment rather than on the basis of their impact upon consumption or equity respect to income distribution' (Minksy 2008a: 156). It was, says Minsky, 'a socialism for the rich'.

Here lays the main root of the path followed by Western Capitalism, since the end of the 1960s and the mid-1970s. When the post-war policies became unsustainable the choice was not between a *laisse faire* and a controlled economy; rather it was one between measures, such as a tax and subsidy system, that increased corporate untaxed income, leading to a lower consumption-income ratio, 'to induce private investment, quite independently of the social utility of investment', on the one side, and policies operating 'on distribution of income so as to raise the consumption-income ratio', on the other (Minsky 2008a: 162).

Thus, we agree with Minsky's idea that an alternative economic path should increase the consumption-income ratio, instead of lowering it. It seems to us that the problem was, for Minsky too, and it is of paramount relevance today, as we have already stated in the previous section, the nature of consumption to be developed. The concept of societal needs and demands, or of 'communal consumption', including public expenditures and welfare provisions, not based on monetary transfer payments, is what we are looking for. It is therefore logically coherent to criticize the joyless affluence and the poverty in the midst of plenty, as a result of the post-war consumption strategy, as Minsky did. The problem was and still is not only the level but also the social quality of consumption. It is not by chance, therefore, that the overall social consequences were a never ending consumerism and a permanent instability because 'a high-investment, high-profit strategy for full employment—even with the underpinning of an active fiscal policy and an aware Federal Reserve System—leads to an increasingly unstable financial system, and an increasingly unstable economic performance' (Minsky 2008a: 163). Minsky states that once it is clear that, under capitalist financial institutions, a system depending on private investments is intrinsically unstable, a rational strategy should aim to decrease that dependence in favour of socialized investments. Minsky warns us that whatever we do and we have to do, we will never get a once and for all resolution of the flaws in capitalism; it cannot be achieved because instability is endogenous to capitalism: 'but if capitalism is to be controlled so that the basic triad of efficiency, justice and liberty is achieved, then the design of the controls will have to be enlightened by an awareness of what was obvious to Keynes—that with regard to both the stability of employment and the distribution of income, capitalism is flawed' (Minsky 2008a: 166).

What does it mean today in the EU?

First of all to restore a democratic stance: we refer to the need to rescue a public sphere where, through a public discussion, citizens can decide all kinds of priorities and goals to be achieved, because all kinds of social relations, the economic sphere included, are political issues, that is under the control of democratic decision processes. The divorce of capitalism from democracy (Stiglitz 2012; Streeck 2013; Urbinati 2013) can be characterized through three major processes: 'the expansion of a powerful private domain and the dynamic interaction between a "privatizing" executive and the erosion of citizens' privacy rights' (Sassen 2006: 186); the 'privatization and marketization of public functions' (Sassen 2006: 186) and 'a new formalization of the private sphere, including a strengthening of its representation as neutral and technical, and of the market as a superior ordering from that of government' (Sassen 2006: 186). Without restoring democratic participation to the decision making process, affecting the nature and the quality of our social life, any type of proposals cannot but remain a wishful thinking. In the EU and in the EMU area this means going beyond the national boundaries, asking for the completion of the European unification process through the setting up of new institutions for a democratic government of the EU. We are using the word 'institutions' meaning the government, the regulatory structure, the legal system, and the financial institutions.

Secondly there should be coherence between the required urgent initiatives to end the economic depression—such as reflationary and industrial policies as already quoted from Varoufakis, Holland, and Galbraith (2013) and Simonazzi, Ginzburg, and Nocella (2013) contributions—and the mid- and long-term reforms we are arguing for.

That being stated, a brand new approach to the concept of economic growth should be debated in the form of a new agenda. The basic idea is that the way to reduce endogenous and chronic capitalism instability is to work for a 'low-investment, high consumption, full-employment economy' (Minsky 2008b: 329) and, we can add today, environmentally sustainable. There are multifarious consequences of such a choice, in short:

a. To afford the high level of unemployment, namely youth, through investments in social infrastructure to give an answer to societal needs, also, but not exclusively, with targeted public programmes for job creation, and in programmes for social and environmental activities. These programmes should be medium term designed in order to facilitate a transition from unemployment to a regular work for unemployed youths. The enrolling scheme should be based, as much as possible, on the individual experiences and instruction levels to favour personal development.

b. Setting up EU-wide minimum and common standards for the quality of work and defining a floor for wages, starting from the specific national situations.

c. To support, with the availability of 'patient capitals' and the long-term initiative of 'an entrepreneurial state' (Mazzucato 2013), innovation in the productive sphere, as qualified before, with the explicit target, and consequent constraints, of the decarbonization of our economies.

d. Setting labour intensive criterion as priority for all kind of public support to private investments. Public support, in the form of subsidizing demand, must be severely restricted to new advanced products/services supporting the decarbonization process, such as the development of new mobility patterns (services and vehicles).

e. Eventually the economic sphere will consist of two sectors and modes of production: labour intensive, due to specific public investments and policies, and capital intensive, due to private investments but with specific social and environmental regulations.

References

Barber, T. 2013. 'Europe's Labour Market Reform Takes Shape'. *Financial Times* 14 February.

Bardi, A. 2002. 'Strategie aziendali e modelli organizzativi, linee di sviluppo e tendenze evolutive nel settore dell'auto'. IpL Working Paper No. 8.

Bellofiore, R. and Garibaldo, F. 2011. 'The Global Crisis and the Changing European Industrial Landscape'. *International Journal of Management Concepts and Philosophy*, 5(3): 273–89.

Bender, G., Hirsch-Kreinsen, H., Jacobson, D., and Laestadius, D. (eds). 2005. *Low-Tech Innovation in the Knowledge Economy*. Frankfurt am Main: Peter Lang.

Danninger, S. and Joutz, F. L. 2007. 'What Explains Germany's Rebounding Export Market Share?' IMF Working Paper No. WP/07/24.

Galgóczi, B., Keune, M., and Watt, A. (eds). 2008. *Jobs on the Move: An Analytical Approach of 'Relocation' and Its Impact on Employment*. Frankfurt am Main: Peter Lang.

Georgescu-Roegen, N. 1971. *The Entropy Law and the Economic Process*. Cambridge, MA: Harvard University Press.

Kalecki, M. 1943. 'Political Aspects of Full Employment'. *The Political Quarterly*, 14(4): 322–30.

Mazzucato, M. 2013. *The Entrepreneurial State. Debunking Public vs. Private Sector Myths*. London: Anthem Press.

Minsky, H. P. [1975] 2008a. *John Maynard Keynes*. New York: McGraw Hill.

Minsky, H. P. [1986] 2008b. *Stabilizing an Unstable Economy*. New York: McGraw Hill.

Sassen, S. 2006. *Territory, Authority, Rights: From Medieval to Global Assemblage*. Princeton: Princeton University Press.

Simonazzi, A., Ginzburg, A., and Nocella, G. 2013. 'Economic Relations between Germany and Southern Europe', *Cambridge Journal of Economics*, 37: 653–75.

Sinn, H. W. 2006. 'The Pathological Export Boom and the Bazaar Effect. How to Solve the German Puzzle'. *The World Economy*, 9: 1157–75.

Stiglitz, E. J. 2012. *The Price of Inequality*. New York: W.W. Norton and Company.

Streeck, W. 2013. *Tempo guadagnato. La crisi rinviata del capitalismo democratico*. Milan: Feltrinelli.

UNCTAD (United Nations Conference on Trade and Development) 2013. 'Regulatory Review of Cross-Border M&As: Safeguarding Public Interests or Resorting to Protectionism'. *Investment Policy Monitor*, no.10.

Urbinati, N. 2013. *La mutazione antiegualitaria*. Rome and Bari: Laterza.

Varoufakis, Y., Holland, S., and Galbraith, J. K. 2013. 'A Modest Proposal for Resolving the Eurozone Crisis, Version 4.0', July. Available at: <http://yanisvaroufakis.eu> (last accessed 7 November 2013).

3

Industrial Competition between Countries in the Eurozone

Michel Aglietta

Industrial competition differs greatly between countries in the Eurozone. In particular, competition between France and Germany is creating economic dislocation and compromising Europe's success as it competes on the international stage. Corporate governance has become more financialized under the shareholder value principle. It has discouraged productive investment in setting financial return requirements much higher than the economic return on productive assets. It has encouraged leverage to boost the return on equity via share buybacks and leveraged buyouts (Aglietta and Reberioux 2005, 2012). In France, corporate strategy has largely followed the Anglo-Saxon way in adopting shareholder value (Lazonik and O'Sullivan 2000). By contrast, in Germany the well-entrenched system of stakeholder value promoting co-determination between capital and labour has resisted. It is still blossoming in the Mittelstand, an ecosystem of intertwined firms, institutes of technologies, local banks, and local public involvement. This brand of governance fosters a long-run horizon thanks to the stability of ownership and autonomous strategy in a network of firms that pursue incremental innovation called 'perfection of the common'. This strategy allows small and medium-sized enterprises (SMEs) to be world industrial champions in electro-mechanics and industrial equipment.

Besides, France's industrial performance has been deteriorating over the ten years prior to the publication of the Gallois report (Gallois, Lubin, and Thiard 2012). Placing the blame on the increase in salaries and shrinking profit margins is a convenient way to move culpability away from management. The labour market is seen to be responsible, since competitiveness is viewed purely as a reflection of payroll costs. Discrepancies in competitiveness have magnified after the 2008 financial crisis, and more so after the burst of the

Eurozone public debt crisis. Member countries are pitched against one another because wage deflation is viewed as the only way to recover competitiveness. This is the so-called internal devaluation that has brought the Eurozone to the verge of deflation and Japan style stagnation. Aggregate gross domestic product (GDP) in the Eurozone is still 2 per cent under the 2007 level in mid-2014 and gross productive investment has declined 20 per cent. Lack of domestic demand and deterioration in productivity feed on one another.

There is insufficient research and development taking place in Southern European countries, including France, which the media tends to overlook. Research and development (R&D) in France's private sector hasn't exceeded 1.4 per cent of GDP since 2002, compared with an average of 1.9 per cent in Germany, 2.0 per cent in the United States, 2.5 per cent in Japan, and 2.8 per cent in Sweden. The automation of industrial production processes is an area in which French companies are falling behind, having purchased 3.5 times less robots than Germany in 2001 and seven times less in 2011. A main factor in the decrease in productivity, as research into total factor productivity (TFP) tells us, is the dated assets of companies in France.

France could be falling behind in industrial competitiveness because companies are not prepared to or cannot fund innovative projects. If this is the case then we must consider the kind of corporate governance created by the economy's financialization. If firms are not able to finance innovation, we should look beyond their production capabilities and look at what type of innovation systems they have and how they are being used.

3.1 Strategy, Private Equity, and Governance

Support from central government and aid from the state after the Second World War allowed France to modernize and create capitalistic competition in chemicals, transport, construction materials, and energy. Increased competition occurred after the establishment of the Common Market, with currency devaluation sometimes used to offset a shortfall in competitiveness. With the progression of financial deregulation, the rules were changed, and a passive trend towards neoliberalism occurred as a result of the 1983 watershed for competitive disinflation. This progression became active in 1995 when a huge flood of US and UK shareholders in CAC40 companies caused disruption in corporate governance and capitalistic interests started to fall apart. Pro-shareholder governance was embraced by French capitalism, whereas in Germany the stakeholder view was prevalent. Managers were not encouraged to pursue an innovative approach with regards to product investment, due to the focus on raising share prices and following the well-established French tradition of a pyramid style, hierarchical approach to running a company.

Business strategies were left at the mercy of the stock market, because management incentives are aligned on shareholders' interests through stock options and the threat of takeovers in the market for control. Private equity ownership (PE) was an option rather than being a publicly owned company, but the fact that more than 70 per cent of a buyout can be financed by debt rather than real equity can lead to problems with long-term strategies in the future. The assets and future revenue of the businesses targeted is used to secure the loans of the private equity funds. However, lending banks spread risks amongst investors by using asset backed securities (ABS). Current managers from the target company, as well as private equity fund representatives, run the company with the aim of making as much profit for themselves as possible in three to five years in order for debts to be repaid, using leverage to secure returns of more than 20 per cent. However, despite the fact that this might be a successful method to generate a burst of start-ups, these strategies can be detrimental to the workforce and can destroy rather than create value, with the stripping down of assets and dividing profits amongst a financial elite.

It is common for firms to be governed by shareholders like this, although it is taken to the extreme in the private equity model. In 2008, an average of 37 per cent of company shares across twenty-one European countries was held by foreign shareholders, whereas in 2003 it was 29 per cent. Core shareholders are disappearing due to the change in European shareholding, which became popular in the UK and the US, and will eventually result in a loss of majority ownership. The sole key shareholder is the community of potential shareholders via the stock market. This has had a devastating effect on approaches to corporate governance. Investors seek to capitalize on their returns through realized capital gains, and companies are seen as a group of assets that can be sold on the stock market, as per the Wall Street model, rather than as entities that require long-term commitment and strategic investment. As a consequence, average holding times has declined tremendously over time in the OECD (Organisation for Economic Co-operation and Development) countries, from seven years in the end of the 1960s to seven months in later years.

3.2 The Key to Competitiveness and Multi-Stakeholder Governance

Long-term commitment with venture capital and strategic guidance helps small and medium-sized companies clear debt and learn to grow whilst exploring new pathways. This is a new governance approach.

In the 1970s the idea developed in the US that introduced the notion of governance in the interests of shareholders alone.[1] The idea attracted even more of a following in the 1980s. This view erroneously fails to differentiate between an actual business, which is a grouping of people whose cooperation is dedicated to producing social value, and the corporation, which is a legal entity of its own. Barring slavery, a human grouping cannot be owned by anyone. The corporation has a legal right to run the business, not to possess it. It owns the profit that is generated collectively. Shareholders own only their shares of equity. Therefore shareholders own some of the company assets. By no means can they claim to represent all the stakeholders of the company and have exclusive rights to determine how the profit should be used (Stout 2007).

Stakeholders are within and outside the firm. Productivity stems from complementarity and cooperation of people who bring specific assets that are partly individual in their competencies and partly collective in tacit knowledge creation due to informal interactions between employees. This is all the more important when the firm is creative. Since productivity is partly due to interrelationships that are not contractualized, it is impossible to pretend that marginal contributions to the output of the firm can be separately measured and valued in market like compensations, so that only shareholders are residual owners. Every stakeholder who participates in producing the profit of the firm has a right to share in it and may have a say on the decisions that can enhance the profit in the future. Therefore the Board of Directors, which is the political organ of the corporation, in the sense that it defines the collective interest of the firm and the strategies to achieve it, must reflect the interests of all stakeholders and make them compatible in creating a sense of common belonging (Kaufman and Englander 2005).

It is up to the board of directors to oversee the running of the company to make sure that it conforms to governance standards. Company policy and strategic objectives are set by the board, which should act in the interest of the corporation as a whole and not on behalf of individual stakeholders, and governance has to ensure that stakeholder coordination is not taken over purely by management interests. If there is multi-stakeholder governance then checks and balances are made internally—management performance is measured, power between the chief executive officer (CEO) and the chairman is separated, and internal audit committees report to the board of directors as opposed to the management.

The key to competitiveness has to be multi-stakeholder governance since it draws on the skills and resourcefulness of the people within that company. Skills are enhanced internally with team members learning from each other,

---

[1] See the seminal paper by Fama (1980).

and employees are motivated through their own creativity and knowledge. The cultivation of collective skills to enhance production is something that only multi-stakeholder governance can achieve, with employees recognized as stakeholders and represented on the board. The efficiency of the labour force is achieved by corporate social responsibility. Managed well, this collective asset can increase productivity.

3.3 Innovation Systems and Extended Stakeholder Governance

We must, however, look into this further. As clearly outlined, private ownership rights for intangible assets do not exist, since no one can sell bonds or shares on one's own capabilities. Only services produced by renting the use of those assets are tradable. Competitiveness based on these assets considers stakeholders to be beyond the legal limitations of the corporation. The intangible assets are a source of external benefits for the corporation. They are non-rival and, in creating a social network, it results in products and business solutions that are in tune with the community and social priorities, including urban renovation and health. Quality standards and efficiency are improved. As the capital invested increases, these intangible assets offset the drop in the marginal productivity of fixed capital, since these assets are not destroyed through use and knowledge is incorporated. Innovation systems are created by networks to internalize externalities due to their relationships with each other. The governance required to capitalize on this coordination is one of extended stakeholder governance; a means of governance that recognizes diversity, innovation, and the mobilization of human resources.

Many different innovation systems exist depending on various cultural traditions and ideologies; there is not one system that is greater than the rest. The well-known venture capital funding to the innovation system in the USA makes individualism a powerful characteristic of the business approach. Entrepreneurs are offered funding by business angels who help them on their way towards growth and innovation, and private equity firms with the Nasdaq paving the way for success or failure.

In Asia, traditional practices differ when it comes to industrial organization. For instance, in Japan, SMEs are seen as partners on industrial projects and an integral part of the value of larger corporations. They are not viewed as subcontractors for outsourcing. In China, ethical standards are maintained through a network of connections including family ties and mutual support and understanding, which is the basis of Guanxi capitalism, deeply rooted in Confucian tradition.

3.4 The German Mittelstand Model and the French Business Approach

Competitive excellence in Europe is measured by the Mittelstand benchmark, which is in complete contrast to the method of industrial organization in France following withdrawal from the state. It is interesting to see the way in which leading companies have reacted to tougher conditions due to globalization. While there has been slow deindustrialization in France since the euro was introduced, Germany has increased in strength as an exporter. In order to enhance competition in innovation systems in their homeland, German companies have invested a great deal into Eastern European countries and have integrated their foreign investments into their industrial systems in the German federal states. However, France has been floundering somewhat and has even offshored its research facilities.

The Mittelstand is a model that encourages the improvement of the quality of intangible assets, a system that is respected and does not venture into radical change but rather focuses on incremental innovation. This self-regulating system allows competitive advantage which can lead to healthy profit margins and solid market share. Mittelstand firms are able to use cash as their main source of investment thanks to good trading accounts. In this way, companies can remain partly run by families, leaving management free to maintain their focus on achieving efficiency in innovation and market share, and developing business strategy.

The German practice brings three matters to the forefront that we can learn from. Firstly, only if you have a solid industrial grounding can you then have incremental innovation. Secondly, small, niche domestic markets can become lucrative exports in the global playing field. Thirdly, an innovation policy which builds on people skills and strengths can protect businesses against competition from emerging countries.

To improve competition, the main factor is social innovation, where governments introduce resources to retrain individuals, endorsing apprenticeships with close associations between schools and businesses. In Scandinavia, men and women are also offered equal career opportunities, and the government provides pre-school childcare.

To ensure a self-sustaining method for industrial growth, policies need to be introduced that are devoted to innovation systems, including industrial strategy, as well as a requirement for a balance between the power of stakeholders and public authorities. French regions should encourage a new business approach and choose firms that can pursue pilot initiatives with private-public backing, increase regional industrial competition, and recognize promising industry sectors. Introducing a particular status for SMEs with good financial solutions could encourage small and medium enterprises to innovate and export. A sustainable development strategy could be used both in Europe and nationally to repatriate industry and encourage incremental innovation.

References

Aglietta, M. and Reberioux, A. 2005. *Corporate Governance Adrift: A Critique of Shareholder Value*. Cheltenham: Edward Elgar.

Aglietta, M. and Reberioux, A. 2012. 'Financialization and the firm'. In M. Dietricht and J. Krafft (eds), *Handbook on the Economics and Theory of the Firm*. Northampton, MA: Edward Elgar, 308–23.

Fama, E. 1980. 'Agency problems and the Theory of the Firm'. *Journal of Political Economy*, 88(2): 288–307.

Gallois, L., Lubin, C., and Thiard, P.-E. 2012. *Pacte pour la compétitivité de l'industrie Française, Rapport au Premier ministre Paris: Commissariat Général à l'Investissement*.

Kaufman, A. and Englander, E. 2005. 'A Team Production Model of Corporate Governance'. *Academy of Management Executive*, 19(3): 1–14.

Lazonik, W. and O'Sullivan, M. 2000. 'Maximizing Shareholder Value: A New Ideology of Corporate Governance'. *Economy and Society*, 29(1): 13–35.

Stout, L. 2007. 'The Mythical Benefit of Shareholder Control'. *Virginia Law Review*, 93(3): 789–809.

4

Financialization, Dependent Export Industrialization, and Deindustrialization in Eastern Europe

Joachim Becker, Predrag Ćetković, and Rudy Weissenbacher

Ten years after the first eastern enlargement of the European Union (EU), recent development trajectories of Europe's eastern periphery—that set in with the late 1990s—have bifurcated. While the Visegrád countries and Slovenia became closely integrated into the German export oriented productive system and only partially relied on financialization, the pre-crisis growth model of the Baltic and Southeast European countries relied in a rather one-sided way on 'dependent financialization'. We follow arguments of external dependency from the Latin American Dependency school, and try to adapt them to the era of financialization (since the crisis of the 1970s). Very briefly, the system of global capitalist accumulation and reproduction once again entered a phase of over accumulation which put pressure on profitability in the productive sectors and therefore shifted investments to the financial sectors. This produced new types of external dependencies driven by financial channels. The main characteristic of dependent financialization is its dependence on capital inflows. These inflows stimulate internal credit growth. In many cases, a significant part of the credits is denominated in foreign currency. Thus, informal dollarization or euroization is often a key feature of dependent financialization (Becker et al. 2010; Becker 2014). Informal euroization is fairly advanced in the Baltic and Southeast European Countries. In many cases, it is foreign banks that control a major part of the financial sector in dependent economies. This feature is particularly pronounced in Eastern Europe. Insofar as Eastern European countries embarked on processes of export industrialization as it has been the case in the Visegrád countries (Czech Republic, Hungary, Poland, and Slovakia) and Slovenia, this process has usually been highly dependent on foreign investment. Therefore, dependent export industrialization is a fitting characterization of their recent industrialization experience. The reliance on capital inflows and, in the case of the more industrially orientated countries, on exports entails significant vulnerabilities to crisis. The strongly financialized economies proved to be particularly vulnerable to the present crisis.

Starting with an overview of the historical trajectories of uneven development in Europe, our analysis will be three pronged: it will analyse the accumulation strategies of foreign and domestic capital (particularly in industry and finance); the policies of the EU, its member states and international financial institutions; and, the policy responses of the states in the region. We will compare the two sub groups of the region identified in this section, namely countries that followed a growth trajectory characterized by export industrialization together with financialization, and those where financialization dominated the growth model.

4.1 Historical Trajectories: From Antiquity into the Twentieth Century

Differences in the development trajectories of countries within Europe's eastern periphery go back to early patterns of uneven (industrial) development. While industrialization began relatively early in parts of Central Eastern Europe, the Baltic countries, and large parts of south-eastern Europe experienced their main industrialization push during the state socialist era. This chapter outlines the historical processes which have had an influence on the development patterns of the last two decades. East–west patterns of uneven development within Europe have historical roots that go back many centuries. The end of the Western Roman Empire, the 'feudal synthesis' of ancient Roman civilization with the Germanic clan system, and the pressures placed on former Roman territory by the south and east shifted the centres of power in Europe to the north-west. Primitive accumulation in Europe and colonial exploitation enabled a transformation to a capitalist system, spreading from early enclaves in Northern Italy to England and Western Europe, and became a global phenomenon in the twentieth century.

In the sixteenth century Eastern European regions were integrated into the Western European 'world economy' as grain exporters (Weissenbacher 2007). Britain's mercantilist policies laid the ground for its accession from the European periphery to the pinnacle of European and global industrial capitalism (Chang 2002). Starting with the era of British industrial revolution, the 'Great Divergence' (Pomeranz 2000) rapidly widened differences in the extent to which capitalist development took place, making it harder for countries within the periphery to overcome the gap between itself and the centre. Be that as it may, certain political economic constellations seem to have enabled regions of Eastern Europe to gain ground in (industrial) development. The Habsburg Monarchy, the Council of Mutual Economic Assistance (Comecon), and the Socialist Federal Republic (SFR) of Yugoslavia to some extent shielded regional development from world market influences (Weissenbacher 2007).

In general, latecomers to industrial development 'were obliged to evolve their national economies as . . . parts of the capitalist world economy' (Berend and Ránki 1982: 160). As policies of import substitution and extensive industrialization, that were being pursued, reached their limits, world market processes impaired the process of catching-up with gross national product (GNP) levels of the industrialized West. Comecon countries failed to enact some form of 'Socialist Fordism' based on intensive production or consumer goods industries. The flipside of infant industry protection afforded by Comecon was, as argued by Berend (1996: 82), that it 'killed the technological inspiration of the competitive milieu of the world market'.

Eastern European economies could not have chosen a more inopportune time to open up. The period since the 1970s has been marked by a downward swing of the global economy with the first global recessions after World War II occurring in 1974 and 1980. The results are known: Comecon countries tried to acquire Western technology and faced Western protectionism (due to global crisis). Furthermore they were vulnerable to Western credit that was available due to the expansion of the financial sector: Shrinking profits of Western companies in the 'real' sector poured money into the international banking sector, a tendency that was reinforced by OPEC's (the Organization of the Petroleum Exporting Countries) 'Petro-dollar-recycling' (Weissenbacher 2007). In addition, Yugoslavia became caught in a debt trap. 'Windfall profits' of the 1970s' international financial liquidity frenzy turned into Washington Consensus austerity after the Volcker shock induced credit crisis in 1979. Hungary, Poland, and Yugoslavia were among the first countries to negotiate with the International Monetary Fund (IMF), trading credit for conditionalities. The bitter consequences of the 1980s' crisis decade for Yugoslavia are well known and amounted to disintegration of the Yugoslav state and deindustrialization of most of its regions (Weissenbacher 2005). Even though Yugoslavia was ahead of the pack in beginning its efforts to counter regional development gaps in the 1960s, it was already too late for them to reap benefits from the post-war boom as it came to its end.

With the start of the capitalist transformation process in the early 1990s, both Western European capital and Western political institutions gained influence over the development trajectories and economic policies in Eastern and south-eastern Europe. Some of the initial economic policy decisions, exchange rate policies in particular, had a lasting impact on future development trajectories. With the commencement of EU accession talks, the EU and Western European capital began to shape the development trajectories of the region in a more decisive way than in the first phase of political economic transformation.

4.2 The Early Transformation Phase of the 1990s

The Eastern European countries entered the early transformation phase with different degrees of economic crisis and external room for manoeuvre. Several countries, such as Hungary, Poland, or Yugoslavia, had contracted substantial external debts since the 1970s. In these countries, international financial institutions, particularly the IMF, gained significant leverage potential over transformation policies (Myant and Drahokoupil 2011: 88). However, in many cases it was not necessary to exercise this leverage since domestic technocrats with ideas close to those of the Washington Consensus held significant influence within the domestic political arena (Drahokoupil 2009: 92). Nevertheless, most states in the region took IMF loans so that IMF 'advice' could easily be evoked in domestic policy conflicts. External policy experts played a similar legitimizing role.

For both external and internal actors, issues of privatization took priority over the issue of the future development model. While Hungary, with its relatively long history of structural adjustment programmes, banked strongly on foreign direct investment (FDI) almost from the beginning, most of the other states actively nurtured the emergence of domestic capitalist groups with state owned banks providing key financing (Pasti 2006; Drahokoupil 2009; Družić 2009; Myant and Drahokoupil 2011). The attempt to control the privatization process seems to have been a key motive of the dominant political economic forces in the break-up of the multinational states of Czechoslovakia, Soviet Union, and Yugoslavia (Barša 1999: 139; Samary 2008: 56). In these multinational states, political forces had strong roots at the level of the constituent republics. It was from the commanding heights of the republics that alliances between technocrats, managers and the top of the political parties wanted to control the privatization process. This entailed the disintegration of existing multinational states with rather strong federal or even confederal structures.

Most of the liberal technocrats who usually predominated in formulating economic policies assumed implicitly that the market would define the course of the development model. Thus, most governments did not adopt active industrial policies. Liberalization, austerity, and privatization policies had a profound and lasting impact on the productive capacities and structures of Eastern European countries. Trade and exchange rate policies proved to be of particular importance. The so-called Europe Agreements of the early 1990s focused on trade issues and reflected asymmetric negotiation power. These policies sheltered sensitive Western European subsectors in which Eastern European exporters were relatively strong, but not the other way round (Andor 2000; Vachudova 2005). Thus, they favoured Western European trade expansion into Eastern Europe, but not the strengthening of Eastern European trading structures. 'A slower pace of external liberalization would have improved the survival chances of domestically oriented producers that were threatened by imports' (Myant and Drahokoupil 2011). Exchange rate policies often proved to have a detrimental impact on industrial development, the trade balance, and the current account, as many countries opted consistently, or at least temporarily, for overvalued exchange rates.

Slovenia was the only country to consciously avoid an overvaluation of the currency. The Slovenian government introduced a mild form of temporary capital controls in order to prevent currency appreciation (Becker 2007). This exchange rate policy was clearly beneficial to the country's manufacturing industry. The Slovenian government successfully fostered industrial development in a neo-corporatist framework (Bohle and Greskovits 2012). Both industrial interests and the labour movement were relatively strong in Slovenia. After surmounting the early transformation depression in 1993, Slovenia's development model relied primarily on the productive sectors and was characterized by greater social cohesion than in any other country of the region until a switch to financialization in 2004 (Mencinger 2012). In the Czech Republic, Poland, and Slovakia, the mode of development also tended to be industry centred for most of the 1990s (Drahokoupil 2009). However, there was hardly any conscious industrial policy. If there was any direct support for manufacturing, 'the greatest help was given not to domestically owned firms but to inward investors that bought more successful established enterprises in Poland, Czechoslovakia and Hungary' (Myant and Drahokoupil 2011: 116). Thus, their policies were less consistent and more oriented towards foreign-owned companies than in Slovenia. In the southeastern European countries, the transformation crisis was more prolonged than in the Visegrád states, the balance of social forces was more volatile, development priorities were less defined, and administrative state capacities were lower than in Central and Eastern Europe (Bohle and Greskovits 2012). It is an indicator of the economic and social malaise that the rural population increased in Romania because agricultural semi subsistence production served as a social security net of the last resort. In most of the successor states of former Yugoslavia, the disintegration of the Yugoslav economy, wars and, in the case of Serbia, sanctions, resulted in deep economic and social problems. Whereas development trajectories were not clearly defined in most of South East Europe, the Baltic States opted for a relatively clearly defined accumulation model early on. Almost from the beginning they moved in the direction of financialization. Soon after introducing their national currencies, the governments of the Baltic countries opted for currency boards or hard pegs resulting in overvalued currencies. This was done in order to wane their economies away from Russia and to capture international capital flows (Feldman 2006, 2008; Becker 2007). These policies had a devastating effect on manufacturing and made the three countries highly dependent on high capital inflows. With the exception of the war ravaged post-Yugoslav countries, the Baltic States recorded the steepest decline of industrial production in Eastern Europe. At times, their reduction of industrial output surpassed 30 per cent per annum. The south-eastern European countries suffered from a stronger decline of industrial production than the Visegrád countries and Slovenia during the 1990s, particularly during the transformation depression at the beginning of that decade (wiiw 2007). Thus, late industrializing countries in Eastern Europe fared worse economically in early capitalist transformation than those countries where industrialization had been initiated earlier and the industrial base tended to be stronger. The transformation depression and policies during the early transformation phase also had a negative impact on technological capabilities. According to Tiits et al. (2008: 72), '(a) closer look at the change in the share of medium and high technology in manufactured exports (reflecting international competitiveness) and at industrial value added (reflecting the quality of the industrial structure) reveals that the new EU member states were more competitive in 1980 in terms of production capabilities than in 2000'.

4.3 From (Pseudo) Boom to Crisis: Development Trajectories since the Late 1990s

In the late 1990s, Western European capital started to expand more aggressively towards Eastern Europe, and accession talks between the EU and Eastern European states commenced. These two processes were closely interrelated. The Western European financial sector almost completely took over banking in Eastern Europe. With the exception of Slovenia, where the state retained an important stake in the banking sector (Štiblar 2010; Žitko 2011: 112), Western banks gained a predominant position in Central, Eastern and south-eastern European countries with controlling between 63 per cent and close to 100 per cent (e.g., Czech Republic, Slovakia, Estonia) of the sector in 2006 (Frangakis 2009: 72; Ćetković 2011). Foreign direct investment in manufacturing has been more selective. The share of FDI in manufacturing has been particularly high in the Visegrád states and in Romania, with Slovakia topping the list with manufacturing accounting for 34.5 per cent of inward FDI stock in 2009.

Likewise, in the Czech Republic, Poland, and Romania, the share of manufacturing in the FDI stock slightly surpassed 30 per cent in 2008/ 2009 (Hunya 2012: 55). The Visegrád countries, Slovenia, and the Transylvanian region of Romania have become relatively closely integrated into the German export sector and the Western European industry more generally (Kulikova and Lobanov 2011: 170). In most of the Baltic and south-eastern European countries, the manufacturing share in FDI is relatively low—and the share of financial intermediation and of real estate and business activities relatively high. In that regard, Estonia and Latvia are extreme cases. In 2009, financial intermediation and real estate activities had a share of 60.6 per cent in inward FDI stock in Estonia. In Latvia, the figure was 48.5 per cent in 2010 (Kulikova and Lobanov 2011: 170). Thus, FDI shows divergent patterns of subordinate integration into the European economy.

The beginning of EU accession negotiations facilitated a more decisive shift among the domestic power blocs towards forces favouring the indiscriminate opening of the economies to foreign capital (Drahokoupil 2007: 90). Slovenia was the only country where such a decisive shift did not occur at that juncture. In countries such as Slovakia or Romania, euro-liberal domestic forces and their external political allies used the prospect of EU integration as leverage against more nationalist forces which were depicted as obstacles on the march towards the West (cf. Vachudova 2005). Drahokoupil (2009: 125) characterizes the 'managerial and administrative elites' that 'translate structural dependence on foreign capital into concrete political processes' as a 'comprador service sector'. It includes state official from FDI related bodies, local branches and some domestic consultancy and legal advice firms. In the Visegrád countries (and later partially Romania), the drive for attracting FDI coincided with the relocation strategies of Western European manufacturing companies. Industrial policy consisted primarily of attracting manufacturing FDI—through low taxation, specific incentives, infrastructure provision and low wages (Drahokoupil 2009). After a decline in the 1990s, industry stabilized in the Visegrád countries. Bohle and Greskovits (2012: 45) show that complex manufacturing (mainly chemicals, machinery, electrical, optical and transport equipment) increased in the Visegrád countries and 37 per cent in Slovenia on average from the period 1989–1999 to 2000–2007. In the Baltic and South East European countries complex manufacturing output even tended to decline (Bohle and Greskovits 2012: 45). Likewise, complex manufacturing exports (chemicals, machinery, and equipment) increased in the Visegrád countries and in Slovenia between the two periods (Bohle and Greskovits 2012: 45). These figures make Bohle and Greskovits (2012: 170) even coin the term 'manufacturing miracle' for the Visegrád countries.

However, these global figures conceal considerable structural weaknesses of the restructured manufacturing sectors. In the Visegrád countries, manufacturing has almost assumed a dual structure with a relatively productive, and usually foreign owned, export sector and a 'national', and mostly inward looking, sector that has fallen behind (Baláž, Kluvánková-Oravska, and Zajac 2007; Kulikova 2012: 11f). Most of the export production consists of outsourced assembly production, which is of a rather shallow nature. Research and development activities are not usually relocated to Central East Europe. However, existing research and development (R&D) activities have at times been continued, for example in the case of the Škoda car manufacturing in the Czech Republic (Myant and Drahokoupil 2011: 297). Since Transnational Companies (TNC) controlled firms hardly have any cooperative links with national firms, technological diffusion is weak (Kulikova and Lobanov 2011: 176). The Czech Republic came with a share of 1.85 per cent of R&D expenditure in the gross domestic product (GDP) at least close to the EU average of 2.03 per cent in 2011, whereas Hungary reached 1.21 per cent, and Poland and Slovakia trailed far behind with shares of 0.76 per cent and 0.68 per cent respectively. In the group of the export industrializing countries, it was only Slovenia with its more domestically owned manufacturing sector that surpassed the EU average and devoted 2.47 per cent of its GDP to R&D expenditure (Eurostat 2013). Not only the low R&D share, but also low private share in R&D expenditure is similar to the peripheral Southern economies of the EU (Baláž and Sabo 2011: 11). With the exception of Poland, the specialization of the export industries tends to be very narrowly concentrated in a few subsectors, mainly car production. Though the trade balance improved, it remained—with the exception of the Czech Republic and Hungary—negative in the pre-crisis years. The current account suffered from increasing profit remittances. In 2008, the deficit of the income balance already reached about 8 per cent of the GDP in Hungary and the Czech Republic. Except for the Czech Republic, the current account deficit hovered around 5 per cent of the GDP what is regarded as a critical limit (Becker 2010: 521).

Export industrialization has, however, not been the only pillar of the growth model of the Visegrád countries and Slovenia. Dependent financialization has been the second one. It has primarily taken the form of credit growth, particularly of credits to private households nurturing real estate booms and sustaining domestic demand. In the Czech Republic, Poland, and Slovakia, domestic credit provision to private households increased considerably, but not extremely. Between 2003 and 2006, domestic credits to private sector as percentage of GDP increased by less than 10 percentage points in the three countries, while in Poland it increased by only 4.2 percentage points (Frangakis 2009: 64). Credits were lower than deposits (Czech Republic) or, at least, did not significantly surpass deposits (Myant and Drahokoupil 2011: 263). They were predominantly in national currency (Myant and Drahokoupil 2011: 319). In Slovenia and Hungary, financialization tendencies were stronger. During the right-wing government of Janez Janša (2004–2008), Slovenia's banks increased lending in an extreme way. The exploding credit provision which nurtured a real estate bubble was financed by lending abroad. Whereas deposits still covered credits in 2004, the ratio credits to deposits deteriorated to 1.6 until 2008 (Mencinger 2012: 76). In Hungary, credit growth was not as unrestrained as in Slovenia, but considerably stronger than in the other Visegrád countries. Domestic credits to private sector increased from 41.0 per cent of GDP in 2003 to 54.6 per cent in 2006 (Frangakis 2009: 64). Credits were predominantly denominated in foreign currencies (Myant and Drahokoupil 2011: 319). This informal euroization increased Hungary's financial vulnerability considerably.

The present global crisis hit the economies of the Visegrád countries and Slovenia in different ways. All countries suffered from the steep decline of exports in late 2008 and early 2009—with Poland, which has a more diversified industrial structure, being hit to a lesser extent than the other countries (Kulikova 2011: 15). Thus, the export channel was relevant for the spreading of the crisis for all countries of the group. Slovenia and Hungary were also affected through the financial channel (Becker 2011: 271ff.). In Slovenia, the real estate bubble burst when external funding ceased to fuel credit expansion. Real estate business and construction industry contracted sharply. Banks faced an increasing share of non-performing credits. Some economic subsectors suffer from the lack of liquidity and/or excessive debt (Bole, Prašnikar, and Trobec 2011). In Hungary, the huge domestic foreign exchange debt proved to be the key economic problem. The forint depreciated considerably in autumn 2008 when international liquidity dried up. The currency depreciation put foreign exchange debtors and banks almost immediately under enormous pressure. In Slovenia, the erosion of the neo-corporative arrangements, which had already begun during the right-wing Janša government (Bohle and Greskovits 2012: 249f.), has advanced even further during the crisis. The possibility of an IMF/EU structural adjustment programme has been invoked in order to push through neo-liberal counter-reforms and privatization, particularly in the banking sector. The Slovenian governments, however, have encountered stronger protests, particularly by the trade unions, than other governments in the region (Becker 2013a). Hungary was the first EU country to apply for an IMF credit (Andor 2009; Becker 2010: 532f.). The financial restrictions were much less relevant for countries without substantial domestic foreign exchange credits and relatively low structural external refinancing needs of the banking sector. In the Czech Republic, Poland, and Slovakia, the debt of private households continued to grow even during the crisis (Becker 2010: 522; Kulikova 2011: 28f.).

Among the countries without a substantial domestic foreign exchange debt, Poland, and the Czech Republic, which both had retained the national currency, fared better in terms of the GDP performance than the two Eurozone countries Slovenia and Slovakia. While Poland's GDP growth declined to 1.7 per cent and the Czech GDP declined by 4.2 per cent, in 2009 Slovenia and Slovakia suffered from a GDP decline of 7.8 per cent and 4.7 per cent respectively. The currency depreciation attenuated the impact of the crisis in Poland and the Czech Republic (Workie et al. 2009: 96, 101; Becker 2010: 522; Czekaj 2010: 206). The Hungarian story is somewhat different. The currency depreciation primarily had a highly negative effect on foreign exchange debtors and banks which clearly wiped out any positive effect on the manufacturing sector. Thus, a high degree of informal euroization massively circumscribed the policy options in the crisis. In line with the 2008 agreement with the IMF and the EU, the top priority of the then social liberal Hungarian government was the stabilization of the exchange rate. Its successor, the national conservative Fidesz government, which has aimed at nurturing the upper middle class, changed policies in regard to the banking sector. It has obliged the largely foreign-owned banks to bear at least part of the losses which have stemmed from the foreign exchange credits and has aimed at reducing the levels of domestic foreign exchange debt. This policy has resulted in partial conflict with the banks (Tóth, Neumann, and Hosszú 2012: 147ff.; Bohle 2013: 126f.). However, the Fidesz government has confined its conflicts with foreign companies to banks and some other service sectors. Its anti-labour policies have clearly favoured the largely foreign-owned export industries (Becker 2012).

Economic recovery has hinged to a considerable extent on the recovery of Western European, primarily German, export industries. Local observers have become much more aware of the implications of this one-sided dependence. The Slovakian financial journalists Marcela Šimková and Marek Poracký (2013: 3) conclude: 'Our fate is not only in our own hands. We suffered from a fall jointly with the Germans. And later, we started to slowly grow jointly with them again.' In Slovakia, a debate on the drawbacks of the (over-) reliance on car exports has at least begun. Baláž (2013: 576) warns that Slovakia might repeat the experience of Spain and Portugal, where manufacturing FDI, which had been attracted by relatively low wages and was accompanied by little R&D activities, was later relocated to Central and Eastern Europe when wages seemed to be more attractive there. In Poland, economists like Czekaj (2010: 206) or Żuber (2012: 286) acknowledged that the relatively high importance of the domestic market had an attenuating effect during the crisis. These new accents have not (yet) translated into economic policy changes. Sustaining domestic demand has not proved to be a strategic element of Polish anti-crisis policies. While the liberal Polish government initially continued public investments and accepted relatively high budget deficits (Osiatyńsky 2010: 224), it switched to austerity after winning key elections. As a result, Polish growth substantially slowed down. In the Czech Republic, the austerity policies of the right wing Nečas government even produced a return of the recession. In Slovenia and Hungary, the private debt problems have severely dampened the economic performance until today. Thus, the growth performance is not only dependent on exports, even in strongly export-oriented countries.

In the Baltic and south-eastern European countries, the pre-crisis growth-model was based on dependent financialization in a much more one-sided way. Western European industrial companies have relocated production to these countries in a much more limited way. At the end of the state socialist period, their industrial production structures used to be weaker than in the Visegrád countries. Wars (and partially sanctions) had a devastating effect on manufacturing in most successor states of Yugoslavia. The governments of the Baltic republics consciously aimed at reducing the links to the Russian economy, which had negative consequences for industry. Industrial development was not an economic policy priority in the 1990s. The Baltic countries, particularly Latvia and Estonia, have had an anti-industrial policy bias. In south-eastern Europe, the governments have not devised active or at least supportive policies for the domestic industries that had survived the 1990s (Uvalic 2010; Bohle and Greskovits 2012: 207ff.; Mihaljević 2013: 66ff.). Although the south-eastern European states have tried to attract industrial FDI, these attempts have had, at best, limited success. As far as Western European companies have invested in manufacturing at all, it has been primarily in low wage and low skill sectors (Bohle and Greskovits 2012: 207). In the Baltic States, particularly in Latvia and Estonia, the raw material based subsector of wood products increased considerably in importance. This signals even a re-primarization of the productive structure. Complex manufacturing output has been particularly low in the Baltic countries. It declined from on average 1989–1998 to 1999–2007. The figures for Bulgaria, Croatia, and Romania are better, but display a decline of complex manufacturing output between the two time periods. In line with the industrial profile, R&D expenditures are very low. With the exception of Estonia, their share in GDP was below 1 per cent in the Baltic Countries, Bulgaria, and Romania in 2011. In Romania, they reached just 0.5 per cent (Eurostat 2013). Thus, the pre-crisis (pseudo) boom growth patterns have produced even a further qualitative decline of manufacturing.

High capital inflows and exploding domestic (foreign exchange) debts have been the main driving force of growth in the pre-crisis years. Private household debt increased more rapidly in south-eastern European and Baltic states than in the Visegrád countries during the pre-crisis years. In the Baltic countries, Bulgaria, and Romania, the relationship of domestic credit to the private sector as percentage of GDP more or less doubled between 2003 and 2006. In Estonia and Latvia, the credits reached almost 80 per cent of the GDP in 2006 (Frangakis 2009: 64). In the three Baltic countries, credits outstrip deposits by far whereas the imbalance was not stark in most south-eastern European countries (Myant and Drahokoupil 2011: 263). The higher the imbalance of credits and deposits was, the more dependent was the credit expansion on external financing. This implied an exchange rate risk. The banks were eager to shift this risk to their credit customers which were offered lower interest rates for foreign exchange loans than for credits in domestic currencies. In most countries in this group, domestic credits were predominantly denominated in foreign currency. Again, Baltic countries were the most extreme case, with foreign exchange credits accounting for 85.3 per cent of total credits in Estonia and 89.3 per cent in Latvia in 2008 (Myant and Drahokoupil 2011: 319). Given the considerable domestic foreign exchange debts, the governments were intent to keep the (nominal) exchange rate at least stable. Countries like Estonia, Lithuania, Bulgaria, and Bosnia and Herzegovina had already adopted currency boards in the 1990s, which do not leave any space for national monetary policies. Latvia and Croatia had very rigid exchange rate regimes while Romania and Serbia fixed high interest rates in order to keep inflation low and capital inflows high (Becker 2007: 244ff.). These policies had a very detrimental effect on trade balances and current accounts. The current account deficits usually surpassed 10 per cent of the GDP in pre-crisis years. In Bulgaria and Latvia, the current account deficit even surpassed 20 per cent and in Montenegro 30 per cent of the GDP (Becker 2011: 272; Myant and Drohokoupil 2011). The current account deficits were predominantly financed by external debt which tended to grow very rapidly in the pre-crisis years.

Due to the extreme reliance of the pre-crisis growth model on huge capital inflows, the Baltic and south-eastern European countries were primarily affected by the global crisis through the financial channel. High current account deficits and high proportions of domestic foreign exchange debt rendered them particularly vulnerable to sudden reductions of capital inflows or even a reversion of capital flows. In countries with a flexible exchange rate, the currencies depreciated sharply in late 2008 which put enormous pressure on foreign exchange debtors and banks. The other countries faced severe problems in maintaining their fixed exchange rate regimes (Becker 2010: 525ff., 2011: 273; Kulikova 2011: 24ff.; Myant and Drahokoupil 2011: 317ff.). Plummeting exports exacerbated these problems. It was the Baltic countries and small successor states of Yugoslavia in particular that faced particularly massive declines of exports in 2009 (Kulikova 2011: 14).

In order to preserve the prevailing exchange rates, the governments adopted strongly pro-cyclical austerity policies—partly as part of IMF/EU programmes, partly without direct recourse to the IMF (Becker 2010: 532ff.; Drezgić 2010: 215ff.; Živković 2012). Exchange rate stabilization has been both in the interest of the foreign owned banks and the domestic indebted middle classes. Core elements of the pro-cyclical policies were expenditure cuts (particularly social expenditure), cuts of wages in the public sector, and pensions. Latvia and Romania are the most extreme examples of these cuts. On the revenue side, it was primarily indirect taxes that were increased. The austerity measures mainly aimed to reduce the domestic demand, and hence imports. A reduction of the current account deficit was perceived as a key condition for stabilizing the exchange rate. In some countries, specific support measures for ailing banks have been part of the policy packages as well. Such support was promised to banks in exchange for continued bank lending as part of the so-called Vienna Initiative which brought the EU, European Bank for Reconstruction and Development (EBRD), European Investment Bank (EIB), IMF, World Bank, and key banks of the region (like Unicredit or Austria's Raiffeisen International) together. The foreign owned banks did not fully comply with their 2009 lending commitments and even achieved some regulatory attenuation in later negotiations (Toporowski 2012: 3). In contrast to the support for banking, measures for supporting productive sectors, such as manufacturing, have generally been completely absent. Thus, the weaknesses of the productive sphere have not been tackled at all.

The austerity policies have deepened the recessive tendencies. In the early phase of the crisis, recession was strongest in the Baltic countries, where the GDP in Latvia declined by 18.0 per cent, followed closely by Lithuania with 14.7 per cent and Estonia with 13.9 per cent (Astrov, Holzner, and Leitner 2011: 363). The strong fall of the GDP made the current account deficit plummet. Temporarily, the Baltic countries even achieved a slight surplus of the current account (Astrov, Holzner, and Leitner 2011: 370). The debt situation, however, deteriorated (Becker 2013a). In 2010, or 2011 in the case of Latvia, a recovery began. This recovery, however, rested on shaky foundations. In Latvia and Lithuania in particular, recovery is linked in some extent to credit financed consumption. This time, the capital flows to Latvia have taken the form of deposits of foreigners, particularly Russians (Becker 2013b).

Recovery made the current accounts deteriorate again. This shows the fragility of the growth model. This fragility is not cured by the flight into the Eurozone—Estonia joined in 2011, and Latvia will do so at the beginning of 2014. The relatively high inflation rate in Estonia—2011 almost the double of the Eurozone average (Holzner and Astrov 2013: 416)—will not help with Estonia's chronic current account problems.

In south-eastern European countries, the recession in 2009 was not as deep as in the Baltic countries, but recession or at least stagnation have proved to last longer (Becker 2013a). Current account deficits have been reduced through the depression of domestic demand. Recession has aggravated debt problems. The share of nonperforming credits is particularly high in Romania (29.9 per cent at the end of 2012; Szigetvari 2013: 25). While domestic demand continues to be depressed, the outlook of exports is hardly brighter in south-eastern European countries. They used to export a lot to southern Europe (particularly Italy) where import demand is depressed due to austerity. In some south-eastern European countries, exports declined even nominally in 2012 (Holzner and Astrov 2013: 417). Both Baltic and south-eastern European countries seem to be in a developmental cul-de-sac.

4.4 From Transformation and Transition to European Integration: Manufacturing Industry in Eastern and South Eastern European Countries

Transformation and transition did considerable harm to the industrial production ability of the Eastern and south-eastern European countries. Modality and speed of privatization has heavily contributed to the production crisis in these countries. Compared to 1989, industrial production was significantly downsized until 1993, particularly in South East Europe and the Baltic countries (Table 4.1). Individual industrial sectors were hit even harder like total industrial production, for example steel production in Bulgaria, the Czech part of Czechoslovakia, Hungary, Poland, and Romania (Berend 2011: 75). In the former Yugoslavia as a whole, the situation was more dramatic due to a crisis stricken decade in the 1980s under pressure of IMF enforced austerity programmes as a prelude to violent disintegration (Weissenbacher 2005).

Industrial production started to increase again from 1994 onwards. However, by 2008 only the Visegrád countries as well as Slovenia and Estonia reached an industrial output which was higher than in 1989. The crisis period 2009–2012 had distinct effects on the countries of the region with Slovenia and Croatia losing the highest amount of industrial output. From Table 4.1 it can also be seen that the manufacturing industry lost a high fraction of its

Table 4.1. Industrial Production and Manufacturing

	Total real industrial production, index (1989=100)				Share of the manufacturing sector in total gross value added, %				
	1993	2000	2008	2012	1990	1995	2000	2008	2012
Czech Republic	66.5	80.6	123.5	121.7	26.2	23.1	25.9	24.3	24.7
Slovakia	67.5	87.9	179.3	186.2	22.5[2]	25.0	23.8	22.4	21.7
Hungary	70.3	134.2	209.1	197.5	21.5[1]	21.3	22.9	21.6	22.7
Poland	76.3	130.2	213.2	246.1	28.0[2]	20.2	17.2	17.7	17.3
Slovenia	66.2	80.2	108.0	95.9	33.0	25.0	24.4	21.4	20.8
Croatia	50.9	56.8	77.8	65.0	–	22.0	19.9	15.8	16.8
Bulgaria	48.9	44.1	75.2	66.2	–	15.6	14.0	15.4	16.7
Romania	46.9	57.6	72.8	79.9	39.0	25.2	22.0	22.0	24.7[3]
Estonia	48.6	65.2	116.0	130.5	36.3[1]	19.9	17.0	15.7	15.4
Latvia	44.6	44.1	67.2	73.1	32.1[1]	20.4	14.4	10.8	14.5
Lithuania	45.7	38.4	70.1	70.8	44.4[1]	18.6	18.8	17.5	20.8

Source: wiiw Handbook of Statistics (wiiw 2013); United Nations Economic Commission for Europe (UNECE 1999); Croatian Bureau of Statistics (CBS 2014).
Notes: Index of industrial production based on real growth rates of gross industrial production from wiiw Handbook of Statistics (HBS NACE Rev 1 until 1999, NACE (Nomenclature statistique des activités économiques dans la Communauté européenne) Rev 2 from 2000); real growth rates of industry for Estonia and Lithuania for 1990 from United Nations Economic Commission for Europe (UNECE 1999); manufacturing-data for Croatia from Croatian Bureau of Statistics (CBS 2014).
[1] 1991, [2] 1992, [3] 2011.

share in total gross value added in most of the countries. Only in the Czech Republic, Slovakia, and Hungary it remained more or less stable.

Along with production, employment in the manufacturing sector decreased significantly from the early 1990s to the early 2000s (Table 4.2). The decline was most heavily pronounced in Romania and the Baltic countries. Downsizing of manufacturing employment was slightly reversed in many countries until 2008, but with the outbreak of the financial and economic crisis at the end of 2008, manufacturing—employment has been reduced again. The share of manufacturing employment in total employment more or less reflects the trend of manufacturing gross value added.

Within this scenario of obvious decline in industrial production, the structure of manufacturing changed during the years after transformation and transition. Tables 4.3.a and 4.3.b provide insight into the structure of gross value added of the manufacturing sector for 1995 and 2012 (for some countries the first available year is 2000 instead of 1995). For all countries mentioned, *food products, beverages, and tobacco* had the highest share in manufacturing gross value added in 1995. Most of the countries showed a significant decline during nearly two decades of integration into a Western European integration model which has always been designated to subsidize its own agro-industries. The decline was most pronounced in the Baltic countries where this sector was the largest in 1995. In the Visegrád countries and Slovenia, where the initial share of this sector was much lower than in the

Table 4.2. Employment in the Manufacturing Sector

	Employment manufacturing, index (1996=100)				Share of the manufacturing sector in total employment, %				
	1990	2000	2008	2012	1990	1995	2000	2008	2012
Czech Republic	142.7	93.2	97.9	89.7	–	26.2	27.0	26.4	24.8
Slovakia	130.2[1]	87.6	95.1	84.3	–	26.2	24.5	23.9	21.6
Hungary	131.2[2]	110.2	100.2	93.9	–	22.0	23.0	21.3	20.2
Poland	98.7[2]	88.3	106.4	98.9	–	21.1	18.2	20.4	18.6
Slovenia	138.6	94.9	87.8	73.1	40.3	30.9	27.2	23.0	20.4
Croatia	–	97.5	99.1	82.0	–	20.7[3]	20.0	19.3	17.4
Bulgaria	–	75.9	84.1	67.1	–	–	20.1	18.9	17.6
Romania	158.3	81.5	77.5	66.6[4]	–	21.2	18.6	20.3	18.0
Estonia	143.1	86.1	90.2	77.6	27.2[1]	24.8	22.2	20.7	19.0
Latvia	204.0	87.6	85.9	76.2	25.5[1]	20.4	17.0	14.2	13.9
Lithuania	172.9	91.3	98.2	75.6	26.8[1]	19.7	18.1	17.1	15.7

Source: wiiw *Handbook of Statistics* (wiiw 2013); wiiw Industrial Database (wiiw 2010); Eurostat 2014.
Notes: For Czech Republic, Hungary, and Slovakia, the index is based on data from wiiw industrial database (ID, NACE Rev 1) until 1995 and from wiiw *Handbook of Statistics* (HBS, NACE Rev 2) from 1996, data for manufacturing share from HBS NACE Rev 2 from 1995; for Estonia and Slovenia HBS NACE Rev 1 (until 1995) and HBS NACE Rev 2 (from 1996); for Latvia and Lithuania HBS NACE Rev 1 (until 2000) and HBS NACE Rev 2 (from 2001); for Croatia HBS NACE Rev 1 (until 2008) and HBS NACE Rev 2 (from 2009); for Bulgaria ID (until 2000 for index) and HBS NACE Rev 2 (from 2001 for index and from 2000 for share); for Poland ID (until 1995 for index), HBS NACE Rev 1 (from 1996 until 2004 for index and from 1995 until 2004 for share) and HBS NACE Rev 2 (from 2005); for Romania ID (until 1995 for index) and Eurostat NACE Rev 1 (for share in 1995) and Eurostat NACE Rev 2 (index and share from 1996).
[1] 1991, [2] 1992, [3] 1996, [4] 2011.

Baltic countries, the decrease was generally smaller. The south-eastern European countries retained more or less a stable food, beverages, and tobacco industry, with a share of more than 20 per cent.

Another sector which experienced a significant downsizing was the *textile industry*. This has been true for all countries except Romania and Bulgaria, although for the latter the first period shown is 2000 and thus does not reflect the initial transformation period. The share of the *chemical industry* in gross value added of the manufacturing sector shows also a decline for most of the countries during the period 1995–2012. Particularly the chemical industry of Slovakia was faced with a massive decrease.

Keeping in mind the overall negative development of manufacturing, some sectors kept or gained importance as share of manufacturing. For example, *fabricated metal products* (except machinery and equipment) increased its importance in most of the countries although to a different extent. *Electrical equipment* is another sector which in most cases shows an increasing importance. The sector of *Machinery and equipment* is also gaining ground.

The Baltic countries seem to have used a natural resource for a niche sector. *Wood and products of wood and cork* as an industry increased its share in manufacturing industry in Estonia and to a lower extent in Lithuania. In Latvia, this sector remained on a high level in the period 2000–2012 (more than 20 per cent). Hungary in particular, but also Slovakia, experienced a

Table 4.3.a. Share of Individual Sectors in Gross Value Added of the Manufacturing Sector (in %), Visegrád Countries and Slovenia

Sector (NACE Rev 2)	Czech Republic		Slovakia		Hungary		Poland		Slovenia	
	1995	2012	1995	2012	1995	2012	2000	2011	1995	2012
Food, beverages, tobacco	14.7	9.9	13.0	7.8	18.5	9.7	19.0	16.6	11.5	7.1
Textiles, wearing apparel, leather	7.3	2.6	7.7	4.3	9.8	2.3	6.9	3.4	12.7	3.8
Products of wood and cork; articles of straw and plaiting material	3.7	2.6	3.2	4.4	2.8	1.1	4.2	3.7	4.0	3.5
Paper and paper products	3.2	1.6	4.6	2.6	2.1	1.7	3.0	2.9	2.7	2.5
Printing and reproduction of recorded media	1.3	1.6	2.5	1.1	2.2	1.3	3.0	2.0	4.0	2.2
Coke and refined petroleum products	2.5	0.4	8.2	1.2	9.7	6.3	3.3	5.0	0.4	0.0
Chemicals and chemical products	5.6	3.7	11.2	2.3	6.7	3.3	5.8	5.4	4.3	5.4
Basic pharmaceutical products and pharmaceutical prep.	2.4	1.6	2.3	1.2	4.5	7.1	1.1	1.6	6.3	10.7
Rubber and plastic products	1.9	8.1	4.2	6.7	3.8	6.5	5.6	7.1	5.1	6.6
Other non-metallic mineral products	7.3	4.8	5.2	4.3	5.2	3.0	8.2	6.4	4.9	3.7
Basic metals	11.0	3.7	8.5	5.5	3.5	2.2	3.8	3.0	3.6	4.2
Fabricated metal products, except machinery and equipment	9.8	11.5	6.7	13.9	7.3	6.9	7.5	11.2	10.3	14.0
Computer, electronic, and optical products	1.9	2.8	2.0	4.7	3.8	8.2	2.5	2.4	4.3	3.2
Electrical equipment	3.7	7.4	2.4	4.2	4.4	4.2*	4.2	4.1	7.5	9.7
Machinery and equipment n.e.c.	9.0	9.6	7.1	7.0	5.5	14.9*	5.3	5.4	3.9	6.8
Motor vehicles, trailers, and semi-trailers	5.4	18.0	2.4	20.3	5.7	15.2	4.1	8.2	4.6	8.4
Other transport equipment	1.2	2.0	1.3	0.9	0.3	0.7	2.3	2.1	0.4	0.4
Furniture; other manufacturing	4.7	3.6	3.1	3.3	3.0	3.1	5.1	5.5	6.5	3.7
Repair and installation of machinery and equipment	3.5	4.5	4.4	4.4	1.3	2.3	5.2	4.0	3.0	4.1

Source: Eurostat 2014.
Notes: * The high increase of the share of the sector machinery and equipment n.e.c from 5.5% in 1995 to 14.9% in 2012 may be partly the result of reclassifications between the NACE-sectors and should be viewed with some caution. The sector machinery and equipment n.e.c. increased its share slightly to 5.8% until 2008. By the end of 2009, the share increased to 13.3% while at the same time the share of the sector electrical equipment fell from 9.1% in 2008 to 4.2% in 2009. This may indicate a reclassification between these two sectors in the data for national accounts. However, data on industrial production from the Hungarian national statistical institution does not indicate a significant up- or downturn in sales values for the two sectors from 2008 to 2009.

Table 4.3.b. Share of Individual Sectors in Gross Value Added of the Manufacturing Sector (in %), South-Eastern European and Baltic Countries

Manufacturing sector (NACE Rev 2)	Croatia		Bulgaria		Romania		Estonia		Latvia		Lithuania	
	1995	2012	2000	2012	1995	2012	1995	2012	2000	2010	1995	2011
Food, beverages, tobacco	24.2	25.5	20.9	22.9	26.3	24.7	27.5	12.9	*	*	31.5	22.4
Textiles, wearing apparel, leather	11.5	5.7	14.7	13.6	11.7	11.5	15.4	6.3	*	5.8	18.0	7.8
Products of wood and cork; articles of straw and plaiting material	3.2	2.8	1.5	1.9	3.0	5.1	8.3	14.6	21.0	21.5	4.8	6.5
Paper and paper products	2.7	1.6	1.1	1.8	1.4	0.9	1.0	2.4	2.5	1.6	3.0	2.2
Printing and reproduction of recorded media	2.9	2.4	1.3	1.8	0.6	2.0	2.9	3.0	3.2	3.5	1.9	2.0
Coke and refined petroleum products	9.3	15.6	14.5	2.6	3.8	3.8	0.4	6.1	*	0.0	*	*
Chemicals and chemical products	5.0	3.0	7.1	4.4	5.9	1.9	7.6	4.9	*	3.7	7.1	11.3
Basic pharmaceutical products and pharmaceutical prep.	6.5	5.0	3.2	2.4	1.8	0.4	0.3	0.5	1.7	*	0.5	1.2
Rubber and plastic products	2.5	3.0	2.3	4.3	2.4	2.3	1.7	3.6	1.6	2.5	1.0	5.1
Other non-metallic mineral products	4.8	5.1	4.5	5.3	5.2	2.3	5.1	5.0	2.7	6.0	5.7	3.4
Basic metals	2.0	1.3	7.8	5.6	7.1	6.5	-0.1	0.3	5.1	3.7	0.6	0.6
Fabricated metal products, except machinery, and equipment	6.8	9.6	4.5	8.5	4.3	2.8	5.9	9.6	4.0	7.1	2.3	4.7
Computer, electronic, and optical products	2.3	2.8	1.9	2.4	4.5	4.0	2.0	5.8	1.4	1.7	3.6	2.2
Electrical equipment	3.9	3.6	2.2	3.7	2.9	5.3	3.0	6.0	1.6	1.6	2.2	1.4
Machinery and equipment n.e.c.	4.8	3.8	5.8	7.7	7.1	3.2	3.2	3.8	2.7	2.0	2.1	2.7
Motor vehicles, trailers, and semi-trailers	0.8	0.7	0.9	2.3	3.8	14.3	3.0	3.8	0.4	1.2	1.0	1.1
Other transport equipment	2.1	3.1	1.0	1.2	1.5	1.8	0.1	1.0	2.1	1.0	1.5	1.1
Furniture; other manufacturing	3.7	3.1	2.4	4.0	5.1	2.7	7.9	6.5	–	–	4.3	10.6
Repair and installation of machinery and equipment	1.2	2.2	2.5	3.7	1.7	4.5	4.9	3.9	–	–	3.3	2.7

Source: Eurostat 2014, Croatian Bureau of Statistics (CBS 2014) for Croatia.
Notes: * Eurostat does not provide data of gross value added for these sectors. Since gross value added of the total manufacturing sector is not equal to the sum of gross value added of those sectors for which data is available, the shares for Latvia or Lithuania does not sum up to 100%.

boost in the *computer, electronic, and optical products* sector, maybe indicating a kind of regional specialization.

The new kid on the block is certainly the car industry (*motor vehicles, trailers, and semi-trailers*). It is a well-known example for the integration of the region into Western European (but also Asian) industries' value chains. In 2012, this sector's share took 15.2 per cent of manufacturing gross value added in Hungary, 20.3 per cent in Slovakia, 18 per cent in the Czech Republic, 14.3 per cent in Romania, and more than 8 per cent in Poland and Slovenia. Let alone the dependency on international production networks and an already saturated market, productivity, and employment in relation to overall manufacturing industry display the two sides of the coin in this sector. According to data from the wiiw industrial database (2010), Slovakia seems to have shown the most extreme divergence in labour productivity in this sector, with a value of 365.1 per cent in relation to the total manufacturing sector in 2007. It is followed by Slovenia (266.3 per cent), Hungary (233.8 per cent), Poland (220.9 per cent), and Romania (188.0 per cent). In 2007, Slovakia's car industry employed 6.3 per cent of overall manufacturing workers, Slovenia's 4.5 per cent, Hungary's 8.1 per cent, Poland's 5.2 per cent, and Romania's 4.2 per cent. This shows that, though the car industry has a very high share in gross value added in these countries, its employment potential is significantly lower.

4.5 Conclusions

The Eastern European growth models and industrial trajectories have displayed a bifurcation for the last 15 years, mostly losing ground to the more industrially advanced European region which they had gained before. In the Visegrád countries, dependent financialization and industrial export industrialization have been the two pillars of the growth model. In the Baltic and south-eastern European countries, the pre-crisis growth model was extremely dependent on financial inflows and rapidly increasing domestic foreign exchange debts. An overvalued exchange rate was a central economic policy element of this growth model. While the exchange rate regime was well fitting for dependent financialization, it aggravated already existing industrial weaknesses. Indeed, the bifurcation replicates to some extent the divergence of earlier industrialization processes. In south-eastern Europe and the Baltic countries, industrialization tended to assume a relevant scope later than in the Visegrád countries. Transformation policies and political conflicts in the early 1990s had a significant impact on later economic trajectories. It was only Slovenia that followed early on relatively consistent pro-industrial policies. The Slovenian situation was particular as both industrial interests and trade unions were relatively strong and resulted in a neo-corporatist compromise with industrial underpinnings. The Baltic countries were the polar opposite of Slovenia in the early 1990s. The new politically nationalist governments made the reduction of the economic links with Russia one of their top priorities. They perceived rigid (and overvalued) exchange rates as a key element for establishing their national currencies. They introduced policies of financialization from the very beginning. Deindustrialization was particularly strong in the Baltic countries in the early 1990s. In the other countries, the character of the development model was not a subject of debate. Industries in the Visegrád countries coped better with the short-term orientation of economic policies than those in the South East of the continent where post-Yugoslav industries paid a heavy tribute to war.

When the Eastward expansion of Western European capital started in earnest in the late 1990s, and the EU accession talks facilitated interests of Western European corporations, industrial investors clearly favoured the Visegrád countries over the Baltic countries and most areas in south-eastern Europe. Industrial policies of the Visegrád countries have been primarily limited to compete for industrial FDI. Although more complex industrial patterns had emerged from FDI, production processes have often remained shallow, R&D has been almost nil and the export structures usually narrow (particularly in the small countries). The car industry is the key industry of several countries of this group. Since there are significant international overcapacities in this subsector and it hardly has a bright future given the ecological constraints, this particular specialization profile involves serious vulnerabilities. The early phase of the present crisis in 2008/2009 revealed serious external vulnerabilities of the export oriented model. In Hungary and Slovenia, these vulnerabilities were aggravated by particularly strong pre-crisis tendencies of dependent financialization. Although there are timid beginnings of a debate on the drawbacks of the narrow export model, its strategic orientation has not been questioned. The main thrust seems to rest on upgrading existing production chains (Baláž 2013: 579). Social and political forces which would strive for a more diversified, inward looking and ecologically sustainable industrial model have so far hardly emerged, although a few alternative proposals have been made that point towards such paths (Švihlíková 2011).

The Baltic and south-eastern European countries attracted either little industrial FDI, or foreign industrial investors preferred low wage and low skill industries. Rather inward looking industries hardly developed a strong lobby and were neglected. Exchange rate policies that favoured dependent financialization were not conducive to industrial recovery. The pre-crisis growth model produced very high current account deficits which made the economies structurally dependent on high capital inflows. High reliance on capital inflows, a high degree of informal *euroization*, and weak productive structures have led to particularly devastating effects of the present crisis. In the interest of (foreign owned) banks and domestic indebted middle strata, the governments made exchange rate stabilization their top priority. Extreme austerity policies aimed at reducing domestic demand and imports have been the main economic policy ingredient, either under IMF/EU guidance or in more home grown programmes. Domestic industries have suffered from depressed demand. The same is true for export industries, which relied heavily on demand from the crisis ridden Mediterranean countries. Productive capacities have not been strengthened. In the successor states to Yugoslavia, workers have locally reacted with (desperate) protests against the closing down of factories. Presently, the social and political forces that would favour reindustrialization seem to be weak. A realistic industrial strategy probably would have to be inward looking and would necessitate a strong push from the state (or, in the case of Serbia, a revitalized 'social' industrial sector). Such industries would require a sort of protection, at least through an appropriate exchange rate policy. Presently, exchange rate policies are constrained by the high degree of informal euroization, particularly in the form of foreign exchange debts. De-euroization would seem to be a decisive step in regaining room for manoeuvre towards more active exchange rate and industrial policies (Zdunić 2010: 201). A different set of policies would necessitate a change in the balance of forces.

References

Andor, L. 2000. 'Trends and Strategies in the East-West Integration in Europe'. *Kurswechsel*, 15(3): 24–32.

Andor, L. 2009. 'Hungary in the Financial Crisis: A (Basket) Case Study'. *Debatte, Journal of Contemporary Central and Eastern Europe*, 17(3): 285–96.

Astrov, V., Holzner, M., and Leitner, S. 2011. 'Stabilisierung des verhaltenen Aufschwungs in den MOEL'. *Wifo-Monatsberichte*, 84: 361–73.

Baláž, V. 2013. 'Od montažnej dielne do inteligentnej ekonomike'. In M. Bútora et al. (eds), *Odkial' a Kam. 20 rokov samostatnosti*. Bratislava: Kalligram/Inštitut pre verejné otázky, 566–81.

Baláž, V., Kluvánková-Oravska, T., and Zajac, Š. 2007. *Inštitúcie, a ekonomická transformácia*. Bratislava: VEDA.

Baláž, V. and Sabo, Š. 2011. 'Finančie toky vo výskume a vývoji v členských štatoch Európskej únie'. *Nová ekonomika*, 4(2/3): 5–19.

Barša, P. 1999. 'Národnostní konflikt a plurální identita'. In P. Barša and M. Strmiska (eds), *Národní stat a etnický konflikt*. Brno: CDK, 9–172.

Becker, J. 2007. 'Dollarisation in Latin America and Euroisation in Eastern Europe: Parallels and Differences'. In J. Becker and R. Weissenbacher (eds), *Dollarization, Euroization and Financial Instability: Central and East European Countries between Stagnation and Financial Crisis?* Marburg: Metropolis, 223–78.

Becker, J. 2010. 'Krisenmuster und Anti-Krisen-Politiken in Osteuropa'. *Wirtschaft und Gesellschaft*, 36(4): 519–42.

Becker, J. 2011. 'Wachstumsmodelle und Krisenmuster in Osteuropa'. *WSI-Mitteilungen*, 64(6): 270–7.

Becker, J. 2012. 'Neo-Liberalism's New Cloth: National Conservatism in Hungary and Turkey'. *Sendika.org*, 14 April. Available at: <www.sendika.org/english/yazi.php?yazi_no=44311> (last accessed 11 September 2013).

Becker, J. 2013a. 'Krise, Anti-Krisen-Politiken und soziale Proteste in Osteuropa'. *Z—Zeitschrift für marxistische Erneuerung*, 24(96): 114–36.

Becker, J. 2013b. 'Latvijski antimodel'. *Le Monde Diplomatique—Hrvatsko izdanje*, 1(2).

Becker, J. 2014. 'Finanzialisierung und globale Peripherie'. In M. Heires and A. Nölke (eds), *Politische Ökonomie der Finanzialisierung*. Wiesbaden: Springer VS, 181–96.

Becker, J., Jäger, J., Leubolt, B., and Weissenbacher, R. 2010. 'Peripheral Financialization and Vulnerability to Crisis: A Regulationist Perspective'. *Competition and Change* 14 (3–4): 225–47.

Berend, I. 1996. *Central and Eastern Europe, 1944–1993. Detour from the Periphery to the Periphery*. Cambridge, Melbourne, and New York: Cambridge University Press.

Berend, I. 2011. *From the Soviet Bloc to the European Union*. Cambridge: Cambridge University Press.

Berend, I. and Ránki, G. 1982. *The European Periphery and Industrialization 1780–1914*. Cambridge: Cambridge University Press.

Bohle, D. 2013. 'Europas andere Peripherie: Osteuropa in der Krise'. *Das Argument*, 55(1/2): 118–29.

Bohle, D. and Greskovits, B. 2012. *Capitalist Diversity on Europe's Periphery*. Ithaca, NY: Cornell University Press.

Bole, V., Prašnikar, J., and Trobec, D. 2011. 'Crisis and Contagion: Banks and the Real Sector'. In J. Prašnikar (ed.), *The Slovenian Economy: Stranded in Recovery*. Ljubljana: Časnik Finance, 51–73.

Chang, H. J. 2002. *Kicking Away the Ladder: Development Strategy in Historical Perspective*. London: Anthem Press.

Ćetković, P. 2011. 'Credit Growth and Instability in Balkan Countries: The Role of Foreign Banks'. Discussion Paper No. 27. London: Research on Money and Finance.

CBS. 2014. Data on National Accounts; Zagreb: Croatian Bureau of Statistics. Available at: <http://www.dzs.hr/default_e.htm> (last accessed 25 August 2014).

Czekaj, J. 2010. 'Wpływ światowego kryzysu gospodarczego na polską gospodarkę'. In G. W. Kołodko (ed.), *Globalizacja, kryzys i co dalej?* Warsaw: Poltext, 189–209.

Drahokoupil, J. 2007. 'From National Capitalisms to Foreign-Led Growth: The Moment in Central and Eastern Europe'. In J. Becker and R. Weissenbacher (eds), *Dollarization, Euroization and Financial Instability: Central and Eastern European Countries between Stagnation and Financial Crisis?* Marburg: Metropolis, 87–108.

Drahokoupil, J. 2009. *Globalization and the State in Central and Eastern Europe. The Politics of Foreign Direct Investment*. London and New York: Routledge.

Drezgić, S. 2010. 'Fiskalna politika tranzicijiskih zemlja u uvjetima rececesije'. In Radošević, D. (ed.), *Kriza i ekonomska politika. Politika i ekonomija razvoja Hrvatske*. Zagreb: Jesenski i Turk, 2015–224.

Družić, G. 2009. *Croatian Economic Development and the EU. Potential and Perspectives.* Zagreb: Croatian Academy of Sciences and Arts.

Eurostat. 2013. Europa 2020 Indicators. Available at: <http://epp.eurostat.ec.europa.eu/portal/page/portal/europe_2020_indicators/headline_indicators> (last accessed 14 November 2013).

Eurostat. 2014. Data on National Accounts. Available at: <http://ec.europa.eu/eurostat/data/database> (last accessed 25 August 2014).

Feldman, M. 2006. 'The Baltic States: Pacesetting on EMU. Accession and the Consolidation of Domestic Stability Culture'. In K. Dyson (ed.), *Enlarging the Euro Area: External Empowering and Domestic Transformation in Central Eastern Europe.* Oxford: Oxford University Press, 127–44.

Feldman, M. 2008. 'Baltic States: When Stability Culture Is Not Enough'. In K. Dyson (ed.), *The Euro at 10: Europeanization, Power and Convergence.* Oxford: Oxford University Press, 243–57.

Frangakis, M. 2009. 'Europe's Financial System Under Pressure.' In J. Grahl (ed.), *Global Finance and Social Europe.* Cheltenham: Edward Elgar, 53–90.

Holzner, M. and Astrov, V. 2013. 'Mittel-, Ost- und Südosteuropa von der EU-Krise voll erfasst'. *Wifo-Monatsberichte*, 86(5): 415–23.

Hunya, G. 2012. wiiw Database on Foreign Direct Investment in Central, East and Southeast Europe 2012. Short-lived Recovery. Vienna.

Kulikova, N. 2011. 'Ekonomika w tiskach krizisa'. In N. Kulikova (ed.), *Central'naja i Vostočnaja Evropa: Uroki mirovogo krizisa.* St Petersburg: Aleteia, 10–42.

Kulikova, N. 2012. 'European Integration and Experience in Catching-Up Development of CEE Countries—New EU Members: Lessons for Emerging Markets'. In M. Antevski and D. Mitrović (eds), *Western Balkans: From Stabilisation to Integration.* Belgrade: Institute of International Politics and Economics, 9–30.

Kulikova, N. and Lobanov, M. 2011. 'The Role of FDI in the Economic Modernization of Central and Eastern European EU Member States: View from Russia'. In M. Antevski (ed.), *Development Potentials of Foreign Direct Investment: International Experiences.* Belgrade: Institute of International Politics and Economics, 51–70.

Mencinger, J. 2012. 'Slovenija med slonom socializma in krizo kapitalizma'. In J. Prunk and T. Deželan (eds), *Dvajset let slovenske države.* Maribor: Aristej, Ljubljana: FDV, 57–80.

Mihaljević, D. 2013. 'The Deindustrialisation Process of the Croatian Economy'. *Kurswechsel*, 3: 63–73.

Myant, M. and Drahokoupil, J. 2011. *Transition Economies: Political Economy in Russia, Eastern Europe, and Central Asia.* Hoboken, NJ: Wiley.

Osiatyński, J. 2010. 'Strategia makroekonomiczna Polski w warunkach światowego kryzysu i jej wyzwania na progu 2011 roku'. In G. W. Kołodko (ed.), *Globalizacja, kryzys i co dalej?* Warsaw: Poltext, 210–29.

Pasti, V. 2006. *Noul capitalism românesc.* Iaşi: Polirom.

Pomeranz, K. 2000. *The Great Divergence. China, Europe, and the Making of the Modern World Economy.* Princeton: Princeton University Press.

Samary, C. 2008. *Yougoslavie de la décomposition aux enjeux européens*, Paris: Éd. du Cygne.

Šimková, M. and Poracký, M. 2013. 'Slovensko ťahá európsky ekonomický gigant'. *Hospodárske noviny*, 20 September.

Štiblar, F. 2010. *Bančistvo kot hrbtenica samostojne Slovenije*. Ljubljana: Založba ZRC.

Švihlíková, I. 2011. 'Systémové alternativy kapitalismu. Analýza současné krize: základní načrt nového systému'. In P. Dinuš and L. Hohoš (eds), *Svet v bode obratu. Systémové alternativy kapitalizmu. Koncepcie, stratégie, utópie*. Bratislava: VEDA, 42–56.

Szigetvari, A. 2013. 'Die Wildwest-Manier der Banken im Osten'. *Der Standard* 6 November.

Tiits, M., Kattel, R., Kalvet, T., and Tamm, D. 2008. 'Catching Up, Forging Ahead or Falling Behind? Central and Eastern European development 1990–2005'. *Innovation: The European Journal of Social Science Research*, 21(1): 65–85.

Toporowski, J. 2012. 'Vienna Initiative: Regulatory Capture and Policy Confusion.' *Bankwatch Mail*, 52 (May): 3.

Tóth, A., Neumann, L., and Hosszú, H. 2012. 'Hungary's Full-Blown Malaise'. In S. Lehndorff (ed.), *A Triumph of Failed Ideas. European Models of Capitalism in Crisis*. Brussels: ETUI, 137–53.

UNECE. 1999. *Economic Survey of Europe*, Statistical Appendix. Geneva: United Nations Economic Commission for Europe.

Uvalic, M. 2010. *Serbia's Transition: Towards a Better Future*. Basingstoke: Palgrave Macmillan.

Vachudova, M. A. 2005. *Europe Undivided. Democracy, Leverage and Integration*. Oxford: Oxford University Press.

Weissenbacher, R. 2005. *Jugoslawien. Politische Ökonomie einer Desintegration*, Vienna: Promedia.

Weissenbacher, R. 2007. 'Historical Considerations of Uneven Development in East Central Europe'. In J. Becker and R. Weissenbacher (eds), *Dollarization, Euroization and Financial Instability. Central and Eastern European Countries between Stagnation and Financial Crisis?* Marburg: Metropolis, 35–83.

wiiw. 2007. *wiiw Handbook of Statistics 2007*. Vienna: Vienna Institute for International Economic Studies.

wiiw. 2010. *wiiw Industrial Database 2010*. Vienna: Vienna Institute for International Economic Studies.

wiiw. 2013. *wiiw Handbook of Statistics 2013*. Vienna: Vienna Institute for International Economic Studies.

Workie, Menbere T. et al. 2009. *Vývoj a perspektívy svetovej ekonomiky. Globálna finančná a hospodárska kríza. Príčiny – náklady – východiská*. Bratislava: Ekonomický ústav SAV.

Zdunić, S. 2010. 'Posebnosti hrvatske monetarne politike'. In D. Radošević (ed.), *Kriza i ekonomska politika. Politika i ekonomija razvoja*. Zagreb: Jesenik i Turk, 183–203.

Žitko, M. 2011. 'Tranzicija financijskog sektora u Hrvatskoj i Sloveniji'. In A. Veselinovic, P. Atanckovic, and K. Žjelko (eds), *Izgubljeno u tranziciji. Kritička analiza procesa društvene transformacije*. Belgrade: Rosa Luxemburg Stiftung, 103–15.

Živković, A. 2012. 'Povratak o budućnosti—tranzicija o Balkanu'. In M. Jadžić, D. Maljković, and A. Veselinović (eds), *Kriza, odgovori, levica. Prilozi za kritički diskurs*. Belgrade: Rosa Luxemburg Stiftung, 188–219.

Żuber, P. 2012. 'The Need for Change—National and Regional Consequences of the Crisis in Poland 2008–2010'. In G. Gorzelak, C. C. Goh, and K. Fazekas (eds), *Adaptability and Change: The Regional Dimensions in Central and Eastern Europe*. Warsaw: Scholar/Euroreg, 284–98.

5

Financialization of Global Value Chains and Implications for Local Development

Nicolas Balas and Florence Palpacuer

5.1 Introduction

The fieldwork research reported in this chapter takes as a starting point the breakdown of the Crolles 2 Alliance (C2A),[1] an inter-organizational arrangement contracted between three lead chip manufacturers of the global microelectronics industry—STMicroelectronics, NXP (formerly Philips Semiconductors), and Freescale (formerly Motorola Semiconductors)— over the period 2002–2007, and localized in the south-east of France (Grenoble area).

The development of R&D activities in microelectronics in Grenoble rests on the exemplary nature of the local industrial base in terms of economic, technological, as well as scientific development (De Bernardy 1999; Druilhe and Garnsey 2000; Lawton Smith 2003). Coined the French Silicon Valley, the Grenoble cluster counted more than 160 companies and a workforce of more than 20,000 individuals in 2009 in the microelectronics industry. In line with the idealized image of local development provided by Porterian *'clusters'* (Porter 1998), it reproduces locally the various segments of the microelectronics value chain: vertically integrated firms

---

[1] The name comes from the small city of Crolles, near Grenoble, the R&D facility and the manufacturing pilot line of the c2a were dedicated to the production of advanced silicon chips.

that design, manufacture, and market silicon chips; firms specialized in the design of subcomponents; suppliers of design and manufacturing tools, public research centres as well as suppliers of materials and associated services. The organizational arrangements driving the social fabric of the cluster draw on an old tradition of cooperation between the scientific, industrial, and political communities dating back to the early 1960s. Since the C2A agreement in 2002, which represented at that time the largest industrial investment in France for the last ten years, the Grenoble area became one of the main flagships of the French cluster policy. Although the consortium between the three partners was based on a five-year agreement, the size of the initial investment—approximately three and a half billion euros—as well as the fact that only three other similar sites existed worldwide,[2] suggested that the C2A might have been the beginning of a more ambitious and longer-term programme of technological development between the three partners. However, in December 2006, NXP's chief executive officer (CEO) announced the withdrawal of its company from Crolles, scheduled for the end of the following year, imitated by its *Freescale* counterpart one month later. Such a decision significantly challenged the model that had served for developing the cluster since the early 1990s, in which the *'upgrading'* of the local industrial base in general (Humphrey and Schmitz 2002), and STMicroelectronics in particular, should provide the backbone of the whole local economy. Such a challenge put into question the rather determinist approaches of innovation embedded both in cluster theory and in its ramifications under the industrial upgrading paradigm of global value chain analysis (GVCs). The first section of the chapter will thus provide a critical stance on the determinist readings of the local innovation systems and global innovation networks literatures, when dealing with the topic of territorial embeddedness of innovation (Section 5.2). After having presented the grounded theory methodology adopted to complete our fieldwork research (Section 5.3), we will explore empirically the various options envisioned for this microelectronics cluster by local or global actors (Section 5.4), as well as the political compromise developed as a solution to this crisis (Section 5.5). The final section of the chapter will discuss the potential political lessons to be derived from such analysis (Section 5.6).

---

[2] Moreover, the C2A R&D and manufacturing facilities have been unveiled by the French President Jacques Chirac on 27 February 2003, arguing that the Grenoble area reached at that time an international stature.

5.2 From Clusters to Global Value Chains: Questioning the Territorial Embeddedness of Innovation

Academic scholars of innovation share the assumption that by expanding the competitive landscape, globalization reinforces the need for continuous innovation in order for both firms and places to reach or maintain competitive advantage. We will first review the main theoretical contributions along such lines, pertaining to the *local innovation systems* and *global innovation networks* literatures. We will then infer from their shortcomings the necessity to refine our understanding of the ways in which the process of globalization operates in the empirical context of innovation, by introducing a more political reading of such process in order to account for the influence of the recent phenomena of financialization.

5.2.1 *Innovation as the Offshoot of Local Innovation Systems*

For the local innovation systems literature, the very features of innovation processes explain their strong spatial embeddedness. The mastery of complex, intangible, and high value added research and development (R&D) activities entails that innovative labour is strongly localized by nature (Porter 1998). Econometric studies have emphasized the importance of such a geographic concentration of high-tech firms (Moreno, Paci, and Usai 2005), and opened the way to the diffusion of territorialized views of innovation. According to these approaches, technology constrains the internationalization of R&D because of its knowledge dependent nature, and physical proximity is considered as a facilitator for the creation, diffusion, and exchange of complex knowledge (Malmberg and Maskell 2002). When activities involved in a given industrial project are co-localized in a cluster, local actors come to share a common set of knowledge, values and standards. The relational embeddedness of actors consequently renders the creation and circulation of tacit knowledge easier inside a local network than beyond its frontiers (Uzzi 1997; Ferrary and Granovetter 2009). In recent years, the basic principles coming from the local innovation systems literature have been widely adopted by policymakers trying to '*jockey for position*' in a context of competition between places (Malecki 2004). Innovation has been seen as the only way to differentiate vis-à-vis other regions and thus, a mean to transform the local into a '*sticky*' place for firms (Markusen 1996). The expansion of cluster-based policies all around the world, since the popularization of the concept of '*cluster*' by management guru Michael Porter, embodies this turn towards localized innovation as a way of thinking local adaptations to globalization (Martin and Sunley 2003). Recent critics have pointed out the over territorialized view of these approaches. Their arguments are twofold. First, the success of the

Porterian cluster tends to naturalize knowledge creation as an intrinsically local matter, whereas a growing stream of literature tends, on the contrary, to show that limits to knowledge circulation can be overcome by knowledge codification and the emergence of global epistemic communities unconstrained by co-localization imperatives (Breschi and Lissoni 2001). Second, critics point out that by focusing on relationships of knowledge creation between organizations in a delimited spatial arena, the local innovation system literature has failed to account for the fact that local inter-firm networks could be embedded within a broader, extra-local organizational field, and that such 'vertical' power relations could influence the spatial organization of innovation (Bair and Peters 2006; Bair 2008). We will see in section 5.2.2 how a recent literature has attempted to go beyond these shortcomings by capturing the global scope of innovation processes.

5.2.2 The Global Innovation Networks Literature

More recently, a critical literature on the spatial embeddedness of innovation has emerged, underlining the limits of co-localization for innovative activities and highlighting the existence of organizational forms by which firms could recreate at a distance the advantages of proximity (Coe and Bunnel 2003). These approaches built on conceptual advances attributable to empirical studies on global commodity chains (Bair 2009), global value chains (Gereffi, Humphrey, and Sturgeon 2005), and global production networks (Ernst and Kim 2002; Henderson et al. 2002). Drawing on the concept of 'modularization', this stream of literature showed how the increasingly complex nature of technological innovation offered enhanced possibilities to divide and vertically disintegrate innovative labour (Arora, Gambardella, and Rullani 1997; Lüthje and Ernst 2006). Coordination between different steps of the innovation process could become formalized around technical standards limiting the need for rich information exchanges between loosely coupled organizations, and making it possible for firms to disintegrate and disperse their value chain beyond geographical borders (Ernst 2005b). However, the globalization of innovation embodies more than mere technical advances enabled by modularity. It is, according to this literature, an institutionalized process in the sense that the formation of global innovation networks is supported by strong market- and standard-building institutions—'industry-level codification schemes' (Sturgeon 2009: 132), 'epistemic communities' (Hakanson 2005), 'Trade Related Aspects of Intellectual Property Rights agreement'[3]—that are largely autonomous vis-à-vis traditional political institutions such as states, national

---

[3] Cf. World Trade Organization (1995), Agreement on Trade-Related Aspects of Intellectual Property Rights, Annex 1C of the Marrakesh Agreement Establishing the World Trade

research agencies, and regional governments (Hamilton and Gereffi 2009). However, recent research contributions have argued that physical proximity still proved necessary at particular stages of the innovation process (Ernst 2005a; Sturgeon 2007). Thus, although this stream of research has conceptualized the ways in which firms could modularize and organize innovative labour on a global scale, as well as the global institutions and governance patterns making it possible, it says little about what is going to be globalized and what should remain localized in global value chains. In other words, modularity seems to provide a strong incentive to outsource and geographically disperse innovative labour, but it does not explain situations in which existing technical and modular capabilities are not submitted to such choice. This important aspect of the spatial dynamics of innovation still remains unexplained.

5.2.3 How Does Innovation Go Global?

The concept of *'industrial upgrading'*, as coined by Humphrey and Schmitz (2002), offered an attempt to take into account the interplay between local clusters and global networks. These authors have highlighted the role of governance patterns of the GVC[4]—ranging from *'market'* to *'hierarchy'*—in offering opportunities for local firms and clusters to upgrade their organizational skills, products, and functional position within the chain. The authors conclude to the necessity for local firms of adapting their strategies and innovation practices to the dominant modes of governance of the GVC they are embedded in, even if such governance patterns might endanger the local industrial base because of asymmetrical power relations. In line with the idea of *'institutional isomorphism'* (DiMaggio and Powell 1983: 147), they depict and promote a growing convergence between organizational forms at the global scale. They prompt organizations to conform to emergent norms emanating from the lead firms of the value chain, or industry level standards (Sturgeon 2009). Local organizations—firms and regions—are framed in a rather determinist environment where they could only act to enhance their competitive position within the iron cage of a given hierarchy (Sassen 1999). The same line of argument can be found in Gereffi, Humphrey, and Sturgeon (2005: 83–4), when they maintain that the superiority of the *'modular'* governance pattern, in terms of economic performance for the whole chain and

Organization. Available at: <https://www.wto.org/english/tratop_e/trips_e/t_agm0_e.htm> (last accessed 10 September 2015).

[4] Governance in GVC analysis underlines the particular modes of coordination—regimes of control, value capture, and distribution—between a(n) (extra-local) lead firm and its (local) network affiliates (Bair 2009). In the seminal work of Gereffi (1994) on global commodity chains, governance patterns were ranging from *'producer-driven'* to *'buyer-driven'* chains.

local economic development, should lead local organizations to transform their socially embedded and locally grounded innovation practices into codified and distance based (i.e., dis-embedded) economic exchanges. By taking for granted both globalization and the necessity to study its functioning at both local and global scales, the *industrial upgrading* paradigm, and the *local innovation systems* literature as well, have not well deciphered the processes by which this phenomenon, and the related reconfiguration of the locus of innovation, were actually enacted in local industrial practices. For instance, by demonstrating that major forces and determinants of production were global, they left aside and unaccounted for the critical role played by a larger set of stakeholders embedded at the local and national scales (Spicer 2006).

One of the most important deficiencies of a classical reading of globalization was thus its lack of consideration of the role of relatively fixed and immobile territorial organizations (Brenner 1999). As shown by several authors including Patel and Pavitt (1991), and Fligstein and Freeland (1995), firms could continue to concentrate innovation in their home country's national innovation system for several reasons including (i) states' political strategies to protect national technological sovereignty, employment, or local economic development; (ii)dependency to governments' subsidies and tax credits; and (iii) the still strongly national nature of the social construction of political and economic elites. Such outcomes were congruent with the '*varieties of capitalism*' thesis (Hall and Soskice 1999) stating that organizational models continued to strongly diverge nationally and that therefore, nationally embedded business systems may be far more significant in the making of firm strategy than the process of globalization itself (Whitley 1999). Nevertheless, the role of the national scale, as well as strategies implemented by states or regional governments in the making of globalization, have remained ignored by both the local innovation system and global production network approaches even when authors explicitly sought to bring '*power and institutions back in*' (Sturgeon 2009: 126). This fieldwork research aims to contribute to fill such gap on the basis of an in-depth study of the globalization of innovation within the microelectronics industry.

5.3 Research Methods

The microelectronics industry was chosen to study locational choices because of its ideal-typical qualities. It is sometimes presented as a paragon of co-localized innovation practices, following the model of the *Silicon Valley* as the place of origin of silicon chip manufacturing (Saxenian 1994). This model, by which the Grenoble industry was nicknamed the *French Silicon Valley*, emerged under the strong influence of the State in financing the growth of

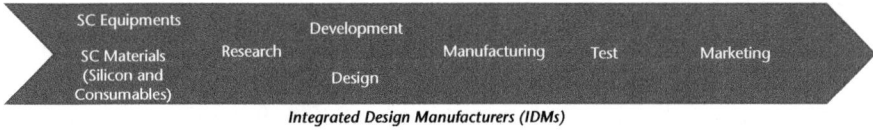

Figure 5.1 State-Led Development of the Semiconductor Value Chain: The Integrated Design Manufacturer Model (1960s–1970s)

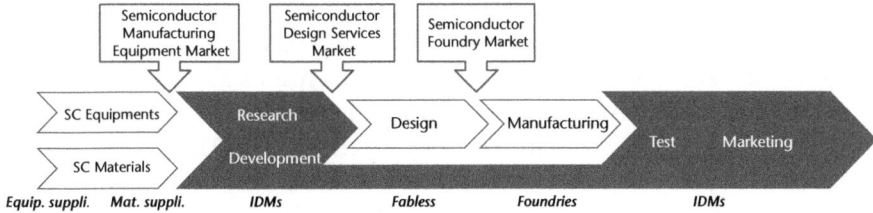

Figure 5.2 Market-Driven Development of the Semiconductor Value Chain: The Fabless/Foundry Model (1980s–1990s)

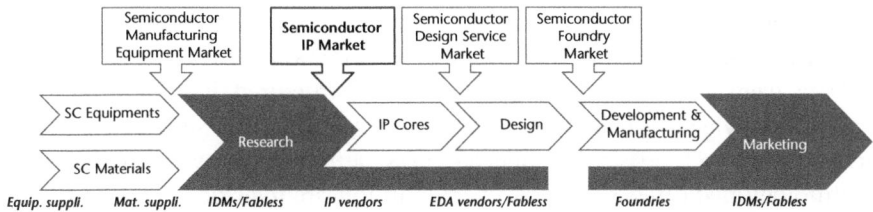

Figure 5.3 Financialization of the Semiconductor Value Chain: The Modular Model (2000s)

the industry in the 1960s and 1970s, and led to the emergence of major integrated design manufacturers in the local industry, working in close interaction with smaller firms, research labs, and local authorities and the government (Figure 5.1).

This industry is also sometimes referred to as a prototype of global innovation network and dispersed R&D teams (Dicken 2007). Indeed, during the 1980s and 1990s a strong vertical specialization and geographical dispersion of distinct nodes of the value chain accompanied the constitution of specialized clusters in North America (Albany-Fishkill, Austin, Santa Clara Valley), in Europe (Grenoble, Dresden, Cambridge), and in Asia (Suwon, Hsinchu, Singapore, Shenzhen) (Figure 5.2). On a global scale, innovation networks have linked together various nodes and categories of industry actors located in separate local clusters specialized in increasingly disaggregated steps of the value chain (Figure 5.3).

This new geography of innovation is often associated with the emergence of a flatter world, where market laws drive a process of convergence by which firms find efficient answers to the new constrains imposed by technical change and globalization (Brown and Linden 2009). But a thoughtful examination of the evolution of the spatial organization of innovation overtime shows that such progression could be much less linear, and also much less driven by the conscious search for efficient answers than by the result of multiple actors' strategies, embedded within different spatial scales, and embodying different logics of action.

The empirical material was collected between 2007 and 2010 during a PhD project (Balas 2011), which aimed at investigating historically (1955–2009) the public, industrial, and technological controversies involved in the development of R&D activities in microelectronics in the Grenoble area. This in-depth study revealed the existence of three major phases in the history of the cluster, with specific spatial implications for innovation. The local innovation network evolved from (i) a technical, state-driven development to (ii) a market-oriented approach in the wake of the 1990s technology bubble, and (iii) a more recent phase of financialization where innovation became strongly globalized and the advantages of proximity were somehow reproduced in distant networks, thanks to a strong standardization of the innovation process itself.

Data were collected from thirty-five semi-structured interviews and an extensive review of 'non-technical' literature (Corbin and Strauss 2008: 38), including press releases, specialized press, annual reports, semiconductor technology dedicated studies, and trade union archives dealing with STMicroelectronics' history and the industrial development of the Grenoble area. They were analysed thanks to a 'constructivist grounded theory' strategy (Charmaz 2006; Corbin and Strauss 2008) enabling us to capture such complex multi-actor, multi-scalar, long-ranging social phenomena.

5.4 The Transformation of the Microelectronics Cluster under the Influence of Financialization

The disruption of plans that the sudden departure of NXP and Freescale had produced in the local cluster opened a period of high uncertainty and intense debate among a variety of stakeholders all concerned with the future of the microelectronics industry in Grenoble, but holding quite distinct views of what this future should be. In this section, we first highlight the influence of financialization in the processes that led to the breakdown of the C2A on 19 January 2007, before considering the industrial compromise eventually adopted in September 2008 under the 'Nano 2012' plan set up by the local industrial and political elite and the State, as a way to incorporate the forces of financialization while accommodating some of its most radical social and industrial consequences.

5.4.1 *The Rise of Market Forces: Microelectronics as a Source of Shareholder Value*

Financialization was a major force underlying the withdrawal of NXP and Freescale, at the core of the very reasons why these partners changed plans towards Crolles 2 and stopped investing in the next generation of silicon chips that the Alliance aimed to develop. Their decision to withdraw was indeed rooted in a paradigm of financialization that industry analysts and institutional investors had been conveying in the microelectronics sector since the beginning of the years 2000, in the face of the market crisis of high tech values. It promoted a specialization of firms along the value chain together with an externalization of production activities by large semiconductor corporations aiming to become *fab-less* as a way to increase shareholder returns. This paradigm was repeatedly emphasized by institutional shareholders and analysts of STMicroelectronics, Philips, and Motorola, since about the same time as the Alliance was established. A French executive commented: 'financial analysts have looked at the accounts and though "this industry is destroying value, and we cannot finance on the long run an industry that destroys value". Why is it destroying value? First, because there are too many corporations, so prices are low. Second, because everybody was doing everything, there wasn't yet an optimization of activities within the chain' (ST former Group Vice-President (VP)).

Philips and Motorola both followed such orientations by selling their semiconductor subsidiaries to investment funds through leveraged buyouts (LBOs) in 2006. Motorola had renamed its semiconductor subsidiary Freescale before the sale, while Philips' subsidiary became NXP (Next Experience). These newly formed entities withdrew from the Alliance as a consequence of externalizing their chip manufacturing activity: NXP formed a technological partnership with the large Taiwanese foundry TSMC,[5] while Freescale joined a competing consortium formed around IBM in the US.

STMicroelectronics had not remained immune to the influence of the financial community where harsh criticisms towards its industrial logics were expressed, as recalled by an executive: 'financial analysts said of us: "they should restructure much more, there's still plenty of factories in Europe,

---

[5] Foundries have emerged from the trend towards vertical disintegration within the semiconductor industry during the 2000s, to focus on the fabrication of semiconductors and the development of the material support (process R&D) needed for the conception of new chips (design R&D). Major foundries are located in Asia, particularly Taiwan, the Taiwanese Semiconductor Manufacturing Co. (TSMC) being the world's largest semiconductor foundry.

what's that mess? They should go to China like everyone else!"' (ST Executive VP). The sales per employee ratio of the firm remained persistently below the norm of 200,000 Euros established by the financial community. Some industry analysts promised ST to a 'slow death', 'a decay that will certainly accelerate with the next semiconductor crisis, perhaps around 2008' (Specialized press, 12 January 2006).

The arrival of Carlo Bozotti as CEO of ST in 2005 signalled a shift in the strategic orientations of the firm, with greater emphasis on vertical specialization and shareholder value. Hence, at the end of the Alliance, the top management of ST emphasized a 'continuous rationalization of the fabs', 'reduction in capitalistic intensity', and 'greater use of foundries' for a 'lighter assets' R&D strategy aimed at increasing 'shareholder value' (ST Executive VP; ST chief technology officer (CTO)). Such strategy departed from the *lab-fab* model that had been at the origins of Crolles 2, in which the phases of conception and fabrication of new chips remained intimately integrated within the innovation process. Here, the development of technological platforms–the so-called *process R&D*–would be externalized to the Taiwanese foundry TSMC while ST would focus on the development of design platform– the so-called *design R&D*, in a further step of segmentation of the phases of fabrication and conception at the core of R&D activities. Such *fab-less* option was considered to provide greater flexibility at lower cost, particularly by the heads of small business units (SBUs) who saw time-to-market as a more important success factor than proprietary or differentiated technology. This option was not endorsed by all of ST management and technological staff, some of whom were in favour of retaining parts of the R&D process in a *fab-light* option by joining the IBM consortium.

5.4.2 The Persistence of the State and Local Authorities: A 'Fab-Light' Compromise with Nano 2012

The *fab-light* compromise that emerged to preserve Grenoble as a strategic centre for both the local and the national economies was established by a broader range of stakeholders including the State, local elected officials, labour unions, industrial leaders, and the main scientific laboratories in what has been described as a *'chaudron grenoblois'* (ST former executive VP) in reference to the dense synergies that had developed between these various spheres and actors to build the microelectronics cluster. It did not challenge the contemporary *doxa* of globalization, insofar as it accepted that global competition rendered fabrication activities unprofitable both in France and Europe. However, it did not adhere to the radical option of entirely externalizing *process R&D* under a *fab-less* scenario. The *fab-light* option rather consisted in maintaining part of the R&D process in Grenoble, but feeding its activity with the

R&D design platforms developed by IBM in its Albany-based consortium. This choice had the support of ST engineers that favoured retaining in house at least part of the firm's historical know how and activities, and would be responsible for transferring into Grenoble the *technology platforms* developed in Albany. It also granted local scientists access to the cutting-edge research carried by IBM with the College of Nanoscale Science and Engineering at the University of Albany, thus allowing them to pursue the research orientations launched under the Nanotec 300 programme that would have been compromised by a *fab-less*/TSMC option. An agreement was signed in April 2009 that gave a major local laboratory, the LETI (Leti, innovation for industry), a central role in ensuring technological transfers between ST and the University of Albany.

For local elected officials, suppliers and labour unions, this choice presented the strong advantage of saving at least part of the jobs that a fab-less option would have led to suppress. 'Local suppliers have progressively withdrawn, and that's the biggest danger when you see delocalization in an industry like this one. When you see all these fab closure announcements, one does not realize the impact on all the local suppliers and subcontractors that are around . . . the next step is that support teams start to downsize, and they start to be difficult to find. You have all this vicious circle that starts to develop' (local chip manufacturer Executive VP). Elected officials such as the Mayor of Crolles, have thus engaged in a massive battle to retain the support of the State, as recalled by a local public official: 'As far as I remember, there's been a lot of worries and interrogations . . . despite the ecosystem, suppliers, and all the chain that existed with subcontractors, despite all this environment, there was a feeling that if the drivers of innovation were no longer sustained, something would fall apart. François Brottes intervened in particular, at the level of the government, the Department of Industry, to remobilize the government and France on this issue, and try to weight against the top management of ST' (member of the local General Council). Local elected officials committed to remain involved in financing the local microelectronics industry in return for a renewed commitment of the State. A national publication of the Parliament Office for Scientific and Technological Choices Assessment known as the Saunier report (2008) pleads in favour of financial support from the State to ST, arguing of the need for ST to buy back the production lines abandoned by NXP and Freescale, and to increase the site's overall capacity from 2800 to 4500 wafers per week in order to reach a profitable level of production volume.

The State was not in favour of the TSMC option, and retained an important position in the governance of ST. Although it was initially leaning towards a fab-less, shareholder value oriented scenario, the top management of ST was all the more sensitive to the State view that it searched for protection, in fear of being acquired by investment funds in a fate comparable to NXP or Freescale. Close relationships between the State and ST further took the form of indirect linkages through the seats occupied by the CEOs of France Telecom and Areva in its Board of Administrators, as well as close informal interactions inherited from the public origins of Thomson Semiconductors, the French firm that merged with the Italian SGS (Società Generale Semiconduttori) to form ST in 1987 (ST Executive VP).

Arrangements between local engineers, scientists, elected officials, ST top management and the State thus converged to allow for the signature in September 2008 of the Nano 2012 convention, providing a framework for the relationships between ST, the LETI, and IBM for a five-year period. Against payment by ST to IBM of 315 million euros, ST will use the portfolio of IBM technologies while IBM is granted access to derivative technologies developed at Crolles. The *technological platform* previously developed by the LETI and ST in the Nanotec 300 programme is to be relocated in Albany, where LETI researchers will collaborate with IBM and the College of Nanoscale Science. The *design platform* will be developed at IBM's *fab* in Fishkill. Fifty R&D engineers from ST will develop design subparts to be incorporated in its own circuits in Crolles. ST can access '*competencies to buy*' in this International Semiconductor Development Alliance (ISDA) that presents the particularity of concentrating the foundry's role in IBM's hands while other partners can buy specific technologies and transfer them back home. Most of ST production will remain anchored in Crolles although other ISDA participants can be used as second source for chips fabrication.

Nano 2012 generated a consensus among a significant group of local actors, but its posture consisting in continuing to develop some fabrication by transferring from the US highly complex technological components and skills appear as an attempt to have it both ways—local and global—in an uneasy position where the core distinctive competences of the Grenoble centre are becoming increasingly difficult to identify as sources of competitive differentiation in the global industry. The strategic choice made by the tenants of the '*chaudron grenoblois*' for the future of the local industry failed to convince some critical observers: 'For me, there's not really a plan, at least I do not see a plan that says how to get the industry moving forward, either in semiconductors or in nanotechnologies. Now, there's money being spent... a lot of money, not very well spent' (Equipment supplier Executive VP).

5.5 Discussion and Conclusion

Observing the dynamics of locational decisions in the microelectronics cluster of Grenoble at the time of the breakdown of the C2A was a particularly rich exercise insofar as archetypal figures of GVC governance including not only firms, but also public authorities, could be seen to be at play, underscoring the political processes by which these actors defined, promoted, chose or discarded a variety of routes that the industry—and the chain embedded in it—could have taken in the future. The specific circumstances of the crisis generated by the unexpected departure of NXP and Freescale played a role in steering debates and controversies among local stakeholders about the local strategy of *'globalization under control'* (Balas 2011) that the C2A had come to embody. Because of the persistence of established political alliances at local and national levels, however, such debates did not produce a major reorientation of the development trajectory for the local cluster.

Indeed, the path chosen for the local industry was not based on the kind of strong industrial development policies that gave birth to the so-called Asian Tigers in the 1980s and 1990s, and were celebrated as a path for export-led development in the early global commodity chains (GCC) literature (Amsden 1989; Gereffi 1995). Neither did it fit the *fab-less* scenario echoing the shift towards a paradigm of hypercompetition taken by the GVC literature in the 2000s through the promotion of a so-called *modular model* in which value chain specialization, the externalization of manufacturing, and the promotion of quick-turn capacities for suppliers, were erected as best practices in an increasingly globalized world (Sturgeon 2002; Ernst 2005c). Perhaps more importantly, the industrial compromise of Nano 2012 was not the outcome of any form of technological determinism embedded in the potentially neutral forces of innovation. On the contrary, this political compromise could be casted as an attempt to accommodate both the global forces of competition and financialization, pushing in the direction of externalizing and offshoring *process R&D* activities, and the local forces of industrial development that induced a preservation of jobs, resources, and activities in the so-called French Silicon Valley. This compromise did not incorporate some more radical local voices pushing for an ecological option of exiting microelectronics altogether (Balas, 2011), underscoring the strongly political nature of locational decisions for innovation activities in GVCs, and the unstable, at times conflictual, ways in which compromises are built, challenged, or sustained among local and global actors on these questions.

References

Amsden, A. 1989. *Asia's Next Giant: South Korea and Late Industrialization*. Oxford: Oxford University Press.

Arora, A., Gambardella, A., and Rullani, E. 1997. 'Division of Labour and the Locus of Inventive Activity'. *The Journal of Management and Governance*, 1: 123–40.

Bair, J. 2008. 'Analysing Economic Organization: Embedded Networks and Global Chains Compared'. *Economy and Society*, 37(3): 339–64.

Bair, J. 2009. *Frontiers of Commodity Chains Research*. Stanford: Stanford University Press.

Bair, J. and Peters, E. D. 2006. 'Global Commodity Chains and Endogenous Growth: Export Dynamism and Development in Mexico and Honduras'. *World Development*, 34(2): 203–21.

Balas, N. 2011. 'The (de)Territorialization of Innovation Work; Genealogy of the Alps Silicon Valley (1955–2009)'. Unpublished PhD Thesis in Management Sciences, University of Montpellier 1, France.

Brenner, N. 1999. 'Globalization as Reterritorialization: The Rescaling of Urban Governance in the European Union'. *Urban Studies*, 36(3): 431–51.

Breschi, S. and Lissoni, F. 2001. 'Knowledge Spillovers and Local Innovation Systems: A Critical Survey'. *Industrial and Corporate Change*, 10(4): 975–1005.

Brown, C. and Linden, G. 2009. *Chips and Change. How Crisis Reshapes the Semiconductor Industry*. Cambridge, MA: MIT Press.

Charmaz, K. 2006. *Constructing Grounded Theory, a Practical Guide Through Qualitative Analysis*. London: Sage.

Coe, N. M. and Bunnel, T. G. 2003. '"Spatializing" Knowledge Communities: Towards a Conceptualization of Transnational Innovation Networks'. *Global Networks*, 3(4): 437–56.

Corbin, J. and Strauss, A. 2008. *Basics of Qualitative Research. Techniques and Procedures for Developing Grounded Theory*, 3rd edition. London: Sage.

De Bernardy, M. 1999. 'Reactive and Proactive Local Territory: Co-operation and Community in Grenoble'. *Regional Studies*, 33(4): 343–52.

Dicken, P. 2007. *Global Shift. Mapping the Changing Contours of the World Economy*, 5th Edition. London: Sage.

DiMaggio, P. J. and Powell, W. W. 1983. 'The Iron Cage Revisited: Institutional Isomorphism and Collective Rationality in Organizational Fields'. *American Sociological Review*, 48: 147–60.

Druilhe, C. and Garnsey, E. 2000. 'Emergence and Growth of High-Tech Activity in Cambridge and Grenoble'. *Entrepreneurship and Regional Development*, 2: 163–77.

Ernst, D. 2005a. 'Limits to Modularity: Reflections on Recent Developments in Chip Design'. *Industry and Innovation*, 12(3): 303–35.

Ernst, D. 2005b. 'Complexity and Internationalisation of Innovation. Why is Chip Design Moving to Asia?' *International Journal of Innovation Management*, 9(1): 47–73.

Ernst, D. 2005c. 'The New Mobility of Knowledge: Digital Information Systems and Global Flagship Networks'. In R. Latham and S. Sassen (eds), *Digital Formations. IT and New Architectures in the Global Realm*. Princeton: Princeton University Press, 89–112.

Ernst, D. and Kim, L. 2002. 'Global Production Networks, Knowledge Diffusion and Local Capability Formation'. *Research Policy*, 31(8/9): 1417–29.

Ferrary, M. and Granovetter, M. 2009. 'The Role of Venture Capital Firms in Silicon Valley's Complex Innovation Network'. *Economy and Society*, 38: 326–59.

Fligstein, N. and Freeland, R. 1995. 'Theoretical and Comparative Perspectives on Corporate Organization'. *Annual Review of Sociology*, 21: 21–43.

Gereffi, G. 1994. 'The Organization of Buyer-Driven Global Commodity Chains: How U.S. Retailers Shape Overseas Production Networks'. In G. Gereffi and M. Korzeniewicz (eds) *Commodity Chains and Global Capitalism*. Praeger: Westport, 95–122.

Gereffi, G. 1995. 'Global Production Systems and Third World Development'. In B. Stallings (ed.), *Global Change, Regional Response: The New International Context of Development*. Cambridge: Cambridge University Press, 100–42.

Gereffi, G., Humphrey, J., and Sturgeon, T. 2005. 'The Governance of Global Value Chains'. *Review of International Political Economy*, 12: 78–104.

Hakanson, L. 2005. 'Epistemic Communities and Cluster Dynamics: On the Role of Knowledge in Industrial Districts'. *Industry and Innovation*, 12 (4): 433–63.

Hall, P. and Soskice, D. 1999. *Varieties of Capitalism: The Institutional Foundations of Comparative Advantages*. Oxford: Oxford University Press.

Hamilton, G. G. and Gereffi, G. 2009. 'Global Commodity Chains, Markets Makers, and the Rise Demand-Responsive Economies'. In J. Bair (ed.), *Frontiers of Commodity Chain Research*. Stanford: Stanford University Press, 136–62.

Harvey, D. 1990. *The Condition of Postmodernity*. Cambridge: Blackwell.

Henderson, J., Dicken, P., Hess, M., Coe N., and Way-chung, Y. H. 2002. 'Global Production Networks and the Analysis of the Economic Development'. *Review of the International Political Economy*, 9; 436–64.

Humphrey, J. and Schmitz, H. 2002. 'How Does Insertion in Global Value Chains Affect Upgrading in Industrial Clusters?' *Regional Studies*, 36(9): 1017–27.

Lawton Smith, H. 2003. 'Knowledge Organizations and Local Economic Development: The Cases of Oxford and Grenoble'. *Regional Studies*, 37(9): 899–909.

Lüthje, B. and Ernst, D. 2006. 'Making Moore's Law Affordable—Modularization and Global Networks of Innovation in Chip Design'. Paper Presented at the Workshop 'Bringing Technology Back In', Max-Planck Institut für Gesellschaftsforschung, 10–11 March, Köln.

Malecki, E. W. 2004. 'Jockeying for Position: What It Means and Why It Matters to Regional Innovation Policy When Places Compete'. *Regional Studies*, 38(9): 1101–20.

Malmberg, A. and Maskell, P. 2002. 'The Elusive Concept of Localization Economies: Towards a Knowledge-Based Theory of Spatial Clustering'. *Environment and Planning A*, 34(33): 429–49.

Markusen, A. 1996. 'Sticky Places in Slippery Space: A Typology of Industrial Districts'. *Journal of Economic Geography*, 72: 293–313.

Martin, R. and Sunley, P. 2003. 'Deconstructing Clusters: Chaotic Concept or Policy Panacea'. *Journal of Economic Geography*, 3: 5–35.

Moreno, R., Paci, R., and Usai, S., 2005. 'Geographical and Sectoral Clusters of Innovation in Europe'. *Annual Review of Regional Science*, 39: 715–39.

Patel, P. and Pavitt, K. 1991. 'Large Firms in the Production of the World's Technology: An Important Case of "Non-Globalisation"'. *Journal of International Business Strategies*, 1: 1–21.

Porter, M. E. 1998. 'Competing Across Locations'. In M. E. Porter, *On Competition*. Boston, MA: Harvard Business School Publishing.

Sassen, S. 1999. *Globalization and Its Discontents: Essays on the New Mobility of People and Money*. New York: The New Press.

Saunier report. 2008. 'Report on Science, Society and Parliaments' (account of the meeting of committees and offices for scientific and technological assessment within the Parliaments of the European Union and the European Parliament, 22 September 2008). Available at: <http://www.assemblee-nationale.fr/13/pdf/i1204uk.pdf> (last accessed 17 May 2015).

Saxenian, A.-L. 1994. *Regional Advantage: Culture and Competition in Silicon Valley and Route 128*. Cambridge, MA: Harvard University Press.

Spicer, A. 2006. 'Beyond the Convergence–Divergence Debate: The Role Of Spatial Scales in Transforming Organizational Logic'. *Organization Studies*, 27: 1467–83.

Sturgeon, T. J. 2002. 'Modular Production Networks: A New American Model of Industrial Organization', *Industrial and Corporate Change*, 11(3): 451–96.

Sturgeon, T. J. 2007. 'Modularity in Global Value Chains'. Paper Presented at Workshop 'Governing production, Trade and Consumption: Power and Agency in Global Value Chains and Networks', Danish Institute for International Studies, Copenhagen, Denmark, 19–20 June.

Sturgeon, T. J. 2009. 'From Commodity Chains to Value Chains: Interdisciplinary Theory Building in an Age of Globalization"'. In J. Bair (ed.), *Frontiers of Commodity Chain Research*. Stanford: Stanford University Press.

Uzzi, B. 1997. 'Social Structure and Competition in Interfirm Networks: The Paradox of Embeddedness'. *Administrative Science Quarterly*, 42: 35–67.

Whitley, R. 1999. *Divergent Capitalisms: The Social Structuring and Change of Business Systems*. Oxford: Oxford University Press.

6

Rethinking Financialization in European Banking

An Interconnectedness Approach

Daniela Gabor

6.1 Introduction

With notable exceptions, scholarly accounts of the European sovereign debt crisis rarely consider cross-border financial integration and interconnectedness. Scholars have discussed the fiscal misbehaviour of periphery European governments, the inability of the European Commission to design and police credible fiscal rules, financial contagion between 'weak sovereigns' (De Santis 2014), and the failure of the European political project to keep up with the complexities of a one currency area (De Grauwe and Ji 2012). More critical accounts—notably post-Keynesian—in turn focus on the build-up of imbalances between export led and domestic demand driven countries, sustained by large capital flows (Stockhammer and Onaran 2012). When financial institutions/markets are considered, scholarship offers two accounts. The first focuses on the link between the sovereign and banks. The state is forced to bail out banks despite the moral outrage of its citizens (Woll 2014) and to thus provide banks with implicit subsidies that allow them to become too big too fail (Haldane 2009). Conversely, the worsening outlook for state finances, often the outcome of bank rescues, has a further negative effect on banks that hold government debt (Gabor and Ban 2015). Governments, in turn, may use moral suasion to get home banks to increase their holdings of government bonds. This strategy is particularly effective where myopic markets fail to identify, quantify, and properly price risks attached to the sovereign (Caceres, Guzzo, and Segoviano 2010).

Of the few notable exceptions, Bolton and Jeanne (2010) proposed a model where financial integration can lead to financial contagion through banks' reliance on wholesale collateralized funding. But their argument that financial integration renders sovereign debt assets systemic to cross-border markets and institutions did not gain much traction in public discourses, for both political and theoretical reasons. The policy implications are unpalatable for European institution as well as for European Member States. If government bond markets are systemic to financial stability, then either fiscal union or a market marker of last resort (European Central Bank, ECB) is necessary to stabilize integrated European finance (see Gabor 2014). In part, the fault rests with the continuous theoretical reliance on an outdated conceptualization of European banking as 'boring' relational banking, pervasive in the comparative political literature (Hardie et al. 2013). Before the crisis, this account typically portrayed European banking as falling behind the innovative market based financial systems in the US. Comparative analysis of financial systems contrasted the universal European banking characteristic with the market based system of Anglo-Saxon countries. Implicit in this discussion was the assumption that the universal European banks behaved as patient lenders to European businesses (see Gabor and Ban 2015). Yet International Monetary Fund (IMF) research shows that eighteen out of the twenty-five banks that European governments rescued during the global financial crisis became vulnerable through their trading activity.

Indeed, the crisis revealed that European banks underwent important changes in size, scope, and complexity. Andy Haldane (2009) drew attention to, and later the Liikanen Report (2012) documented the rise of large, globally systemic banks headquartered in Europe, with business models reliant on leveraged creation and trading of risk funded in wholesale markets, enabled by regulatory and tax arbitrage. To conceptualize and explore this transformation in banking, this chapter combines insights from recent scholarship on financial networks and financialization. It proposes a new definition of financialization as the increasingly tradability of risk that generates fragile connections within the financial sector, and new forms of embeddedness for public actors such as governments and central banks. In particular, wholesale funding markets have come to play a systemic role not only for the financial institutions reliant on them, but for governments that stand behind those institutions during crisis. Interconnectedness between financial institutions, across government bond markets and other securities markets, is thus a crucial characteristic of financialization in Europe.

6.2 The Analytics of Interconnectedness

In its spring 2009 meeting, the G20 mandated the IMF, the newly created Financial Stability Board (FSB), and the Bank for International Settlements

(BIS) to design a framework for assessing the global systemic importance of financial institutions, markets and instruments. Six months later, the three organizations jointly presented the results of a survey asking countries to identify fundamental concerns about systemic risk (IMF, BIS, and FSB 2009). Policymakers across the world identified interconnectedness to be the second most important determinant of systemic relevance (after size).

Such policy urgency could not rely on well-established theoretical frameworks. Indeed, economic theories of interconnectedness are quite recent. Gabor (2015) distinguishes the early, narrow approach from the post-crisis critical interconnectedness approach. Thus, the narrow approach initially focused on the risks arising from interactions between banks on the domestic interbank market. For Allen and Gale (2000), highly connected networks on the interbank market distributed risk better. Leitner (2005) in turn proposed that interconnected banks have better incentives to bail each other out in response to market stress. In contrast, Freixas, Parigi, and Rochet (2000) argued that concentrated interbank networks can create 'too interconnected to fail' institutions, thus increasing the lender of last resort burden on central banks. While engaging with the risks underpinning interconnectedness, these economists remained wedded to a traditional view of banking known as 'relational' banking where banks pool savings to lend them out, and in doing so, ignored the specific challenges of transnational, market based banking.

Since the crisis, the narrow interconnectedness school included more explicit concerns with modelling how larger, more interconnected banks increase financial fragility. Gai, Haldane, and Kapadia (2010) argued that fragility is highest, and contagion fastest, where a few large banks suffer liquidity problems. Afonso et al. (2013) documented significant differences in the type of relationships US banks develop through the interbank money market, with most banks engaged in long term, stable relationships that help them withstand exogenous liquidity shocks. In turn, Cont, Mousa, and Santos (2013) argued that it is not size but interconnectedness that renders a bank systemic. Focusing on cross-border exposures, Hattori and Suda (2007) anticipated the post-Lehman contagion between banking systems due to tighter connections. Similarly, Minoiu and Reyes (2013) argued that financial globalization rendered global banking networks unstable and that borrowing countries suffered more from volatile interconnectedness.

Yet such models cannot offer a causal story of what drives interconnectedness or how global banks become key nodes in financial networks. Network analyses of interconnectedness often amount to little more than an ex post exercise of documenting fragile relationships between banks.

In contrast, the critical approach to interconnectedness stresses the spatial, political, and institutional dimensions of cross-border financial networks. In a famous speech, Bank of England's Andrew Haldane (2009) proposed to analyse financial networks as complex, adaptive systems and transnational banks as 'super-spreaders' of systemic risk that arises from a collective migration of their business models from the relational one described earlier to the so-called 'market based' banking model (see Hardie et al. 2013), that is in a way of doing business that entails higher risk, higher yield activities such as trading in complex structured products and off balance sheet. In October 2010, the IMF published its first Understanding Interconnectedness report. Echoing Haldane, the report stressed that financial fragility propagates quickly through global networks that are generated by 'a handful of large, complex financial intermediaries', mostly transnational banks (IMF 2010: 1).

Hyun Song Shin (2009) attributed increasingly complex linkages between financial institutions to financial innovation. Sharp increases in leverage strengthen interconnectedness and financial fragility since banks (and other financial intermediaries) can only increase aggregate leverage by transacting more with each other in short-term wholesale funding markets (Yellen 2013). The converse is true in a downturn, as bank lending and bank leverage are procyclical (Miranda-Agrippino and Rey 2013). This model of leverage *cum* interconnectedness is also relevant for global banking, as the leverage cycle of global banks further determines the pace and volume of capital flows to banks in developing countries (Bruno and Shin 2014). In other words, global banks increasingly organized and dominated international finance through complex, layered, market-based relationships disconnected from the 'real' economy, relationships anchored in tax and regulatory arbitrage (Blundell-Wignall, Atkinson, and Roulet 2012).

6.2.1 *Financialization as (Critical) Interconnectedness*

The critical interconnectedness literature is useful to rethink financialization and to provide a conceptual anchoring that takes explicitly into account the structural changes in global finance. So far, scholars have proposed several definitions of financialization that include the growing structural power of finance in a new, finance-dominated regime of accumulation (Aglietta and Breton 2001; coupon pool capitalism where households' private wealth is managed through capital markets as the state withdraws from its welfare function that hitherto mitigated future uncertainties (Erturk et al. 2008); as processes and technologies that shape new financial subjectivities in everyday life (Langley 2007).

More recently, financial geographers have called for financialization theorists to engage explicitly with the networks of international finance (French, Leyshon, and Wainright 2011), and to examine critically the instruments and processes through which new actors reshape the spaces of international finance (Pike and Pollard 2010). Indeed, this literature offers important insights into the complex spatialities of 'never ending search for yield' that push the frontiers of accumulation to new material assets and subjects that can generate revenue streams (Johnson 2014). However, when financial geographers engage with systemic actors and markets in global finance, they still confine critical scrutiny to sovereign wealth funds or geographies of securitization (see Hall 2013).

Johnson (2014) provides a useful starting point for building theoretical bridges between financialization and critical interconnectedness literature. Examining the market for catastrophe bonds, he asks how space affects the tradability of financial assets and suggests that securitization enables mobile finance to gain yields from 'reframing spatial liabilities as tradable assets' (185). Yet Johnson conceives of risk as something to escape from, to transfer to a new party that is willing to take it on given precise calculations of risk and return. Implicitly, the financial system that this approach imagines is a financial system that innovates new practices to minimize and displace risks.

But this only reflects one side of the story. (Large) financial institutions seek risk in order to generate higher returns. To capture the dynamics of financialization in modern financial systems, it is not the tradability of assets per se that matters, but the tradability of risk. In other words, new financial instruments and connections emerge not solely for the purpose of transferring risk, but to produce it, to move it around and manage it for profit. Consider the recent structural changes in banking. Traditional banking involved closely monitored relationships with borrowers. In extending a loan, the bank would calculate the risks that the borrower would not be able to repay, pricing those risks to include the inherent informational asymmetries in the interest rate. Once the asset (loan) is created, the bank rarely trades it or prices it (Hendricks, Kambhu, and Mosser 2007). On the funding side, the bank would worry against about the risks that interest rates it had to pay on deposit would rise, forcing it to fund long term assets with increasingly expensive short(er)-term liabilities. Indeed, the point of banking was to gain return from assuming the risk for the maturity mismatch between its on balance sheet assets and liabilities.

Over the past thirty years, bank business models have changed markedly from close relationships with borrowers towards market based trading activities. Banks trade on their own account and make securities and derivative markets 'by standing ready to buy and sell, and capturing bid ask spread by doing so, and by providing market infrastructure' (Lindo 2013: 154). Trading in financial assets and leverage are intimately connected because financial institutions' ability to trade financial assets and risks relies on their ability to raise cheap funding.

Securitization is often used to illustrate the originate and distribute mode of banking where new loans are issued in order to be rapidly removed off balance sheet and packaged into tradable securities. Thus, securitization can be understood as the transformation and fragmentation of credit risk that can be then packaged and traded by investors searching for yield. For Jobst (2007: 199), 'the tradability of credit risk facilitates the synthetic assembly and dynamic adjustment of credit portfolios via secondary markets, but numerous counterparty links established in the commoditization of securitized asset risk also create systemic dependence susceptible to contagion'. But more broadly, the rise of shadow banking—that includes securitization and repo markets (see FSB 2011)—captures a secular shift in financial practices towards increasing the tradability of risk.

The rapid growth in derivative markets captures well the increasing tradability of financial risk. Derivatives allow financial institutions to take a position on the underlying asset without having to physically deliver that asset, thus creating (in the cash settled version) economies of scale/scope that are not possible in outright securities trading (see Lindo 2013). Beyond simple hedging of risk, derivative markets allow financial institutions to structure and specify exactly the desired risk exposure, to unbundle a collection of risks embodied in an asset, and trade the components separately (Hendricks, Kambhu, and Mosser 2007). This makes derivatives a useful tool for hedging and trading risk, since a hedger can choose which risk to hedge and which to leave uncovered.

Derivative markets are largely over the counter (OTC) markets, dominated by a handful of large financial institutions. Markose (2012) shows that the largest sixteen Systemically Important Financial Institutions (SIFIS) together accounted for 97 per cent of the gross notional value of global derivative markets. For those institutions, their bulk of derivative activities took place off balance sheet, at volumes many multiples of their assets. Consider the example of the SIFIs headquartered in Europe. Royal Bank of Scotland held USD76 trillion gross notional derivatives, almost forty times its on-balance-sheet assets, Deutsche Bank USD71 trillion, thirty-five times its on-balance-sheet assets, and BNP Paribas USD60 trillion, twenty times its on-balance-sheet assets. Together, SIFIs headquartered in the EU generated around half of global gross derivative volumes.

After 2008, the G20 pledged to mitigate the systemic interconnectedness in the OTC derivative markets. In Europe, reforms focused on increased transparency and lower counterparty risks have been implemented through EMIR (European Markets Infrastructure Regulation). EMIR rules include reporting to a trade repository, clearing standardized derivative contracts through a central counterparty (CCP) and collateral requirements for non-cleared OTC derivatives. These last two initiatives require financial institutions to have collateral agreements in place and sufficient collateral available for non-cleared OTC derivatives.

Yet the increasing collateral requirements for derivative transactions may sharpen, rather than mitigate, systemic interconnectedness by moving fragile connections onto the markets where collateral is sourced.

6.3 Systemic Interconnectedness through Collateral Intermediation Markets

Financial institutions can borrow or lend collateral, or fund securities, through repo and securities lending markets. These offer a perfect example of financialization as new practices for producing and trading risk that create new, complex, and deeply fragile connections. A repo transaction involves the exchange of an asset for cash (if for another asset the transaction falls under securities lending), with the commitment to reverse that transaction at a later date (a day, a week, a month). That asset is usually described as collateral, and that transaction a repo transaction. In theory, any asset can be 'repo-ed' as long as the lender (the counterparty) accepts it. What distinguishes a repo from other, functionally equivalent transactions is that the practices of risk management have evolved to enable the two counterparties to agree on turning (theoretically) any asset into collateral, as long as its risks can be priced (see BIS 1999). That risk management framework is at the core of shadow interconnectedness.

Consider this example. Santander Spain wants to get exposure to high yielding Spanish BB rated corporate bonds. To finance these, it can attract new deposits or issue its own securities. While both take time, Santander has at its disposal a cheaper alternative. It can use the BB-corporate bonds as collateral to raise funding in repo markets and pay for the purchase of those bonds. Put differently, the assets fund themselves while allowing Santander to realize the gains from its decision to buy corporate bonds.

Thus, Santander enters a repo contract with Deutsche Bank, who accepts the corporate bonds as collateral in return for euro cash. In this contractual relationship, Deutsche Bank is a buyer, and Santander a seller. But the relationship does not end here because the *economic* interpretation of a repo is distinctive from the *legal* one. In economic terms, a repo is a collateralized *loan* from Deutsche Bank to Santander. Santander has to pay a repo interest rate on the cash borrowed, a rate which is typically the lowest in funding markets since the cash loan is fully collateralized.

Although Deutsche Bank is now the legal owner of those corporate bonds until the end of the repo transaction, the two parties remain involved on a daily basis. Connections have a distinctive time dimension that is analytically relevant, since it capture the impatient character of financialization. Risk is made tradable through practices that are inherently impatient.

Thus, collateral management in repo transactions with maturity longer than one day are impatient in the sense that repo parties remain connected throughout the duration of the repo through margin call practices. In the previous example, if Santander Spain defaults, then Deutsche Bank has to sell the collateral in order to recover its cash. To ensure that it does not lose in the process—when, for example, that collateral falls in market price—Deutsche Bank calculates the market value of those corporate bonds on a daily basis (marking them to market) and, on repos with maturity beyond overnight, makes margin calls: if the price of corporate bonds falls, Santander has to post additional collateral to Deutsche Bank to match the difference to the cash loan. In turn, Santander retains the corporate bonds on its balance sheet and with these, the associated risks and return: Deutsche Bank has the obligation to transfer any coupon payments to Santander (Comotto 2012).[1] For this reason, reps and securities financing are used interchangeably: Santander uses the corporate bonds as collateral to finance them in the repo market, while retaining the underlying exposure to the risk and returns of those BB-bonds.

The distinction between the economic and legal interpretations is crucial for interconnectedness. It makes repo different from other forms of secured lending (see BIS 1999). A repo cash borrower is a seller of collateral because the transfer of ownership is crucial to protect the cash lender (the buyer of collateral) in case of default.[2] In other words, the legal status of a repo transaction morphs the counterparty risk—that Santander defaults—into collateral risk; that the collateral provided by Santander falls in price below the value of the cash loan. This is repo 'magic': the move form counterparty risk to collateral risk means that both parties care most about 'the volatility . . . in the value of collateral' than about the other's credit worthiness (BIS 1999). Yet this does not imply that counterparty risk disappears altogether: riskier counterparties may have more difficult access to repo funding, or pay higher haircuts (Comotto 2012). This is particularly the case during periods of market stress, when uncertainty about asset valuations rises, and expectations of collateral quality worsen.

Furthermore, collateral intermediation strengthens interconnectedness through a second channel: reuse or re-hypothecation. This is crucial to understand why repo transactions are intimately linked to cycles of private leverage

---

[1] Not all accounting regimes require the repo-ed assets to remain on balance sheet. In the US, for instance, the failure of both Lehman Brothers and MF Global was linked to off-balance sheet repos that allowed these institutions to present smaller balance sheets and lower levels of leverage (see Comotto 2012).

[2] This is the case for repo agreements outside the US; where transfer of legal ownership is not possible, but substituted by exemptions from safe harbor bankruptcy procedures, see Comotto (2012) for details.

(FSB 2012). In the previous example, Santander used repos to increase leverage. Conversely, Deutsche Bank accepts those corporate bonds because it needs it to settle a short position, to hedge an interest rate exposure, or because, as a market-maker, it can relend those securities at more favourable rates in the same market. These various functions imply that collateral managers can lend and borrow the same piece of collateral repeatedly, if there are no legal restrictions that constrain reuse (re-hypothecation).

Singh (2011) describes these as collateral chains: the same asset can move between various counterparties in different repo transactions, so that all these counterparties have a common exposure to the variation in the market value of collateral. The European Commission, alongside the FSB (2012), took this further, arguing that 'dynamic collateral chains' generated leverage and systemic risk through the shadow banking sector:

> If this collateral is lodged in cash, it can be re-invested. These strategies generate dynamic collateral chains in which the same security is lent several times, often involving actors from the shadow banking system. This mechanism can contribute to a surreptitious increase in leverage and strengthens the pro-cyclical nature of the financial system, which then becomes vulnerable to bank runs and sudden deleveraging.   (European Commission 2012)

Singh and Stella (2012) estimated that before the 2008 crisis, a high quality asset typically sustained three different repo transactions. Put differently, three different financial institutions were connected through one financial instrument and exposed, in a chain like fashion, to its price volatility. The lower the haircuts, the higher the leverage that can be built on a single piece of collateral reused repeatedly. If haircuts are pro-cyclical, that is, if they are low when markets are confident, then repo markets enable the production and trading of risk through increasingly complex connections (see BIS 1999; also FSB 2012).

Yet there are legal limits to reuse. Some jurisdictions, such as the US, may put restrictions on reuse in repo transactions involving an intermediary (a tri-party repo, see FSB 2012). Faced with shortages of collateral, potential sharper following the post-crisis regulatory reforms that require financial institution to collateralize OTC relationships (such as derivative contracts), (shadow) banks have developed three strategies to improve the availability of collateral. These embed 'socially useful' financial institutions, governments and central banks in repo architectures.

a. collateral *mining*: collateral managers identify pools of assets in ownership of asset managers—hedge funds, sovereign wealth funds, pension funds, insurance companies or mutual funds—and borrow them through repo transactions (see Pozsar and Singh 2011). Collateral mining sharply sharpens interconnectedness between financial institutions that own assets and are willing to lend them. Many pension funds do so in order to gain some additional returns on buy-to-hold portfolios of low-risk, low-return assets.

b. collateral *transformation*: crisis of interconnected finance play out in asset markets and through collateral market values. As liquidity disappears and prices fall, repo parties no longer accept the now illiquid assets as collateral. This can easily trigger contagion across repo networks, prompting central banks to offer collateral swaps: exchanging low quality for high quality 'safe asset' collateral that can be used to tap private repo markets (Gabor and Jessop 2014).

c. collateral *manufacturing*: Pozsar (2011) documents a third response to collateral shortages: innovations to manufacture new pools of collateral. A closer look at the preferences for collateral is useful to clarify this channel. Private repo transactions typically rely on sovereign debt instruments: around 75 per cent of the collateral flowing through repo markets both in the US and Europe comes from highly rated governments (Hordahl and King 2008; ECB 2012). What explains the preference for government debt as collateral? For Giovannini (2013), this is a story of costs and profitability: when using government debt, repo actors impose low or no haircuts and thus economize on financial transactions costs.

In other words, government bonds markets are intimately linked to repo markets because their risk profile—supported by the guarantee of the sovereign to pay its debt—that cannot be matched by the private sector. That is, the increasing tradability of private risk relies on the promise of the sovereign to meet its commitments.

Before the crisis, Pozsar (2011) argues, governments did not generate sufficient debt to satisfy the appetite for leveraged trading of risk and the associated demand for collateral. Shadow banking met supply shortages with financial innovation. In doing so it became, according to Giovannini, 'a collateral factory'. Through securitization, shadow banking produced highly rated, private debt instruments that had low haircuts and enabled leverage. From this perspective, securitization is a subset of collateral intermediation activities, and functions to connect distinct financial institutions through new collateral chains. Collateral management through the repo market thus connects securities markets, derivative markets, and interbank money markets.

6.4 Financialization and Interconnectedness in Europe

Before the crisis, large European banks engaged in an aggressive expansion of balance sheets through trading and warehousing risks. Consider the uneven pace of financial integration before 2008, one of the key concerns of both the ECB and the European Commission. Integration occurred fast in the markets that supported leveraged risk trading. In turn, traditional banking remained a largely national affair.

Thus, European retail banking remained highly segmented, whereas securities and wholesale money markets—where financial institutions exchange liquidity, issue debt, trade, or hedge risk—integrated the fastest (Kalemli-Ozcan, Papaioannou, and Peydro 2010). Measured by volumes, by 2008, around 40 per cent of interbank borrowing took place in cross-border interbank markets, shifting from the unsecured to the collateralized (repo) segment. Similarly, one of every two EU bonds belonged to portfolios of institutions residing elsewhere in Europe. In contrast, Eurozone banks lent 85 of every 100 euros to domestic (non-financial) borrowers, 12 in cross-border loans to Eurozone residents, and only 3 outside the Eurozone (ECB 2013). In price terms, the introduction of the euro was accompanied by a rapid convergence in funding costs for banks and sovereign in Europe.

Scholars explain the differentiated pace of European financial integration as a consequence of informational asymmetries or turn to political economy aspects of the market-regulation nexus. It is thus argued that the pace of integration depends on the ability of financial institutions to gather readily available information about the financial solvency of governments, businesses, or individuals that require loans or issue assets (Degryse and Ongena 2004). Securities markets entail less information gaps since issuers are typically governments, large banks, or large corporations who disclose the criteria necessary for evaluating and pricing risks. In contrast, retail banking involves a more information intensive relationship that can be more effectively sustained in conditions of close proximity between banks and borrowers. Cross-border integration in retail financial services requires foreign ownership of domestic banking units in order to address these asymmetries. But, Grossman and Leblond (2011) point out, political priorities at global and European level matter and play out differently in the integration of wholesale and retail financial markets. Thus, European governments remained guided by national interests in the regulation of cross-border retail financial services, often discouraging further integration (i.e., cross-border ownership) in order to protect national banking champions. Internationalization and cross-border integration was encouraged in securities and money markets as a strategic priority for the competitiveness of European finance, including banking, faced with the rapid growth of US finance.

The Liikanen Report (2012) provided a detailed account of how European banks had become key players in the global shift to trading based banking. By 2007, the ten largest banking groups in Europe had balance sheets larger than the GDP of the country where they were headquartered (as for example ING

Bank, BNP Paribas, Santander, RBS, and HSBC) and combined, larger than the EU gross domestic product (GDP). Their off balance sheet derivative positions increased to large multiples of their assets (Markose 2012). The increase in scale went hand in hand with rapid internationalization: large cross-border banking groups with lending and trading activities in a multitude of countries. This translated into higher organizational complexity—several large groups had, and continue to have, over 1000 affiliates (subsidiaries and branches)—that relied increasingly less on domestic funding sources, substituted for an active internal capital market where resources were allocated centrally depending on the relative profitability of banking activities across the group (Cetorelli and Goldberg 2011; Kudrna and Gabor 2013) and for wholesale funding markets, including the repo market. Before the crisis, EU banks held only one third of their assets in the domestic market, whereas another third was held in Europe and the rest outside the EU. The Liikanen report further highlighted the role that 'excessive trading and market based activity' played in the European crisis. Indeed, eighteen of the twenty-three banks bailed out by European governments throughout 2008—2009 had become vulnerable through their substantial trading activity (Chow and Surti 2011).

The shift to market based banking also energized a rapid growth in short-term collateralized interbank markets, and repo markets. As European banks became globally systemic, the repo market on which they relied to grow balance sheets gained systemic importance. The European repo market tripled in value between 2000 and 2008, to around EUR 6 trillion euros. According to ECB figures, more than half of private repo transactions involved cross-border counterparties and collateral (Gabor and Ban 2015).

European institutions played an important role in supporting the cross-border integration of the repo markets (see Gabor and Ban 2015). In 2002, the ECB (2002) noted that repo markets had been growing faster in comparison to other money markets, evidence of successful market-regulator cooperation. Since 1999, the ECB had thrown its support behind initiatives to accelerate repo integration and put it on an equal footing with the traditional market for liquidity, the unsecured interbank market. For the ECB, integration mattered because the institution itself used the repo instrument in its daily liquidity management operations (known as open market operations) that provided refinancing to the Eurozone banking system. According to the ECB, a well-functioning private repo market would enable European banks to source collateral necessary to access ECB liquidity, and improve the transmission mechanism of monetary policy. In parallel, the European Commission also made the integration of the European repo market a priority. Following the 1999 report of the Giovannini Expert Group on Repo Markets, the Commission introduced a series of European legislative reforms that would harmonize the legal frameworks for cross-border repos (see Gabor and Ban 2015).

The favourable attitude of European legislators thus removed important obstacles to the growth of private repo markets. But repo markets did not grow because European policymakers wished them to. Instead, that repos became the fastest growing segment of European wholesale money markets reflects two systemic repo features at different junctures in the financial cycle: a market supportive of leverage trading during periods of market confidence, and a 'preferred habitat' for interbank transactions during periods of financial distress.

First, repos constitute an important funding instrument for banks that move away from the traditional balance sheet structure where assets are dominated by loans to non-financial corporations and liabilities by retail deposits. Thus, 2012 figures for European banks show that loans to non-financial corporations only accounted for around 30 per cent of bank assets, with deposits of non-financial institutions amounting to around 30 per cent of total liabilities, with some heterogeneity depending on the size and degree of internationalization of the banking group (ECB 2012; see also Hardie et al. 2013). In other words, banks financed risk trading through wholesale money markets, in particular the repo market.

Indeed, large European banks made extensive recourse to repos to grow balance sheets: by 2008, the twenty largest European banks—that is, those now described as global SIFIs—generated between themselves around 80 per cent of repo transactions (Hordahl and King 2008; Gabor 2014). Repo-reliance is thus a distinguishing feature of global systemically important banking, making them systemic players in the shadow banking universe (see Singh 2011; Singh and Stella 2012; Gabor 2014; Gabor and Ban 2015). Furthermore, in the European financial system, repos cemented the interconnectedness of large financial institutions that built a pyramid of financial claims against each other funded through repo markets. The recent debates on the European Financial Transactions Tax highlighted the systemic importance of repo activities for European banks with significant trading activities. Goldman Sachs estimations indicate that the biggest loss to European banks—in the sample analysed by Goldman Sachs mostly French, German and Italian banks—stem from their repo portfolios, four times higher than losses from derivative activity, equities, and government bond books.

Second, the fall of Lehman Brothers highlighted that banks prefer secured to unsecured interbank markets during crisis. In Europe, the traditional market where banks traded liquidity with each other, the unsecured interbank market, contracted rapidly (ECB 2012). Banks' reluctance to lend to each other without collateral reflects well the difficulties that banks face in evaluating counterparty risk when that counterparty has growing rapidly both on balance sheet and off balance sheet activities. Indeed, unsecured interbank markets are an institutional feature of relationship banking: a banking business model where banks gather information about each other's balance sheets (and about non-bank lenders), build trust, and thus lend to each without the security of a collateral. However, the shift to large-scale, cross-border banking renders this informational effort far more complicated—indeed, post-crisis research argues that a significant degree of uncertainty about exposures exists *within* large banking groups, let alone *between* banking groups.

Collateralization partly addresses informational gaps. By involving collateral in trading relationships, banks can overcome the informational complexity that makes the evaluation of counterparty risk more difficult. As long as the bank can sell (liquidate) the collateral portfolio at a market price close to the cash it has lent out, counterparty risk is no longer the key risk of an interbank lending agreement. While counterparty risk does not disappear altogether, a collateralized relationship moves some of that risk onto the collateral. Furthermore, the risk management techniques underpinning repos seek to mitigate the risks associated with collateral. For lower rated collateral, repo lenders will ask for a haircut (the difference between the market value of the collateral posted and the cash). On repos with maturity beyond overnight, collateral portfolios are marked to market and subject to margin calls. If the market price of the security posted as collateral falls, the repo borrower posts additional collateral (margin maintenance) to keep collateral and cash close in value.

6.5 The European Crisis as a Crisis of Financialized Connections

One important feature of pre-crisis financialization was that banks mobilized a growing share of their securities portfolios as collateral to trade and manage risk. In this context, the concept of tradability of risk (and assets) encompasses liquidity, that is, ease of changing risk positions without large price changes and subsequent losses. The fragility of connections forged through collateral materializes in the markets where collateral is traded. If liquidity disappears in collateral markets as risk makes room for uncertainty, relationships supported by that collateral unravel. Lower liquidity and falling prices trigger fire sales and liquidity spirals for collateral reliant financial institutions, with contagion propagating through markets (see Brunnermeier and Pedersen 2009; Gorton and Metrick 2012). Put differently, when the distinction between risk and uncertainty collapses, the tradability of a wide range of assets diminishes and the illusion of liquidity is rapidly eroded. Financialization becomes disruptive as risk warehousing becomes uncertainty warehousing. A new language emerges to capture systemic connections: wrong-way risk, between (collateral) market and institution.

The dynamics in the European repo market illustrate well financializaton in its disruptive phase. Within a few days of Lehman's collapse, repo-reliant financial institutions began differentiating between Greek and German sovereign debt collateral, hitherto considered as functionally identical collateral (Hordahl and King 2008). Thus, financial institutions raised haircuts or even refused to accept Greek collateral, concerned about potential volatility in the Greek sovereign debt market. By the end of 2012, contagion from the Greek sovereign crisis combined with an ECB reluctant to intervene directly meant that collateral issued by 'Southern' countries no longer circulated through European repo markets.

Bolton and Jeanne (2010) first theorized the possibility that repo markets would lead to a fragmentation of collateral markets in a monetary union. In their model, financial integration allows banks to use government debt of any country as collateral in repo markets. But financial integration creates different incentives for sovereigns. Those with recognized fiscal probity—the providers of 'safe assets'—benefit by restricting the supply of safe assets whereas sovereigns with a poorer credit outlook benefit because European banks, both domestic and foreign, treat their debt as good collateral. In turn, integrated repo markets act as a conduit for financial contagion: the default of a risky country impairs the balance sheet of banks in 'safe' countries that can no longer use the debt of the risky country as collateral.

Through a financialization framework, the Bolton and Jeanne (2011) model has two shortcomings. First, it fails to ask an important question: is the default of a 'weak' sovereign analytically related to repo markets? In other words, the model only recognizes one component of repo-induced pro-cyclicality in government bond markets: during the upswing of a financial cycle, banks increase their cross-border holdings of government debt, and thus improve the market liquidity of weak sovereigns. But conversely, if banks rely on government bonds to increase leverage, shouldn't crises of (de)leveraging affect government bond markets? Gabor and Ban (2015) and Gabor (2014) argue that this is an important, if neglected, aspect of the Eurozone sovereign debt crisis.

Consider the example of highly leveraged Irish banks, funded through short-term repo markets, against Irish government collateral. Crisis hit Irish banks once their repo lenders suddenly become concerned about the viability of highly leveraged business models. Immediately, repo lenders increase haircuts or withdraw funding, forcing Irish banks to either find new cash or new collateral. In both scenarios, Irish banks have no choice but to fire-sale some assets—including Irish government bonds. Even if the Irish government's fiscal position is exemplary (notably better before the crisis than Germany's), a repo run involving highly leveraged Irish banks increases interest rates on government debt, trigger further margin calls and eventually a sovereign debt crisis. Put differently, the repo market can introduce volatility in government bond markets that supply collateral, and pose further systemic risks to the financial sector. A sovereign's viability in financial markets depends on its banking sector as much (more?) than on its spending and revenue decisions.

The Irish example highlights the second problem of the Bolton and Jeanne (2010) model. It pays limited attention to the banks of the 'weak' sovereigns, downplaying the fragility arising from the growing interconnectedness in European banking through what financial institutions describe as 'wrong-way' risk: that the collateral and the institution that provides it may be simultaneously affected by a market development. Such a correlation can for example influence the terms on which a Greek (Irish) bank can raise repo funding against Greek (Irish) sovereign bond collateral, as the default of the bank may put the sovereign in a precarious position and vice-versa. In such a scenario, the Greek bank may have to pay a higher haircut (to provide more collateral than the cash it receives) or non-Greek assets as collateral. This can generate a run on collateral markets—including on the home sovereign—as described above. Indeed, there is a small but growing literature that shows the European sovereign debt crisis was a crisis of repo the form of runs on sovereign collateral Gabor 2014; Gabor and Ban 2015). The ECB tolerated runs as long as these occurred in sovereign bond markets that played a marginal role as suppliers of collateral to the European SIFIs dominating the European repo market. However, once collateral contagion threatened to spread to Spanish and Italian government bonds that together collateralize around 30 per cent of outstanding repo transactions, Mario Draghi stepped in with the promise to do 'what it takes' (see Gabor 2014b).

Both wrong-way risk and runs on repo collateral markets are distinctive features of interconnected, leveraged banking. Both were at play during the various stages of the European banking, and then sovereign debt crisis (see Gabor 2013). Banks can significantly increase the distress of the home or other European sovereigns when forced to deleverage and liquidate assets rapidly. In other words, the rapid integration of government bond markets through repo markets has a pronounced cyclical component, moving with the rhythms of leveraged banking. The standing of a sovereign in financial markets is evaluated through the collateral quality of its debt, in turn influenced by a series of factors outside its control: the expansion strategies of its banks and vulnerability to short-term funding shocks, the portfolio decisions.

6.6 Conclusion

This paper stressed that the analytics of financialization in European banking should include banks' business models and the connections these forge across markets and across borders. In this context, financialization is understood as the increasing tradability of risk—a concept that encompasses the increasing tradability of assets as well as banks' (market making) activities in securities and derivative markets. The increasing tradability of risk in private markets relies on the sovereign's promise to meet its obligations, thus embedding governments in financial markets, and creating new mechanisms of disruption. This conceptualization further captures the cyclical nature of financialization. When the distinction between risk and uncertainty collapses, the tradability of a wide range of assets diminishes, dispelling quickly illusions of liquidity created through risk appetite. Financialization becomes disruptive as risk warehousing becomes uncertainty warehousing. If/when liquidity disappears in collateral markets as risk makes room for uncertainty, relationships supported by that collateral unravel or becoming increasingly fragile.

References

Afonso, G., Kovner, A., and Schoar, A. 2013. Trading partners in the interbank lending market. *FRB of New York Staff Report*, 620.

Aglietta, M. and Breton, R. 2001. Financial systems, corporate control and capital accumulation. *Economy and Society*, 30(4): 433–66.

Allen, F. and Gale, D. 2000. Financial contagion. *Journal of Political Economy*, 108: 1–33.

BIS (Bank for International Settlements). 1999. Implications of repo markets for central banks, CGFS Papers, no. 10, March.

Blundell-Wignall, A., Atkinson, P., and Roulet, P. 2012. The business models of large interconnected banks and the lessons of the financial crisis. *National Institute Economic Review*, 221: R31–R43.

Bolton, P. and Jeanne, O. 2010. Sovereign default risk in financially integrated economies. Paper presented at the 11th Jacques Polak Annual Research Conference, Washington, D. C., 5–6 November. Available at: <http://www.imf.org/external/np/res/seminars/2010/arc/pdf/boj.pdf> (accessed 20 March 2011).

Brunnermeier, Markus and Pederson, Lasse. 2009. Market liquidity and funding liquidity. *Review of Financial Studies*, 2201–38.

Bruno, V. and Shin, H. S. 2014. Cross-border banking and global liquidity. Available at: <http://www.princeton.edu/~hsshin/www/capital_flows_global_liquidity.pdf>.

Caceres, C., Guzzo, V., and Segoviano, M. 2010. Sovereign spreads: global risk aversion, contagion or fundamentals? IMF Working Paper No. WP/10/120.

Cetorelli, N. and Goldberg, L. 2011. Global banks and international shock transmission: evidence from the crisis. *IMF Economic Review*, 59: 41–76.

Chow, J. T. and Surti, J. 2011. Making banks safer: can Volcker and Vickers do it? IMF Working Papers, 1–34.

Comotto, R. 2012. Shadow banking and repo. European Repo Council paper. Available at <http://www.icmacentre.ac.uk/images/2011/08/shadow-banking-and-repo.pdf> (accessed 21 June 2013).

Cont, R., Amal, M., and Edson, S. 2013. Network structure and systemic risk in banking systems. In J. P. Fouque and J. Langsam (eds), *Handbook of Systemic Risk*. Cambridge: Cambridge University Press.

Degryse, H. and Ongena, S. 2004. The impact of technology and regulation on the geographical scope of banking. *Oxford Review of Economic Policy*, 20(4), 571–90.

De Santis, R. A. 2014. The Euro Area sovereign debt crisis: identifying flight-to-liquidity and the spillover mechanisms. *Journal of Empirical Finance*, 26: 150–70.

De Grauwe, P. and Ji, Y. 2012. Mispricing of sovereign risk and macroeconomic stability in the Eurozone. *JCMS: Journal of Common Market Studies*, 50(6): 866–80.

ECB (European Central Bank). 2002. Main features of the repo market in the Euro Area. Monthly Bulletin October: 45–67.

ECB (European Central Bank). 2013. Financial Integration in Europe.

European Commission. 2012. European Financial Stability and Integration Report 2011. April.

Erturk, I., Froud, J., Johal, S., Leaver, A., and Williams, K. (eds). 2008. *Financialization at Work: Key Texts and Commentary*. Abingdon: Routledge.

Freixas, Xavier, Parigi, Bruno, and Rochet, Jean-Charles. 2000. Systemic risk, interbank relations and liquidity provision by the Central Bank. *Journal of Money Credit and Banking*, 32(3): 611–33.

French, S., Leyshon, A., and Wainwright, T. 2011. Financializing space, spacing financialization. *Progress in Human Geography*, 35(6), 798–819.

FSB (Financial Stability Board). 2011. Shadow banking: scoping the issues. a background note of the financial stability board. 12 April. Available at: <http://www.financialstabilityboard.org/publications/r_110412a.pdf> (accessed 20 July 2011).

FSB (Financial Stability Board). 2012. Global Shadow Banking Monitoring Report. 18 November 2012. Available at: <http://www.financialstabilityboard.org/publications/r_121118c.pdf> (accessed 22 Feb 2013).

Gabor, D. 2015. The IMF's Rethink of global banks: critical in theory, orthodox in practice. *Governance*. Available at: <http://onlinelibrary.wiley.com/doi/10.1111/gove.12107/full>.

Gabor, D. 2014. Learning from Japan: the European Central Bank and the European sovereign debt crisis. *Review of Political Economy*, 26(2): 190–209.

Gabor, D. and Jessop, B. 2014. Mark my words: discursive central banking in crisis. In B. Jessop, B. Young, and C. Scherrer (eds), *Financial Cultures and Crisis Dynamics*. Abingdon: Routledge, 294–315.

Gabor, D. and C. Ban. 2015. Banking on bonds: on the new links between states and markets. *Journal of Common Market Studies*, DOI: 10.1111/jcms.12309.

Gai, P., Haldane, A., and Kapadia, S. 2010. Complexity, concentration and contagion. *Journal of Monetary Economics*, 58: 453–70.

Giovannini, A. 2013. *Risk-free Assets in Financial Markets*, BIS Papers No. 72, July.

Gorton, G. B. and Metrick, A. 2012. Securitized banking and the run on repo. *Journal of Financial Economics*, 104: 425–51.

Grossman, E. and Leblond, P. 2011. European financial integration: finally the Great Leap Forward? *Journal of Common Market Studies*, 49(2): 413–35.

Haldane, A. 2009. Rethinking the Financial Network. Speech at the Financial Student Association, Amsterdam, March 21.

Hall, S. 2013. Geographies of money and finance iii: financial circuits and the "real economy"'. *Progress in Human Geography*, 37: 285–92.

Hattori, M. and Suda, Y. 2007. Developments in a cross-border bank exposure 'network'. In *Proceedings of a CGFS workshop held at the Bank for International Settlements*, December.

Hardie, I., Howarth, D., Maxfield, S., and Verdun, A. 2013. Banks and the false dichotomy in the comparative political economy of finance. *World Politics*, 65: 691–728.

Hendricks, D., Kambhu, J., and Mosser, P. 2007. Systemic risk and the financial system. *Federal Reserve Bank of New York Economic Policy Review*, 13(2):65–80.

Hordahl, P. and King, M. R. 2008. Developments in repo markets during the financial turmoil. *BIS Quarterly Review*, 23 December, 37–53.

IMF (International Monetary Fund). 2010. 'Understanding Financial Interconnectedness'. Available at: <http://www.imf.org/external/np/pp/eng/2010/100410.pdf> (accessed 22 June 2012).

IMF (International Monetary Fund), BIS (Bank For International Settlements), and FSB (Financial Stability Board). 2009. 'Guidance to Assess the Systemic Importance of Financial Institutions, Markets and Instruments: Initial Considerations. Report to G20 Finance Ministers and Governors.

Jobst, A. A. 2007. A primer on structured finance. *Journal of Derivatives & Hedge Funds*, 13(3), 199–213.

Johnson, L. 2014. Geographies of securitized catastrophe risk and the implications of climate change. *Economic Geography*, 90(2): 155–85.

Kalemli-Ozcan, S., Papaioannou, E., and Peydro, J.-L. 2010. What lies beneath the Euro's effect on financial integration? Currency risk, legal harmonization, or trade? ECB Working Paper No. 1216.

Kudrna, Z. and Gabor, D. 2013. The return of political risk: foreign banking in CEE countries. *Europe-Asia Studies*, 65: 548–66.

Langley, P. 2007. Uncertain subjects of Anglo-American financialization. *Cultural Critique*, 65: 67–91.

Leitner, Y. 2005. Financial networks: contagion, commitment and private sector bailouts. *Journal of Finance*, 60(6): 2925–53.

Liikanen, E. 2012. High-level Expert Group on reforming the structure of the EU banking sector. *Final Report, Brussels, 2*.

Lindo, D. 2013. Political economy of financial derivatives: a theoretical analysis of the evolution of banking and its role in derivatives markets. Doctoral Dissertation, University of London.

Markose, M. S. M. 2012. Systemic risk from global financial derivatives: a network analysis of contagion and its mitigation with super-spreader tax. IMF Working Paper No. WP/12/282.

Minoiu, C. and Reyes, J. A. 2013. A network analysis of global banking: 1978–2010. *Journal of Financial Stability*, 9(2), 168–84.

Miranda-Agrippino, S. and H. Rey. 2013. World Asset Markets and Global Liquidity. Mimeo.

Pike, A. and Pollard, J. 2010. Economic geographies of financialization. *Economic Geography*, 86: 29–51.

Pozsar, Z. 2011. Institutional cash pools and the triffin dilemma of the US banking system. IMF Working Paper No. WP/11/190.

Shin, H. S. 2009. Securitisation and financial stability. *The Economic Journal*, 119(536), 309–32.

Singh, M. 2011. Velocity of pledged collateral: analysis and implications. IMF Working Paper No. WP/11/256.

Singh, M. and Stella, M. P. 2012. Money and collateral. IMF Working Paper No. WP/12/95.

Stockhammer, E. and Onaran, Ö. 2012. Rethinking wage policy in the face of the Euro crisis. Implications of the wage-led demand regime. *International Review of Applied Economics*, 26(2), 191–203.

Yellen, J. 2013. Interconnectedness and systemic risk: lessons from the financial crisis and policy implications. Speech at the American Economic Association/American Finance Association Joint Luncheon, San Diego, California, 4 January.

Woll, C. 2014. *The Power of Inaction: Bank Bailouts in Comparison*. Cornell University Press.

Part II
Finance and Industrial Policy for Post-Crisis Recovery

7

The Crisis of Industrial Financing in Europe

Jan Toporowski

7.1 Introduction

The economic crisis in Europe is a crisis of shifting financial form: one that started with the sub-prime crisis in the US in 2007–2008, to which European banks were exposed due to their holdings of mortgage-backed securities; shifted into a crisis of investment banking in the US that froze up international money markets from 2008, and thereby also affected European money markets; became a crisis of government financing in 2010, as government budget deficits expanded due to increased welfare expenditure and refinancing of failed banks; and is now a generalized crisis of deflation, with inflation undershooting the European Central Bank's (ECB) target rate of 'below, but close to 2 per cent'. Accounts of the financial crisis in Europe therefore usually amount to restatements of this history as background to the core policy dilemma of what to do about the Maastricht Treaty limits on government debt and fiscal balances (e.g., Phillips 2014; Wolf 2014). Now that government debt and the fiscal deficits expanding that debt in most of the European Union exceed those limits, the policy dilemma is whether to accept that the limits are, in effect, a dead letter, or whether to exercise renewed vigour in reducing those excessive deficits and debts.

This policy dilemma is correctly being discussed in terms of economic consequences. On the one side of a gladiatorial academic debate are economists mostly from the German-speaking countries, who are backed by legal opinion reinforcing the legality of the Maastricht Treaty and the illegitimacy of the excessive debts and deficits. They have behind them both theory and the industrial and financial history of Central Europe. The theory is essentially the monetarist view that the private sector finds its own equilibrium, while the disequilibrium of the public sector (manifest in the form of fiscal deficits and rising debt levels) can only, in the long run, increase the rate of inflation. The industrial and financial history behind this is a concentration on export led growth that has historically underpinned the financial stability of Central Europe's central banks, during the period of fixed and semi-fixed exchange rates leading up to the monetary union. However, the recent coincidence of falling inflation with high public debt and deficits levels casts doubt on the monetarist theory behind this outlook.

Critics of this outlook have behind them both theory and some recent economic and financial history of Western Europe. Their theory is that the private sector cannot find its equilibrium without assistance from the public sector, so that inflationary and deflationary 'gaps' (differences between actual and potential output and employment) should be regulated by appropriate fiscal surpluses or deficits. This view has been supported by the recent rising unemployment, associated with efforts to reduce fiscal deficits.

The focus on policy from both sides of this argument has rather distracted attention from what has been happening in the private sector. In particular, the exclusively policy focus has tended towards suggesting that the private sector is 'led' by fiscal and monetary policy, with the policy stance either determining the price level (in the case of monetarists) or the level of economic activity (the Keynesian position). A proto-Keynesian 'business cycle' tradition, from Thomas Tooke, Karl Marx, and Knut Wicksell in the nineteenth century, to Michał Kalecki, John Maynard Keynes, Joseph Schumpeter, and Josef Steindl in the mid-twentieth century, examining systematic changes in industrial and economic activity, has effectively become extinct. By the end of the twentieth century industrial and economic fluctuations came to be deemed either as the usual 'creative destruction' of a market economy or, if systematic, as being due to inappropriate policy stances, including the 'deregulation' that is widely supposed to have caused the recent financial crisis. The earlier models of the political business cycle of Kalecki and Hayek (based on inappropriate fiscal or monetary policy respectively) may be seen, in some sense, as a transition stage to the widespread *perception* that the present economic difficulties are 'policy-led' and have to be solved by more appropriate policies. This may account for widespread conscious (but mostly unconscious) appeals to those political business cycle models on the two sides of the dispute.

This chapter takes a somewhat different approach by looking at what happened in the private sector during the recent financial crisis that contributed to that crisis, deriving the key features of the crisis from corporate finance rather than from policy. This alternative approach then reveals the crisis as one of industrial financing, rather than as a policy-induced failure. The next section examines the corporate finance of the crisis. This is then followed by a section showing the key financial fault lines in the relative stabilization that has been achieved in Europe since 2013. The chapter concludes by arguing that, without industrial policy, European fiscal and monetary policy must remain endogenous to, or determined by, developments in the private sector.

7.2 Corporate Finance and the Crisis

Corporate finance has been largely overlooked in explanations of the crisis, in part because of four decades in which macroeconomists have been hectored about having 'micro-foundations', which entail everyone believing that the key decisions in the economy are made by households. Corporate and business structures are supposed to be mere details of 'principal-agent' inconsistencies between household agents. The neglect of corporate finance is a casualty of this dismissal of the firm as the key economic decision maker in the economy. Hence the part played by corporate finances of large corporations has not really been considered as in the analysis of the financial crisis (a rare exception here is the study of Cemex given in Vargas y Albino Luna (2012)).

In examining the role of corporate finance in the financial crisis, or indeed in any economic conjuncture a distinction needs to be made between non-financial business corporations and small and medium sized enterprises. The defining feature of business corporations that their corporate treasurers have access to the full range of financial markets, from banks, through capital markets, right up to derivatives markets. At the extreme, in the case of multinational corporations, they have access to financial markets in all parts of the world where they are not excluded by capital controls (as in China or India). This allows such corporations to take full advantage of long-term debt markets, to stabilize their financing costs, for example through the issue of shares on which payments and repayments, in the form of dividends and share buy backs, are at the discretion of the management, rather than determined by inflexible financial contracts. Long-term obligations like this also avoid the need to roll over debt.

At the other extreme are small and medium sized enterprises. They usually operate with finance borrowed from a bank, finance that is usually of a limited term, payments on which are contractually determined. Access to a limited range of other financial services, for example, leasing or foreign currency, is usually obtained through a given bank. In many countries (most notably in Germany) there exists a stratum of local banks specifically designated to provide financial services to small and medium sized firms. However, limited access to long-term debt markets makes firms in this sector vulnerable to changes in interest rates on financing and potential difficulties with rolling over shorter-term debt. This limited access to financial services by smaller companies, sometimes referred to as a 'financing gap', is the subject of a large literature, and policies to encourage 'venture' capital and capital market like facilities (a particular enthusiasm in the European Union under the Lisbon Agenda (see Frangakis 2009). Although this is not the place to give any comprehensive treatment of the topic, it is commonly forgotten in the discussion that the amount of risk capital in an economy at any one time is limited by the size and structure of the liabilities of long-term investment institutions (Toporowski 2010). The provision of unlimited capital to all enterprises would require a massive inflation of the capital and long-term debt markets that, without a corresponding inflation of intermediary institutions to maintain the liquidity in those markets, would increase financial instability well beyond anything that has been experienced so far in the capitalist world. In effect, the restriction on access to the capital market is a stabilizing factor in an otherwise unstable financial system.

Apart from access to the capital market, there is another economic distinction to be made between corporations and small and medium sized enterprises. This is that, despite the existence in some countries of an important segment of medium sized enterprises that engage in fixed capital investment and even technological innovation, in general it may be said that in virtually all capitalist countries, large industrial corporations account for the vast bulk of fixed business investment. Since such investment is the key private sector determinant of the business cycle, it is usually this (rather than government policy) that creates a given macroeconomic conjuncture of boom or recession. This is further explained in section 7.3 of this chapter in the context of the current difficulties of the Eurozone. Nevertheless, in virtually all capitalist countries, it is the small and medium sized enterprises that account for the majority of non-agricultural private sector employment. Thus, in the private sector, large corporations, through their investment, determine aggregate demand and employment, but small and medium sized enterprises actually employ most workers in that sector. This now gives us a framework for understanding how the present economic crisis was created in the sphere of corporate finance.

The corporate finance mechanism initiating the crisis was described in a report in the Business section of *The Economist* on 13 December 2008. The report revealed the key relationship between debt, capital market inflation, and investment in the economy in a review of the accounts of six of the largest industrial multinational companies. These companies had incurred net debts of $136 billion. The usual financial cycle analysis, drawn from Hayek, Keynes, Fisher, and Minsky, would suggest that this arose because of those companies' enthusiasm for fixed capital investment. In fact, the report states that four fifths of this debt was spent on mergers and acquisitions, driving the leverage ratio (ratio of net debt to equity) of these companies to an average of 2.6

(4.4 in the case of the acquisition-hungry Cemex, 4 in the case of Lafarge, and 3.5 in the case of Tata Steel).

With borrowing at an unsustainable level, what could the companies do? 'Raising equity is tricky since investors had been sucked dry by capital-hungry banks' (confirmation that the supply of equity is not as elastic as theory would suggest (see Toporowski 2010)). Nor would asset sales generate much cash inflow: 'disposals could occur only at miserly prices, if at all, because most potential buyers have no access to funds themselves' (*The Economist* 2008). The report concludes by identifying the mechanism that appears to the companies, and the author of the report, to be the most effective way of cutting their debt: 'in the fight to survive, the biggest weapons are cuts in production and capital spending. ArcelorMittal has led the way on the former with a reduction of output by one third that even its chairman, Lakshmi Mittal, calls "very aggressive". The cuts to investment plans are as dramatic: ArcelorMittal, Lafarge and Cemex have sliced their budgets for next year by between one third and one half, and on December 10th Rio (Tinto) cut its planned capital expenditure in 2009 from $9 billion to $4 billion. Xstrata has yet to announce its plans, but a 50 per cent reduction is possible.' (In the event, Xstrata cut its planned capital expenditure by $3 billion, leaving capital expenditure of $3.2 billion.)

The report concluded that these expenditure cuts 'would mean a $15bn boost in annual cash flow—equivalent to about 18 months' worth of interest costs...It is a glimmer of hope during these bleakest of times.' One may forgive a journalist for failing to see beyond the balance sheet that a corporation is trying to repair. But those familiar with the analysis of Fisher, Keynes, Kalecki, Minsky, and Steindl, know that this way of dealing with excess debt is the mechanism of economic depression in a finance driven economy.

Subsequent reports of the debt problems of large companies (i.e., companies with access to the capital markets) have confirmed that it is not their fixed capital investments, but their capital market operations that have driven those companies into difficulties. A report on Tata Motors, promoting its latest venture in car production in India (*The Economist* 2009) could not overlook the financial difficulties of this branch of the Tata empire. The report revealed that Tata Motors had a financial deficit that was expected to be at least $3.4 billion in 2009. 'About $1.4bn of that is in the form of short-term loans raised for working capital.' This working capital requirement arose due to current production costs exceeding sales revenue. The remaining '$2bn relates to the bridging loan taken out last year (i.e. in 2008) to finance its $2.3bn purchase of Jaguar Land Rover (JLR), a British premium carmaker, which must be either repaid or refinanced in June (2009)'. At the end of 2008, 'an attempt to raise $885m through a rights issue ended up with Tata Sons, the group holding company, taking up 61 per cent of the ordinary shares' (*The Economist* 2009).

In other words, the capital market was unable to provide most of the equity capital that the company needed.

Perhaps the most curious relationship between a large company and the capital markets is that of General Electric. This relationship is curious not only because it reveals so much about how large corporations use financial markets. It also demonstrates the willingness of management experts and economists to accept the claims of business leaders made charismatic by the financial boom. Under Jack Welch its chief executive from 1981 to 2001, General Electric was supposed to be managed in accordance with profit targets requiring quarterly increases in those profits. These were enforced by management techniques that bewitched the business press and the prestigious *Harvard Business Review*. Another recent report revealed that these profit increases were in fact largely due to the financial operations of General Electric's financial subsidiary GE Capital (*The Economist* 2009). GE Capital had been set up in 1932 as the General Electric Contracts Corporation to assist in financing the company's industrial activities. However, by the 1980s, GE Capital was in effect operating like a bank, raising funds through bond issues and commercial paper to invest in various financial assets. During the period of financial market inflation, GE Capital became a useful source of additional profits: if General Electric was due to miss its profit target, GE Capital would sell financial assets to generate the profits required. It was not the much touted efficient management of industrial resources that made General Electric so profitable, but the operations of its banking subsidiary GE Capital in the 'shadow banking system'.

In 2008, General Electric was plunged into difficulties when GE Capital found itself unable to roll over commercial paper due for repayment, and holding assets that could not be sold except at a loss. As a bank GE Capital benefitted from US government measures to support banking. However, the company lost its valuable AAA credit rating, which was cut in March 2009 to AA+, and was forced to cut its quarterly dividend by two thirds, the first time the dividend had been reduced since 1938. General Electric was forced to raise $15 billion of new capital from a consortium that included Warren Buffett's Berkshire Hathaway.

7.3 Stabilization and Deflation

The illiquidity of multinational corporations, and construction companies in Ireland and southern Europe, inevitably showed up in bank balance sheet as non-performing loans, or simply a lack of demand for credit, along with a failure of the credit turnover between bank accounts that occurs with investment and other forms of inter-company expenditure. At the same time, the crisis of government finances in its turn drained what little liquidity was left in banks, if only because government bonds that cannot be sold at a fair price must be held to maturity in order to preserve their value. It was recognition that a crisis of government finances could not be confined to government borrowing that finally persuaded the ECB to emulate belatedly the 'quantitative easing' of the US Federal Reserve and the Bank of England. In December 2011, and in the following March, the ECB allotted a total of just over €1 trillion of three year loans to banks at rates of interest of just under 1 per cent, virtually doubling the size of the ECB's balance sheet. These Long-Term Refinancing Operations (LTROs) were a very effective move. Not only did it relieve the liquidity of banks in Southern Europe. It also offered European governments the next best facility to central bank financing of a fiscal deficit, namely central bank financing of commercial banks' lending to governments. As long as the yield on government bonds exceeded the rate on central bank borrowing, it was going to be profitable for banks to finance governments.

The LTROs came in the wake of the Vienna Initiative of 2009 that showed the limitations of managing private sector liquidity by trying to influence bank lending. The Vienna Initiative was a much less formal arrangement under which European banks engaged in cross border lending (Italy's Unicredit, France's Société Générale, Austria's Raiffeisen International) were given 'financial support packages' by the World Bank, the European Bank for Reconstruction and Development (EBRD), and the European Investment Bank (EIB) in return for commitments not to reduce their lending in Central and Eastern Europe. Close to €33 billion of public money was lent to the commercial banks. Far from keeping their lending to Europe's new member states constant, the banks reduced their lending and managed to secure a postponement of required capital increases (Toporowski 2012).

In many respects, the Vienna Initiative showed how fatally compromised the long standing strategy of standardizing bank regulation was in Member States of the European Union, in the face of the deflation that was spreading through Europe. The parallels with attempts at international coordination of bank regulation were obvious. In difficulty, banks have to be rescued if a run on the financial system is to be avoided. But bank rescue also makes banks less dependent on regulators, whose inconvenient demands can be pushed down the agenda until after the crisis has been overcome. The only way out of the dilemma is macroeconomic management to ensure cash and income flows in the economy are adequate to meet debt obligations and that requires management of the business cycle in an open economy, rather than just management of debt.

Meanwhile, corporations in Europe have been building up their liquidity. *The Economist* reported on the 6 October 2012 that Arcelor Mittal was closing its blast furnaces at Florange in eastern France, due to reduced production by three of its key customers, the car makers PSA Peugeot-Citroën, Fiat, and Opel. But it also reported figures from Bloomberg which showed that the cash holdings (actually bank deposits) of the 300 largest companies in Europe had tripled since the crisis started to an average of US$9 billion (€7.25 billion), or US$2.7 trillion (€2.175 trillion) for the companies taken together (*The Economist* 2012).

The counterpart of this build-up in liquid assets is the 'forced indebtedness' of government and small and medium sized enterprises. Governments are forced to borrow to refinance banks and provide welfare support for the unemployed and those forced into poverty. The plight of small and medium sized enterprises is worse, because their size usually gives them a weaker position in their markets. Their borrowing, because of shrinking markets and squeezed profit margins, is inevitably more risky because it is more likely to be incurred to cover current costs, rather than building up assets.

With European governments forced into programmes of debt reduction, the prospects for the European economy depend on what the large corporations do with their liquid assets. The current deflation spreading through Europe makes it rational for those corporations to hold onto their bank deposits, or use them to repay debt, rather than speculating on an economic recovery. The engagement of the private sector in an industrial strategy planned and implemented by governments and the European Commission, with finance from the EIB, could give those corporations the incentive to start throwing their liquid assets into industrial and commercial circulation. In this way bank deposits are converted into income for firms, households and the government, instead of being locked up in bank accounts that require repeated central bank intervention for their liquidity. The extra €1 trillion of liquidity that the ECB announced, on 6 November 2014, that it would provide for bank balance sheets is a way of making banks more liquid. But it cannot make that liquidity circulate in the economy in the way in which firms can, through their expenditure, make their liquidity circulate among firms and households.

7.4 Conclusion

Without an industrial strategy led by government, fiscal and monetary policies are left more or less passively accommodating the business cycle determined by firms' expenditure. In this situation, automatic stabilizers in the fiscal deficit serve to moderate (but not eliminate) booms and slumps. There is a widening consensus, from the International Monetary Fund through the business press to conservative and progressive political circles, that the disabling of those stabilizers by austerity policy has clearly exacerbated the present 'recession'. At the same time, monetary policy (if it ever worked at all, since inflation targeting may just as well have made monetary policy endogenous to the business cycle) has been disabled by the failure of inter-bank markets in the recent crisis, and the bringing of those markets into the balance sheets of central banks. In this situation, industrial policy, beyond the provision of residual incomes and infrastructure through public works, is necessary to initiate and sustain an economic recovery. Mere fiscalism is not enough.

References

The Economist. 2008. 'Riding the Rollercoaster', 13 December: 73–4.

The Economist. 2009. 'General Electric: Losing Its Magic Touch', 19 March.

The Economist. 2009. 'The Tata Nano, The New People's Car—Why the Nano Alone Cannot Solve Mounting Problems of Its Maker', 26 March.

The Economist. 2012. 'Companies and the Euro Crisis', 6 October: 70–1.

Frangakis, M. 2009. 'EU Financial Market Integration Policy'. In J. Grahl (ed.), *Global Finance and Social Europe*. Cheltenham: Edward Elgar, 91–114.

Phillips, T. 2014. *Europe on the Brink Debt Crisis and Dissent on the European Periphery*. London: Zed Books.

Toporowski, J. 2010. 'A Theory of Capital Rationing'. Working Paper No. 166, Department of Economics, The School of Oriental and African Studies, University of London.

Toporowski, J. 2012. 'Vienna Initiative: Regulatory Capture and Policy Confusion'. *Bankwatch Mail*, 52 (May): 3.

Vargas y Albino Luna, G. 2012. 'El papel de la incertidumbre en la crise de Cemex'. *Economía Informa*, January–February (372): 34–50.

Wolf, M. 2014. *The Shifts and the Shocks*. New York: Penguin Press.

8

The Myth of the 'Meddling' State

Mariana Mazzucato

Policymakers have been asking themselves a burning question for a long time—well before the recent global economic crisis. That question is: where are the 'European Googles'—the innovators, the risk takers?

The answer we have heard to this question is that the US economic model is more 'entrepreneurial' than that in many parts of the globe. This is supposedly due to the prevalence of economic actors such as 'venture capitalists', who provide high risk funding to genius 'garage tinkerers' in their endless pursuit of innovation.

We are even told that Americans somehow have a greater entrepreneurial spirit, which makes them more tolerant of the occasional failures that go hand in hand with the occasional successes—like the Internet—that result from an endless experimentation process (Schramm 2013).

In general, there seems to be a consensus that the US model is more successful because it is more market driven. The perceived heavy hand of the state in Europe has made it slower, less efficient, less innovative—putting its growth, even before the crisis, under threat. And inside the US, the current battle in Congress over how large the state should be often resorts to claims that a larger state would wipe out the innovative drive of the economy.

Of course, economists understand that markets sometimes fail—with 'big-time' failures most recently. But in the end the state is still viewed, even by progressive economists, as a backseat player (Stiglitz 1993). Important for 'fixing' market failures but not for creating or shaping markets actively; guiding the capitalist engine.

But what if the image we are constantly fed—of a dynamic business sector contrasted with a necessary but sluggish bureaucratic, often 'meddling', state—is completely wrong? What if the revolutionary, most radical, changes in capitalism came not from the invisible hand of the market but the very visible hand of the state?

8.1 Changing the Narrative on the Role of the State

Indeed, the real story behind Silicon Valley is not the story of the state getting out of the way so that risk taking venture capitalists—and garage tinkerers—could do their thing. From the internet to nanotech, most of the fundamental advances—in both basic research but also downstream commercialization—were funded by government, with businesses moving into the game only once the returns were in clear sight (Block and Keller 2011). Indeed, all the radical technologies behind the iPhone were funded by government: the internet, GPS, touchscreen display, and even the new voice activated Siri personal assistant (Mazzucato 2013a).

These investments were not just about the government providing the 'basics'—like funding upstream research. The state funded both the basic and applied research and, in some cases, went as far downstream as to provide early stage risk finance to companies themselves that were deemed too risky for private finance. Apple initially received $500,000 from the Small Business Investment Corporation, a public financing arm of the government. Likewise, Compaq and Intel received early stage grants not from venture capital but via public capital through the Small Business Innovation Research (SBIR) Program. As venture capital has become increasingly short-term, SBIR loans and grants have had to increase their role in early stage seed finance.

While many of the examples sound as if they are related to the military, they are actually everywhere, including in the US Department of Health and the Department of Energy. Indeed, it turns out that 75 per cent of the most innovative drugs owe their funding not to Big Pharma or to venture capital but to that of the National Institutes of Health (NIH). Since 2000, the NIH invested more than $400bn (2013 dollars) in the biotech-pharma knowledge base, $29bn in 2013 alone.

Although venture capital entered the biotech industry in the late 1980s and early 1990s, all the heavy investments in this sector occurred in the 1950s, 1960s, and 1970s—and were mostly made by the state (Mazzucato and Dosi 2006; Vallas, Kleinman, and Biscotti 2011). Venture capitalists entered twenty years after the state funded the most high risk and capital intensive parts of the industry. And their desire to reap back returns within 3–5 years has also done quite a bit of damage to the industry (Lazonick and Tulum 2011). Today it is filled with productless companies that produce little for the economy beyond the returns earned by private equity in the exit stage.

We are seeing the same pattern being repeated in clean technology. In countries including the US, China, Singapore, Germany, Finland, and Denmark, the state funds the difficult areas that are characterized by high capital intensity and technological and market uncertainty. Business is waiting for future returns to become more certain.

These examples are important for three reasons. First, they tell a very different story about the drivers of capitalism in areas like Silicon Valley—and hence also offer very different recipes for countries that are failing. Is Greece having problems because its state is too large, or because its state is not doing enough? Are Germany and Denmark among the stronger countries in Europe because they have 'tightened their belts' or because their governments have spent more than most EU governments on areas such as research and development (R&D), and have the type of 'patient', long-term committed public finance that China also has?

Is Europe's problem the lack of risk capital, or the lack of a wave of state funding for that risk capital to surf on? Evidence points to the latter. And no matter how much venture capital and private equity we try to muster up, it is the wave that is missing.

Second, they teach us why so many policies aimed at unleashing entrepreneurship are ineffective. Here it is interesting to go to economist John Maynard Keynes, who actually did not talk about innovation. He talked about government and was an expert on what drives private investment. He used the phrase 'animal spirits' to talk about the volatility of investment, driven more by gut instincts and herd behaviour than by rationality. And he used this to justify why you need government investment to stabilize growth.

However, in a private letter to President Roosevelt in the 1930s, Keynes also talked about businesses as 'domesticated animals' (Keynes 1938). And indeed, this distinction, which he did not really delve into, is vital. Are we talking about businesses as lions in cages, who simply need barriers to be taken away for them to roar; or are we talking about pussy cats who need to be groomed into lions? So much of policy today assumes the former. Different types of tax cuts—whether they are capital gains tax cuts, or taxes aimed at reducing the cost of R&D—assume that business is willing and able to spend.

In fact, these stories show us that they are only willing after the state leads the way and takes the risk. Did Pfizer recently move out of Kent in the UK to Boston in the US due to the lower taxes and regulation in Boston? Or due to the $30bn a year that taxpayers in the US fund through the NIH? Many businesses complain about taxes but walk to where the government spending is. Yet the two contradict each other since lower taxes are de-funding the public purse.

This brings me to the third point and the biggest problem. By not admitting to the role of the state as lead risk taker and entrepreneur, what we are increasingly witnessing is a dysfunctional capitalism—where the risk for innovation is increasingly socialized yet the profits are privatized. And this is putting the innovation machine at risk.

If we acknowledge that the state does not only fix markets but creates them through active risk taking, we need to have a more direct mechanism that brings something back into a public 'innovation fund' that can be used to fund the next round. Had only 1 per cent of the direct financial profits from the internet come back to the state to compensate for its seed funding, there would be much more today to spend on Green-tech, which is being starved—and only gently 'nudged' rather than pushed as previous revolutions were (Mazzucato 2013a).

While many argue that this return generating mechanism is the tax system itself, we live in an era in which major global corporations, whose products descend directly or indirectly from state funded research, use legal loopholes to pay hardly any tax (Lazonick and Mazzucato 2013). We socialize the risks, but not the rewards.

In the end, it is about not hyping up myths about innovation 'eco-systems' but admitting who does what in them—and allowing the rewards to be as social as the risks taken. Otherwise, growth might be 'smart', but surely not 'inclusive'. This will hurt not only future innovation (starving the state of funds, despite it being one of the lead innovators) but also the wellbeing of future generations.

8.2 Setting both the Pace and Direction of Change

The state also plays a prime role in financing and directing innovation. Further, finance for innovation must be long-term, committed, and patient (Mazzucato 2013b). It can and will thus only be done by government institutions, but these institutions must be independent of the electoral process.

Countries that have turned out to be successful in public funding of innovation have done so with the help of largely independent public institutions: the US Department of Energy, the Finnish Innovation Fund Sitra, and the Office of the Chief Scientist in Israel's Ministry of Industry. The process works even better when those institutions are decentralized and 'don't get too much attention' (Breznitz and Ornston 2013). Indeed, when these institutions are decentralized and well funded they are more willing to fail because it is less high profile. US president Ronald Reagan, for example, who was against big government, doubled the spending of decentralized government agencies that founded innovation.

However, independence and decentralization are not the only requirements for institutional innovation. It is also crucial for the state to have an innovative drive direction and this requires a vision (Mazzucato, 2015). This has been captured by the notion of 'mission-oriented' innovation policies, such as those behind the Manhattan and Apollo projects (Mowery, Nelson, and Martin 2010; Foray, Mowery, and Nelson 2012).

Until now, the most common view is that of the state coming in to fill the gaps in sectors such as basic research where the private sector stays away because it is difficult to appropriate the returns. Vision is something completely different: it is the state identifying and creating new spaces and setting up entire eco-systems of innovation that will then attract the talent that is needed to move forward.

These eco-systems, where they work well, have certain characteristics. Countries in Europe that are succeeding in growing through innovation like Finland, Denmark, or Germany have patient capital, science–industry links and a great deal of medium sized companies. Germany's development bank KfW, for instance, not only invests in R&D, but these investments are also 'green directed' (Mazzucato and Penna 2014). And green does not only mean solar and wind, it also means really transforming industries. The same goes for China that is spending 1.7 trillion dollars on seven new areas that have been identified by the government and that are all related to some extent to the 'green' transformation of industries.

8.3 Lessons for Europe

Several lessons can be drawn for Europe from the evidence presented here. However, Europe first has to address a problem of internal contradiction. On the one hand, Europe is pursuing an innovative drive. In November 2011, the European Commission announced an 80-billion-euro research, innovation, and competitiveness programme called Horizon 2020. This programme is supposed to provide direct stimulus to the economy and secure our science and technology base and industrial competitiveness core the future, promising a smarter, more sustainable, and more inclusive society.

Although, this programme is promising, on the other hand the treasuries at national level and the commission's Directorate General for Economic and Financial Affairs (ECOFIN) at the cross national level still stick to their macroeconomic theories of where growth comes from: free markets, the ideal locus for the 'revolutionary and innovative' private sector. In particular, the Fiscal Compact and its requirements for national budgets to be in balance have significantly undermined the ability of the state to become a strong economic actor and have deprived it from any meaningful possibility to use deficit financing to promote growth, innovation, and investment. The state is allowed to only address market failures and 'level the playing field' for the private initiative. No vision, no targeted public investments in radical innovations. And no European Googles.

The first thing that Europe needs to do is become much more coherent and have innovation become a central part of macro growth policies. Otherwise innovation policies remain in the 'ghetto', and even when spending increases, if this is not coherent with macroeconomic strategies, it is destined to fail.

Second, it is important to get innovation policy out of that market failure framework where the role of the state is to either just solve the public good problem, or at best, create the conditions for innovation in this really dynamic private sector.

The private sector requires government to be much bolder and directly invest in certain areas and this translates to the need of governments to make a decision where to invest.

The skewed distributions of competiveness in Europe tend to prove this point. The places that are least competitive, Greece and parts of Italy, as well as parts of Portugal and Spain, are those that had no strategic state funding. And Germany's success is based on massive spending on strategic innovation funding, via the state bank KfW, the Fraunhofer Institute, a great network of research institutions with dynamic links to the private sector and the clearly 'green direction' of research. Everybody thinks that Germany became more competitive because it kept wages down; obviously that was part of the strategy, but that would never have been enough to win procurement contracts in the UK. For instance, Siemens is winning procurement contracts in the UK to build trains and this is because they produce greener, faster, more modern trains, as a result of a successful industrial policy framework.

What is the solution to Europe's skewed distribution of competitiveness? Countries like Greece should not do what Germany says it does, but what it actually did: get a proper state investment bank, get the Fraunhofer institute, get the diversified financial structures, spend on research and development and direct it.

Finally, Europeans should learn to cooperate, to rely on each other and to allow a certain division of labour. We should let the Greece do solar panels, Germany machine tools, Italy art, the UK science—not exclusively but to some extent, with this division of labour, Europe could become a competitive hub. This requires not only actively discovering, but also *shaping and creating* 'comparative advantages' (Rodrik 2004). We should think together how we can all work with our capacities and use our tools. The European Investment Bank for example, could help us achieve these areas of serious competitiveness. However, in order for these strategies to be successful we need to get the story right and rid our minds of the image that the state is a place for 'boring bureaucrats'.

References

Block, F. L. and Keller, M. R. 2011. *State of Innovation: The U.S. Government's Role in Technology Development*. Boulder, CO: Paradigm Publishers.

Breznitz, D. and Ornston, D. 2013. 'The Revolutionary Power of Peripheral Agencies Explaining Radical Policy Innovation in Finland and Israel'. *Comparative Political Studies*, 46: 1219–45.

Foray, D., Mowery, D., and Nelson, R. R. 2012. 'Public R&D and Social Challenges: What Lessons from Mission R&D Programs?' *Research Policy*, 41: 1697–702.

Keynes, J. M. 1938. 'Private Letter to Franklin Delano Roosevelt'. In D. E. Moggridge (ed.), *Maynard Keynes: An Economist's Biography*. London: Routledge, 1992.

Lazonick, W. and Mazzucato, M. 2013. 'The Risk–Reward Nexus in the Innovation–Inequality Relationship: Who Takes the Risks? Who Gets the Rewards?' *Industrial and Corporate Change*, 22: 1093–128.

Lazonick, W. and Tulum, Ö. 2011. 'US Biopharmaceutical Finance and the Sustainability of the Biotech Business Model'. *Research Policy*, 40: 1170–87.

Mazzucato, M. 2013a. *The Entrepreneurial State: Debunking the Public vs. Private Myth in Risk and Innovation*. London: Anthem Press.

Mazzucato, M. 2013b. 'Financing Innovation: Creative Destruction vs. Destructive Creation'. *Industrial and Corporate Change*, 22: 851–67.

Mazzucato, M. 2015. "From Market Fixing to Market-Creating: A new framework for innovation policy", Forthcoming in Industry and Innovation: "Innovation Policy – can it make a difference?" also SPRU Working Paper 2015–25 https://ideas.repec.org/p/sru/ssewps/2015–25.html.

Mazzucato, M. and Dosi, G. (eds). 2006. *Knowledge Accumulation and Industry Evolution: The Case of Pharma-Biotech*. Cambridge: Cambridge University Press.

Mazzucato, M. and Penna, C. C. R. 2014. 'Beyond Market Failures: State Investment Banks and the "Mission-Oriented" Finance for Innovation'. SPRU Working Paper Series, No. 2014–21.

Mowery, D. C., Nelson, R. R., and Martin, B. R. 2010. 'Technology Policy and Global Warming: Why New Policy Models Are Needed (or Why Putting New Wine in Old Bottles Won't Work)'. *Research Policy*, 39: 1011–23.

Rodrik, D. 2004. 'Industrial Policy for the Twenty-First Century'. John F. Kennedy School of Government Working Paper Series No. rwp04-047.

Schramm, C. J. 2013. *The Entrepreneurial Imperative: How America's Economic Miracle Will Reshape the World (and Change Your Life)*. New York: HarperCollins.

Stiglitz, J. E. 1993. 'The Role of the State in Financial Markets'. Proceedings of the World Bank Conference on Development Economics Supplement, World Bank, Washington, D.C.

Vallas, S. P., Kleinman, D. L., and Biscotti, D. 2011. 'Political Structures and the Making of US Biotechnology'. In F. Block and M. R. Keller (eds), *State of Innovation: The U.S. Government's Role in Technology Development*. Boulder, CO: Paradigm Publishers, 57–76.

9

Regional Industrial Development

Moving Beyond Specialization

Michele Mastroeni and Alessandro Rosiello

9.1 Introduction

The impact of the current economic crisis is contributing to the reshaping of the industrial structure of various OECD (The Organisation for Economic Co-operation and Development) economies and beyond. Manufacturing sectors are particularly exposed to competition from emerging countries (OECD 2012) and fiscal pressures are pushing governments to reflect on how to invest more strategically in new domains of growth. Regional administrations are increasingly seen as key actors to design resilient economies in the face of global competition (Barca 2009; Hudson 2010; OECD 2011; Birch, MacKinnon, and Cumbers 2010). While this renewed interest in regional development coincides with a shift away from old structuralist or neo-classical approaches to industrial policy, a number of questions regarding the conceptual strength and practical implementation of some recent approaches to regional development and policy need to be addressed. Our central concern is with the strategic approach termed 'smart specialization' (SmSp) and its focus on prioritizing economic activities with greater potential for growth by relying on processes of 'entrepreneurial discovery' (Foray, David, and Hall 2011; Foray and Goenaga 2013), a notion that draws on Hausmann and Rodrik's (2003) view of development as a 'self-discovery process'. However, not enough advancement has been made in either the theory or the practice of SmSp (Mastroeni, Tait, and Rosiello 2013). There are unresolved issues regarding how to deal with the complexity of institutional structures and internal and external networks that make up innovation systems, and does the approach deal with the constantly evolving nature of the institutional structures as new practices are established, new market niches opened, and new functions needed to help the process of innovation to continue. We will put forward the challenges that face regional innovation policy and the features that will be necessary for an effective framework, and illustrate these with empirical examples in the area of venture capital (VC) and risk finance policy.

9.2 Regional Innovation Policy

Policy focusing on regional systems of innovation (RSI) has, for the last two to three decades, been pursued by governments as a way to spur economic growth and prompt high value economic activity. The justification for innovation policy has always been based on the economic growth that innovation is expected to cause through temporary monopolies and the new market spaces created in the process of delivering new products, services, and processes to the market/end user. Initially, policy intervention to promote this kind of growth has been based on market failures and correcting the inability of entrepreneurs to capture a large portion of the benefits of knowledge creation due to its nature as a public good (McCann and Ortega-Argiles 2013). More recently, however, market failure rationales were seen to 'provide important rationales for public sector intervention, but rarely sufficient guidance for the degree of intervention in particular instances; nor do they address the many other potential institutional and connection failures which may arise in an innovation system' (McCann and Ortega-Argiles 2013 quoting Hughes 2012: 38), therefore the rationale for intervention has switched to a systems approach. Systems approaches look at, in addition to market failures, failure of knowledge flows, system lock-in, and institutional incompatibilities that may stifle innovation (McCann and Ortega-Argiles 2013).

Innovation systems, with all their component parts, are complex systems—the complexity means that each system differs from another since the unique characteristics, strengths, history, and structure of each component will impact the whole (Martin and Sunley 2011; Camagni and Capello 2013). Policy therefore needs to be implemented with this in mind: different components of an RSI will evolve along different timelines, and basing policy on the success of other RSIs is not adequate since the unique evolutionary path of such a system does not guarantee similar results if 'best practices' are simply cut and pasted (Uyarra 2010).

A dynamic approach is therefore necessary both to understanding the function of systems of innovation and to plan policy that nudges, pushes, and pulls the features to match strategic objectives. In this regard, it is our view that an effective policy approach will be based on an initial assessment of a region's strengths, capacities, resources and limitations, and cyclical reassessments that track the evolution of the different system features according to how they compare to a strategic outline. In order to do this, a life cycle approach is generally recommended by scholars based on an industry's evolution from an emergent phase through to a growth stage, expansion, stagnation, and reorganization/failure (Avnimelech and Teubal 2006, 2008). As industries evolve business models and behaviour patterns stabilize, and the knowledge, skills, and capital requirements for the industry change from phase to phase; policy needs to take these changes into consideration.

At the same time, the *individual* features of *a region* are crucial to an innovation system's evolution, therefore not only is an industry's life cycle important (which spreads across regions and is generally global for knowledge based industries) but also the life cycle of the local cluster which may ebb, flow, and change to a different rhythm. Martin and Sunley (2011) highlight these differences very clearly noting that there are many diverse evolutionary paths that local clusters or regional systems may take, both in terms of positive growth and development, but also in terms of random change, contraction and/or failure and disappearance. Clusters, and RSIs, are complex adaptive (i.e., evolving) systems that 'are made up of numerous components with functions and interrelationships that imbue the system as a whole with a particular identity' (1303), and with differing levels of connectivity internally but also to external components.

Menzel and Fornahl (2009) also describe how different clusters belonging to the same industry can follow different growth paths, citing Saxenian's 1994 comparison of Boston and Silicon Valley. They also note that some clusters may dissolve if they become too locked-in to a particular path with little flexibility for change, while others can become renewed, depending on the ability of firms to take advantage of exogenous events such as changing technological frameworks or a lead company's restructuring, or on the ability of firms to interact with each other and continue to find related but equally new and profitable pathways to new innovations.

According to Cooke (2012), the ability of clusters to renew themselves depends upon the ability of the actors involved to consider the broad and overlapping activities occurring in the regional economy in a way that allow for the reconstruction of knowledge so that new ideas and new solutions can emerge and facilitate new niches of activity to arise. This echoes Hall and Clark's (2010) statement that successful innovation systems, being complex adaptive systems, are those that allow for 'mobilizing different pieces of information to resolve a changing series of challenges and opportunities' (322). The signature of innovation is no longer a single node of expertise but rather one of multiple nodes of expertise interacting with each other.

Innovative capacity will depend on features such as the mix of extant knowledge (Asheim, Boschma, and Cooke 2011) or older (but related) industries (Birch, MacKinnon, and Cumbers 2010), the resultant absorptive capacity, and other such pre-held features which can have been put in place by 'accident' or through earlier strategic policy. Like Martin and Sunley, Menzel and Fornahl note that it is the specific elements—or functions—that operate within the innovative space defined as a cluster or system of innovation a that determine the ability of the system to evolve, change, grow, or decline.

The policy planning therefore needs to reflect this contextual complexity, identify the unique strengths and weakness of system functions (see also Cooke 2012 and Mastroeni, Tait, and Rosiello 2013), and maintain an analytical viewpoint that moves from the local to national to the global levels of interaction, knowledge exchange, and impact.

9.2.1 *Smart Specialization as the European Approach*

In Europe, the economic crisis of 2008 has meant that policy is being anchored by two principles: (i) long-term growth through innovation, (ii) but with a more frugal and efficient use of resources and public investments. In order to achieve this, the concept of SmSp has been introduced by the Knowledge for Growth working group (Foray, David, and Hall 2011) and adapted by the European Commission (EC) in its Rationale for Action (2010); and further developed by the OECD (2012). For the EC, SmSp is based on the idea that General Purpose Technologies (GPTs such as information technology, biotechnology, and nanotechnology) have become prevalent in society and the economy, and these GPTs are (or are becoming) a factor in increased productivity. In terms of where the GPTs are developed, however, Europe is made up of regions that are research and development (R&D) and innovation 'hotspots' (e.g., Cambridge, UK, the Oresund region of Denmark, and Sweden), and regions that are lagging in the development/absorption of these technologies (and the underlying scientific base). SmSp, therefore, involves the targeting of these current 'hotspots' to further develop the GPTs, sharing this knowledge with other regions of Europe so that more specialized applications of the technologies could be developed in regionally specific industries (i.e., a localized process of incremental innovation), leading to improved productivity and creating an overall and more equitable rate of economic growth across all European regions. Duplication of R&D efforts in GPTs across European regions is seen as an unnecessary waste of resources when synergies of radical and incremental innovation can feasibly be developed across those same regions.

As currently proposed by the Knowledge for Growth Working Group and EC documents, SmSp depends on private sector entrepreneurs discovering and pursuing the opportunities for innovative applications of GPTs in the various European regions, with public policy lending support to these efforts. Such support will include many of the resources often discussed in the innovation studies literature such as education, skills development, and infrastructure, though in a more targeted manner. Supporting entrepreneurial efforts will also include providing finance or facilitating the availability of capital to support the creation of small and medium sized firms, often touted as being important sites of innovative activity and the main locus of entrepreneurial efforts. This is not a new argument or revelation, though SmSp may argue for more specific targeting; however, some key points that must be considered that have not yet been addressed by proponents of SmSp, and are described in the following two paragraphs as challenges or concerns facing RSI policy.

The first concern is that policy emphasis on specialization may induce lock-in effects on the basis of existing path dependencies, rather than strategic differentiation via exploitation of technological convergence and related (knowledge variety (Cooke 2012)). A second concern is the already mentioned potential of relying on a static view of RSI rather than taking a dynamic or evolutionary view of a region's development and the different aspects that make up a functioning innovative milieu (within cluster of RSI). For example, with SmSp, the assumption is that there will be entrepreneurs present in a local economy to identify the opportunities for GPT exploitation and with the capacities to pursue them; it may be that the skills base or local practices are inadequate for the kind of activity necessary for successful SmSp. Policy must therefore reflect and be timed to meet the different system needs, to optimize the investment of resources and minimize the failures of policies, avoiding the commitment of resources where users may be unprepared or incapable of utilizing them. The current thinking around SmSp, beside some few examples, has not shown the necessary acknowledgement of complexity, and seems to default into a static view of policy addressing RSI weakness in a one off manner. This concern is particularly relevant to finance that aids or provides risk capital investment—if a pipeline of opportunities does not exist upon which investors can realistically invest, then the resources may be wasted or misused. According to Foray and Goenaga (2013), identifying windows of opportunity for policy intervention along the regional development cycle represents a key and yet very problematic challenge.

Finally, while SmSp and regional innovation policy in general is targeted at a particular region or local jurisdiction, neglecting the broader national and international links is a third concern, given the importance of knowledge networks and knowledge flows (both within and across regions) for innovation systems to function. Overall, therefore, without a dynamic multilevel approach to planning regional policy, the assorted problems discussed above would not be overcome.

9.2.2 Venture Capital: A (Key) Component of the RSI

In the area of risk finance the complexity of the system is particularly high and the policy challenges seem particularly difficult. When evaluating innovation policy or performing the initial analysis upon which to base policy, at the very least two overlapping cycles or system progressions must be considered: the endogenously driven cluster life cycle and the exogenously (to the local setting) driven industry life cycle. However, the complexity can increase when looking at risk capital as invested in a knowledge intensive sector. Analysing the effect of VC on an emerging tech cluster, let alone planning policy to support it, must contend with the emerging cluster's life cycle, the related industrial life cycle, the global VC cycle of expansion and contraction, and the experience and growth of the local venture capitalists (i.e., the local VC cluster). Risk financing and VC investment on innovation based sectors means that the strengths and weaknesses of the industry receiving investment must be considered (hence consideration of the related industry and cluster life cycles). VC itself, however, is a subsector of the financial industry subject to the expansion and contraction cycles of global finance, as well as the local knowledge base, network connections, and 'smart money' of investors that would be operating in a particular region; as many VC investors tend to operate locally, this means that they can be seen through a 'local cluster' lens as well.

While the complexity of investing in, or supporting through policy, a VC/risk finance market in a region is high, the importance that has been given to the availability of this kind of capital for the knowledge economy has meant that policy will still be directed to it. Much of the attention to VC in the knowledge economy is closely tied to the importance given to small high technology firms as they are seen as important locally based sources of innovative activity and job creation. Sjogren and Zackrisson (2005) explain how such firms display higher risk, few fixed assets (or bricks and mortar), and whose products/services may be problematic for investors to understand, thereby making traditional bank financing or traded stock activity difficult to engage in right away. Bartzokas and Mani (2004) and Pfirrmann, Wupperfeld, and Lerner (1997) all highlight the challenge that small or start up high tech companies face in terms of attracting finance because of the high information asymmetries and associated risk. In terms of building entrepreneurial capacity, VC is therefore important because investors are more willing to engage with this uncertainty than others, many times investing based on their knowledge of the management team rather than the company or product, and working from a different risk/return ratio than more traditional funders.

Moreover, the importance of VC investors is not simply in their provision of funds, but also in their provision of market expertise and networks to the young firms (Lerner 1999; von Burg and Kenney 2000). Financiers not only provide the funds, but also explicitly help to shape the firms that operate in the industry. Financiers often have to rely on tacit knowledge, visceral instincts, and personal trust in their decisions due to information asymmetry, a lack of 'benchmarks' for new product or new market performance, and the inherent risk in innovation (von Burg and Kenney 2000). Financiers manipulate the market and bring to the arena various contacts in different areas of the innovation process. These contacts range from other firms along the production line to researchers and potential clients, effectively creating and shaping markets for the innovative products in which they are investing. North, Baldock, and Ullah (2013) re-emphasize the difficulties small high tech firms face in terms of finance, but also note that because of their particular informational constraints, it is 'reasonable to expect [these firms] to have been particularly adversely affected by the recent financial crisis. Indeed, it has been suggested that those small business most capable of creating new jobs and stimulating economic growth are being prevented from doing so by limited access to investment capital' (238).

Pierrakis (2010) notes the cyclical behaviour of VC investment in the UK, how VC retreated after the dot.com crisis, and a greater retreat and retrenchment with the more current financial crisis (falling each year from 2007 to 2009). New firms in particular faced difficulties, as many investors sought to maintain their existing portfolio of investments. Both crisis periods showed that seed and first round companies (i.e., early investments) were the most vulnerable. North, Baldock, and Ullah (2013) highlight the fact that many VC investors are lowering their risk by investing later in a technology firm's life cycle, less in seed and very early stage investments. North, Baldock, and Ullah describe a 'finance escalator' that in theory should exist in a system of innovation with a functioning risk capital market; the escalator begins with (i) public seed grants, (ii) private equity from business angels and public supported VC, (iii) corporate and institutional VC, and finally (iv) bank debt finance. The implication of venture capital investors moving towards later stage investments means that the finance escalator, at least in the case of the UK studied by North, Baldock, and Ullah, is not functioning as well as it should, again emphasizing the complexity of engaging this sector with policy.

The image that is presented to policymakers looking to enhance growth and move their national or regional economy beyond the difficulties and contractions of the economic crisis is that innovation is still a mechanism to expand the economic sphere of activity of a region, as well as capturing growth and encouraging productivity. We also see the complexity of the innovative process and the system within which it occurs, given its multiple components and constantly evolving nature. The finance of this whole process remains of paramount importance; if anything, however, rather than becoming smoother over time with market failures being removed, the various layers of activity impacting VC provision and the risk perceived by investors means that policy to support or provide VC must take into account, regional, national, and global influences. Most important, as Harrison et al. (2010) state, besides a flow of risk capital,

> there is a parallel requirement for a flow of entrepreneurial capital—individuals and teams able to see and willing to exploit entrepreneurial opportunities—and a pool of managerial talent (human talent) with the experience and expertise to successfully manage the business growth and market development process. To these must be added deep pools of *intellectual capital* (the ideas and creativity on which business is based) and *market capital* (deep knowledge of and experience in relevant markets) (Harrison et al. 2010: 212–13).

As already noted by authors such as Mason and Harrison (2003) and Rosiello and Parris (2009), this means that the different functions and components of an innovation system are intertwined, and the different cycles of evolution must be considered and engaged with appropriately if policy decisions are made to intervene. In particular, entrepreneurs are attracted by money as much as investors are attracted by pools of 'investor ready' opportunities; the two tend to co-evolve in the context of emergent RIS within their areas of specialization:

> emergence coincides with processes of cumulative and collective learning: formal and informal networks and knowledge flows, collective adaptation to changing conditions, forms of coordinated behaviour to deal with transactional problems (dilution and internal conflicts), technical challenges (moving compounds through R&D stages) and managerial risks (high attrition rates and regulatory uncertainty). All of these mechanisms allow learning through direct interaction and apprenticeship (Rosiello and Parris 2009: 204).

In the rest of the chapter, we will be illustrating the points with different empirical examples. Israel will be discussed to illustrate how policy to launch VC can fail yet also spark a learning process that can lead to future success in VC provision to the IT sector. Scotland's experience in the biotech domain will be discussed to illustrate how VC can ebb and flow at different times, and how system adaptations to early challenges can influence the ability of the system to make future change or grow (i.e., initial VC growth and investment followed by retraction; angel funding filling the gap but currently conflicting with expansion capita). Ireland in the period following the dot.com bubble bursting (i.e., *c.*2003) demonstrates the combined impact of practices conditioned by the global VC industry's contraction, as well as the inexperience of the local investors using public funds to reduce or share their risk in the Irish indigenous software sector. Sweden in the period following the dot.com bubble bursting and later in 2010 shows the impact of the local corporate network strengths conditioning investor behaviour in the newly established VC market and the country's specialisms in IT and life sciences. At the same time it shows how it responded to changes in the global economy and in the technology sectors as Small and medium-sized enterprises' (SMEs) innovative performance and importance grew in an economy normally characterized by multinational firms.

9.3 Case Studies

The cases discussed in this chapter have been selected because they represent different attempts to strengthen systems of innovation through government intervention, and the creation of a VC market or provision of risk finance. As a result, they are representative of how similar policy starting points will diverge based on the local conditions, but also how global exogenous factors will have an impact on the system. Furthermore, the cases were selected because of the availability of data from academic literature, grey literature, and interviews which the authors have gathered from 2003 to 2013. The authors analysed the cases of Scotland, Ireland, and Sweden by first reviewing the published data on the innovation systems and investment practices for each case, and then contributed to this data by analysing government and industry documents, and drawing on interviews with regional stakeholders on the issues of innovation policy and investment. The case of Israel as analysed mostly through a literature review, and in this case the authors also drew on insights shared by colleagues on the Israeli innovation system during a European Commission Framework 7 project (TARGET).

9.3.1 Israel

The case of Israel's development of a VC industry demonstrates some of the key points highlighted above: the preceding creation and growth of entrepreneurial activity, the uncertainty of policy efforts and the high chance of risk, the importance of learning in policy, the importance of international networks, and the impact that exogenous events may have on the development of an industry. The VC industry did not develop smoothly in Israel, but ultimately it shows a positive combination of policy learning, and the identification and leveraging of opportunities from very unique characteristics of the Israeli economy.

Jeng and Wells (2000) describe the Israeli VC industry as nascent between 1988 and 1997, with only one fund of 30 million US dollars, and most of the funds coming from large investment holding groups. In 1992, the Likud government set up the Yozma programme both to invest in funds as well as directly into companies; in 1993 Yozma provided 100 million in nine VC funds, by 1996 the VC industry had leveraged this to raise 1 billion and the government decided to leave the market. In doing this, to ensure that investors remained in Israel, the government enacted temporary legislation for tax-free investing in VC funds by large funds that had tax free status in their home (i.e., foreign) country. The growth of the Israeli VC market was not standalone, however; it was intimately connected to the development of the software industry and the nationally specific strengths that allowed that sector to develop.

Avnimelech and Teubal (2004) describe how the Six Day War and the boycott of technological trade by France led to Israeli policymakers emphasizing self-sufficiency, spurring heavy investment and support in R&D. This security-oriented decision led to the simultaneous development of the military and civilian IT sector, with the military having the most resources to invest in the actual R&D but also in human capital development in terms of training and hands on experience. Breznitz (2005) argues that the military not only trained personnel and provided R&D space and experience, but also provided a space for formal and informal knowledge exchange and network development, leading to a well-connected and skilled pool of technicians and engineers. Breznitz (2007) also argues that Israel's development of the IT sector and VC industry was possible from the close links with the US financial and IT sectors. Early Israeli IT firms were developed without risk capital, but had managed access to the US market and managed to 'bootstrap' or self-fund to successful initial public offerings (IPOs), building confidence and momentum in the industry. The period of relative stability of the 1980s meant many engineers were released from the military, and many were immigrating to Israel from the Soviet Union, so that the talent pool increased. The Office of the Chief Scientist continued to invest in IT, and the Binational Industrial Research and Development Foundation (BIRD, US and Israel) supported firms without equity investment, leading to the creation of entrepreneurial opportunity, some of which needed the spark of funding (Jeng and Wells 2000; Avnimelech and Teubal 2004; Breznitz 2007).

What is particularly noteworthy is that the Israeli government attempted to spur VC creation with the Inbal programme in 1992. The programme was set up to guarantee the investment of publicly-traded VC funds, but was too constraining in terms of how funds could invest and how quickly and flexibly funds could operate in their investments (Avnimelech and Teubal 2006). This failure, however, facilitated success later on in that it created a learning process that fed into the subsequent Yozma programme; this programme corrected the errors of the previous programme, required Israeli funds to partner with foreign funds (enhancing their skill set), and provided an environment of learning in terms of due diligence work, deal flow, and exits. The policy intervention in the area of VC creation was therefore inseparable from the decisions made in the sphere of security and industrial policy leading to the development of an internationally connected IT sector. Furthermore, the timing of the programs should be noted in that Inbal and Yozma coincided with the global growth of the IT sector, with sufficient time to build experience and establish a critical mass of firms (both in IT and VC firms) before the dot.com crisis set in.

9.3.2 Scotland

While Israel was able to build a VC industry *in tandem* with an entrepreneurial IT sector which provided the entrepreneurial, intellectual, and market capital necessary for a critical mass to build a growth oriented regional system of innovation, Harrison et al. (2010) note that Scotland has struggled to achieve the same levels of entrepreneurial capital. The Scottish economy has been dominated for a long time by a 'small number of large, international competitive corporations' (213); but these same companies do not provide sufficient traction for an innovation system to develop and create an internal or indigenous dynamic of innovation-based growth.

Scottish policymakers recognized this deficiency and sought to encourage the creation of Scottish start-ups across the knowledge based sectors, in particular ICT and the life sciences. In order to do this, the Scottish public sector, mostly through Scottish Enterprise, launched a set of horizontal (i.e., non-industry specific) policies aimed at providing risk capital to start-up firms such as the Scottish Co-Investment Fund (investing up to £500K per firm), the Seed Fund (£100K per firm), as well as funds to facilitate proof of concept development and to support innovative projects in small firms (Rosiello, Avnimelech, and Teubal 2011). The Scottish case shows policy heterogeneity and a completely different development trajectory of systems of innovation, including components of those systems such as risk finance (Rosiello, Avnimelech, and Teubal 2011).

In Scotland most risk finance is provided by the public sector, London-based VC funds, and small angel investors based in Scotland, rather than locally based private limited partnership funds as the majority of VC providers have become in Israel. While this looked like an adequate alternative development path for Scotland's risk finance, it has also meant that it is less resilient in the face of exogenous shocks—firm failures and downturns in financial markets means that private VC investors in London and abroad are more hesitant than before to invest in new ventures in Scotland (Harrison et al. 2010; Pierrakis 2010; Mason, Botelho, and Harrison 2013). Over the past few years, VC investment over 2 million GBP has been constantly decreasing and almost halved between 2010 and 2011, from 62.8 m to 33.8m, with some large VC being made predominantly in the IT/media, life sciences, and renewables domains (Young Company Finance 2012). Harrison et al. (2010) note that much of the fluctuations in Scotland's risk capital investments after 2001 and 2005 came from large 'blockbuster' deals financed by external investors and their later retreat, while there is a steady rate of investment amongst Scottish angel and public sector investors throughout the period. Moreover, as noted by Harrison et al. (2010), many of Scotland's successful firms grow to a certain size and become acquisition targets for larger firms based elsewhere—maintaining a cycle of firm creation therefore becomes important in order to maintain any kind of local mass of knowledge-based firms.

The current new investments in Scotland, however, are dominated by angel investors whose contribution has been constantly increasing between 2003 and 2011, coinciding with the setting up and implementation of the Co-Investment Fund policy by the Scottish Enterprise (Mason, Botelho, and Harrison 2013), which offers up to 1 million GBP equity funding for deals up to 2 million GBP. However, year–to-year fluctuations in the level of VC investment (with a recent decrease for deals over 2 million GBP) suggest that collaborations with larger and/or specialist foreign or London-based investors—which appeared to be significant especially in the biopharmaceutical and life sciences domains up to 2006 (Rosiello and Parris 2009)—may have recently dropped. Interviews with industry representatives in the life sciences and IT has revealed that angel investors are resisting cooperation with larger investors in follow on funds because of loss of control and valuation. Mason, Botelho, and Harrison (2013) note that newer firms may be increasingly limited to angel only funding from 'cradle to grave' due to this hesitation, and that the paucity of exits is limiting the amount of capital available to be re-invested as well as discouraging more angels to join existing syndicates. The implication is that the risk capital market for new technology companies has become extremely problematic (Young Company Finance 2012).

What are notable are that Scotland's public sector efforts to create risk capital paralleled Israel's to some extent in that funding was meant to lower the risk for private investors and spur an increase in start-up activity from the scientific and technical talent that was already present in Scotland's universities; in contrast to Israel which had a base level of indigenous entrepreneurial activity before a VC market was setup, in Scotland the idea was that the missing entrepreneurial behaviour could be coaxed out of the universities or research base (which is particularly strong in the medical and life science) with seed funds and other Scottish Enterprise incentives. In spite of the success of the Scottish Co-Investment Fund and in contrast to Israel and its development of a VC market, while start-up activity has increased in Scotland, links with foreign investors and mutual learning effects did not occur and the VC market in Scotland has remained fragmented. While knowledge-based firms are marketing themselves internationally, the risk finance is less global (angel dominated), though still subject to the cyclical effects of the global financial markets (ebb and flow of London-based capital), and the growth potential of local Scottish firms is therefore impacted.

9.3.3 *Ireland*

Ireland's government intervention to develop VC was based on the motivation to create indigenous start-up firms, which was seen as a longer-term solution to creating high value employment in contrast to the increasingly footloose foreign manufacturing plants that had initially been courted by the Irish Industrial Development Agency. While the growing number of foreign technology firms in Ireland did little in terms of high value work such as R&D, and kept most operations to simple manufacturing or back office functions, their presence created an opportunity for Irish managers to gain experience, and for local firms to appear that provided software services and bespoke products for the large foreign firms (O'Riain 2004; Mastroeni 2011; Mastroeni 2012). This formed the base for the Irish indigenous software companies which continued to develop their products and look for export markets. Ireland's VC development in the early millennium was tied to the development of the indigenous software sector.

Much like Scotland, government provision of risk finance and the sharing of risk with the private sector was provided to encourage the creation of start-ups, and the software sector was explicitly championed by the Irish government. During the late 1990s up to and including 2003, the convergence of the dot.com success and hype, and Silicon Valley being marketed as an ideal to emulate, meant that Irish policy and industrial stakeholders saw it necessary to try to adopt Silicon Valley's 'standard' format for VC funds in the form of limited partnerships. Repatriated Irish talent, which had built up business and managerial experience in the US, helped to cement this view of how risk finance and the sectors it supported were to be developed (Mastroeni 2011).

Enterprise Ireland (EI), the public sector organization tasked to encourage the growth of indigenous companies, began with the Seed and Venture Capital Fund programme investing €40 million into privately managed funds—matching private investments on a one-to-one basis, while also investing directly into the market.[1] The funds Enterprise Ireland helped create were not limited to any one sector, but initially they were limited regionally to investments in Ireland (*Sunday Tribune* 2010; Mastroeni 2011). As the funds

---

[1] A second Seed and Venture Capital Fund round was launched in 2001–2006 with €95 million of Irish public and EU funds with the objective of leveraging €400 million (having reached €500 million by 2004) (Barry et al. 2012).

have grown, they must still continue to put twice the amount EI has committed back into Ireland, but can invest the rest at the managers' discretion; in 2007–2009 Irish funds invested 27 per cent abroad, up from 19 per cent during the preceding seven-year period (*Sunday Tribune* 2010). EI's direct investments were, in contrast, as first investor—in the nascent software sector this meant essentially establishing company valuations from scratch as there was no previous market benchmark.

EI therefore led the market, reducing the private sector's risk, and the private sector followed. The Irish VC investors saw a way of further reducing their risk encouraging—and effectively limiting their investments to—firms which created a cash flow through consultancy or bespoke product development before moving to off-the-shelf solutions which would have required longer timelines and more development resources. The software sector in Ireland was therefore impacted directly by these interventions in the capital market. Ireland emulated very closely the structures and investment practices of US VC, and invested heavily in the one area of the knowledge economy that Ireland was demonstrating strength during that period of time. The lack of diversity in the economy, however, meant that when the dot.com crisis occurred, followed by the later economic crisis, foreign investment would ebb and flow accordingly, and local investment would look to invest in foreign markets while at the same time 'increasing their due diligence' on local opportunities. Much like VC markets in other regions, Irish VC also shifted away from start-up and seed funding in 2007, dropping from 45 per cent to 29 per cent in seed and early stage companies (IVCA 2007). The director general of the Irish Venture Capital Association (IVCA) explained the drop in investment activity during the financial crisis by stating that 'there isn't a recession in VC or the tech industry at the moment; the question is whether entrepreneurs have the ability to build a business in this environment,' reflecting the impact of global markets on the local economy as well as the risk adjustments local investors made (*Sunday Tribune* 2010). Barry, O'Mahony, and Sax (2012) note how VC investment dropped from over 90 per cent of equity investment in 2002 to just over 30 per cent in 2003, and from just under 90 per cent in 2006 to approximately 20 per cent in 2007; again reflecting the global financial cycles.

Ireland reflects a risk finance market where equity investment through limited partnerships is the most commonly used format, but it was one selected (unlike in Scotland) by policymakers and stakeholders copying the perceived best practices of other economies (i.e., Silicon Valley and Israel). It raises questions, however, about how risk accepting such investors are when it comes to business models and new niches of economic activity that do not correspond to the preferred models developed during the Irish software sector's development. If such financiers are the main source of start-up funding beside informal/public sector seed funding, then the flexibility of the Irish innovation system may be impaired.

9.3.4 *Sweden*

The case of Sweden shows levels of complexity, and corresponding strategic level policy interventions, which cases like Ireland and Scotland do not because of the interconnected nature of the institutional structures related to the innovation system. Sweden's economy was described as having a relatively small stock market and long-term relations between financiers and corporate leaders (Reiter 2003). The system of family owned trust companies—which traditionally had controlling shares in the major Swedish multinational firms and banks—is still evident in the new economy: new spinoffs were supported by large parent companies, and capital resources were provided by traditional industrial financiers and state organizations. Like Ireland and Scotland, Sweden's desire to increase the number of high technology start-ups and spinoff companies was linked to their perceived contribution to economic growth and employment creation. The Swedish economy in the late 1980s and early 1990s was going through a contraction which the traditional social democratic and corporatist system of large indigenous multinationals, cross board power sharing between banks and major firms, and life time employment, was increasingly struggling to deal with. Small high tech firms were therefore seen as part of the solution, and the larger technology firms and the high quality talent and research in the university sector were seen as the source of these companies. What was missing was the entrepreneurial culture, and incentive structures had to be created to spur entrepreneurial activity (Henrekson and Rosenberg 2001; Henrekson and Jakobsson 2003; Mastroeni 2011). To this extent, a series of changes coordinated by the public agencies Nutek and later Vinnova were initiated throughout the mid-1990s to 2003. The first was a series of deregulations in markets, in particular in the stock market, that would allow greater foreign and individual ownership of stocks, and which would create greater capital availability (Henrekson and Rosenberg 2001). Such changes would also create greater exit opportunities for VC investors; like Ireland, Swedish policymakers, investors, and industrial stakeholders saw the limited partnership model of VC as one which should be emulated. Funds were co-created with public money, and the large banks also invested in funds and created their own VC branches which operated under different expectations regarding rates of return (Solvell, Zander, and Porter 1993; Mastroeni 2011).

The public industrial investor Industrifonden, which traditionally provided finance to the large Swedish multinationals for their activities, had their focus shifted along with their expected return on investment (ROI) in order to act as

VC investors and move towards creating a critical mass of capital in the market. According to Industrifonden representatives, while the ROI was lowered to breakeven in order to encourage start-up creation, they also brought 'grey hairs' to the market in terms of experience and network access, only investing in firms that passed extensive due diligence and working with market valuations rather than cutting them.

As mentioned above, there was also a need to ensure that there was a deal flow for investors. The IT sector, among others was seen as one of the best bets due to the high expectations of growth in the 1990s as well as Swedish strength in the area due to anchor firms such as Ericsson. Spinoffs from large firms did begin to occur as capital was made available to them and the underlying incentives were adjusted for people to see entrepreneurialism as an option, multinational firms helped create spinoffs by providing in kind capital in terms of office space and salary for a year in order to determine of ideas developed might later be of interest in terms of acquisition, and the dot.com crisis actually led to more of these kinds of arrangements as companies such as Ericsson narrowed their market focus (Mastroeni 2011). The coordinated shifts in activity between the banks and large anchor firms indicated a shift in how the traditional networks were applied, from large multinationals to a new focus on spinoffs and start-ups; in other words, Sweden's traditional spheres of influence such as the Wallenberg group (Ericsson and SEB bank) were key to facilitating a high tech entrepreneurial system of innovation and the capital market necessary to support it.

Government policy was also used to increase the pipeline, with the universities required by law to begin commercialization activities in addition to their research and teaching in order to remain as recognized universities. This policy resulted in universities setting up their own incubators, holding companies and VC funds so that students and faculty (who owned the IP in the Swedish system) could create start-up companies. The end result of these myriad changes across different institutional systems, and the long-term adjustments, re-evaluation, and readjustment under coordinated guidance has meant that the Swedish VC market has become one of the ten most active VC markets in the world (Lerner and Tag 2013).

Despite this success, however, the Swedish VC market is, like the others, heavily impacted by global financial markets. For example, Sweden's VC investments in the life sciences reflected broader trends in other areas where investors were hesitant to invest in the risky therapeutics subsector. The subsector itself was changing with shifting business models and firm restructuring, so the investor behaviour was reflecting more the limitations in the biotechnology global markets than financial markets and local investors reacting to the perceived risk.

Lerner and Tag note that the capital under management and the number of transactions both dropped sharply in 2001–2003 and later in 2007–2008.[2] A Nordic Venture Association report also shows that venture investment in Sweden dropped in 2008 from just under €400 million to €200 million in 2009 (Menon Publication 2010).

The relative success, yet continued impact of exogenous capital market shocks, means that regardless of how well planned policy is relating to VC creation, public sector funds in Sweden have retained their importance and have remained stable at a level of SEK 1 billion from 2008–2011 (Tillvaxtanalys 2013). Data from the Swedish Private Equity and Venture Capital Association (SVCA) noted that private VC investment continued to show a clear downward trend from SEK 4.8 billion in 2008, falling over 60 per cent to SEK 1.8 billion in 2012 (Tillvaxtanalys 2013). The importance of market intervention policy is evident in the Swedish case; however it must also be emphasized that it would be extremely difficult for other regions to duplicate Swedish efforts without the history of industrial activity and corporate collaboration that are part of the Swedish story, and regardless of the relative success, the impact of global shift and trends on local industrial development must still be accounted for.

9.4 Regional Innovation System Policy in Post-Crisis Europe

In a post-crisis Europe, the harnessing of innovation and the creation of new market niches has not only remained, but increased, in importance. Innovation is seen as necessary to create high value production and manufacturing jobs, stimulate local industry and locally based firms into new competitiveness, and increase their employment requirements. Given innovation's importance, RSIs and government policy to support them are a centre piece of EC strategy, and SmSp is seen as the approach to be used in terms of helping regions harness their economic potential.

While the focus on local capacity is correct, the lack of dynamism in SmSp as currently concerned is problematic; RSI policy requires a constant evolutionary view of changing system needs and the multiple levels of activity impacting RSI's development, from the local to the global. The cases of Israel, Scotland, Ireland, and Sweden illustrate the changing dynamic of the innovation system over time, and how a component of the innovation system—a market in and of itself—changes, ebbs, and flows based on both local VC firms as well as global market aspects.

---

[2] The percentage drop of venture capital as percentage of GDP was from 5.0 per cent in 2001 to 3.0 per cent of GDP in 2003.

The cases also offer lessons on system resilience and learning. Israel demonstrated how the VC industry was inherently tied with other industries (IT) in that it required a healthy pipeline of opportunities to exist for investors to commit to. It also showed, however, the reality of failure as the Inbal programme led to a lack of critical mass and limited investor activity. What is important about the Israeli case, however, is that it provides an example of policy learning—identifying the weakness of the system functions and the fixes that were necessary—that led to the better networked and ultimately successful Yozma programme. By the same token, it also shows how without Israel's military-industrial development of IT and skills, and its links to US markets and investors, the same efforts may not have led to anything.

Sweden's success would not have been possible without its ability to draw on the collaborative culture between government and industry. The policies and institutional changes such as those impacting stock market investment, and university activity in commercialization, occurred at the same time as the VC market was being created and helps to illustrate how RSI policy cannot be isolated to a few issues.

Scotland and Ireland, while successful in their initial build-up of entrepreneurial firms and entry into different innovative sectors through state led provision of risk capital, do not seem to share the same resilience of Swedish and Israeli VC markets and innovation systems. While determining the particular weaknesses that have led to Scotland's dependence on angel investment and entrepreneurial stasis and Ireland's narrow industrial focus and risk averse private investors is beyond the scope of this paper, part of the explanation may be that longer timelines (and locally appropriate solutions) are needed in both case to build up the economic diversity and entrenched collaborative networks that are demonstrated in Sweden and Israel.

This chapter has argued, and the cases have demonstrated, that RSI policy requires a context specific and dynamic approach. Especially in a post-crisis Europe, where resources are constrained, an understanding of local capacity in an innovation system, the missing pieces, and how these elements interact with national and international factors is crucial in order to minimize squandered resources. Analysts and policymakers must consider the local cluster or RSI's development over time, the more international industrial life cycles, and those of related industries. Finally, given that the knowledge economy and the pursuit of innovation by their nature are uncertain and risky, government intervention will always play a role, though it too will have to change according to the dynamic needs of the innovation systems.

References

Asheim, B., Boschma, R., and Cooke, P. 2011. 'Constructing Regional Advantage: Platform Policies Based on Related Variety and Differentiated Knowledge Bases'. *Regional Studies*, 45(7): 893–904.

Avnimelech, G. and Teubal, M. 2004.' Venture Capital Start-Up Co-Evolution and the Emergence and Development of Israel's New High Tech Cluster'. *Economics of Innovation and New Technology*, 13(1): 33–60.

Avnimelech, G. and Teubal, M. 2006. 'Creating Venture Capital Industries That Co-Evolve with High-Tech: Insights from an Extended Industry Life Cycle Perspective of the Israeli Experience'. *Research Policy*, 35: 1477–98.

Avnimelech, G. and Teubal, M. 2008. 'Evolutionary Targeting'. *Journal of Evolutionary Economics*, 18: 151–66.

Barca, F. 2009. 'Agenda for a Reformed Cohesion Policy: A Place-Based Approach to Meeting European Union Challenges and Expectations'. European Commission, Brussels.

Barry, F., O'Mahony, C., and Sax, B. 2012. 'Venture Capital in Ireland in Comparative Perspective'. IIIS Discussion Paper No. 400, May, Dublin, Ireland.

Bartzokas, A. and Mani, S. 2004. 'Introduction'. In A. Bartzokas and S. Mani (eds), *Financial Systems, Corporate Investment in Innovation, and Venture Capital*. Cheltenham: Edward Elgar.

Birch, K., MacKinnon, D., and Cumbers, A. 2010. 'Old Industrial Regions in Europe: A Comparative Assessment of Economic Performance'. *Regional Studies*, 44(1): 35–53.

Breznitz, D. 2005. 'Collaborative Public Space in a National Innovation System: A Case Study of the Israeli Military's Impact on the Software Industry'. *Industry and Innovation*, 12(1): 31–64.

Breznitz, D. 2007. 'Industrial R&D as a National Policy: Horizontal Technology Policies and Industry-State Co-Evolutions in the Growth of the Israeli Software Industry'. *Research Policy*, 36: 1465–82.

Camagni, R. and Capello, R. 2013. 'Regional Innovation Patterns and the EU Regional Policy Reform: Toward Smart Innovation Policies'. *Growth and Change*, 44(2): 355–89.

Cooke, P. 2012. 'Relatedness, Transversality and Public Policy in Innovative Regions'. *European Planning Studies*, 20(11): 1889–907.

European Commission. 2010. 'A Rationale For Action'. Communication from the Commission to the European Parliament, the Council, the European and Social Committee, and the Committee of the Regions, COM 546.

Foray, D., David, P., and Hall, B. 2011. 'From Academic Idea to Political Instrument, the Surprising Career of a Concept and the Difficulties Involved in Its Implementation'. MTEI Working Paper, November.

Foray, D. and Goenaga, X. 2013. 'The Goals of Smart Specialisation'. JRC Scientific and Policy Report, S3 Policy Brief Series (01).

Hall, A. and Clark, N. 2010. 'What Do Complex Adaptive Systems Look Like and What Are the Implications for Innovation Policy?' *Journal of International Development*, 22(3): 308–24.

Harrison, R., Don, G., Glancey, K., and Greig, M. 2010. 'The Early Stage Risk Capital Market in Scotland since 2000: Issues of Scale, Characteristics and Market Efficiency'. *Venture Capital*, 12(3): 211–39.

Hausmann, R. and Rodrik, D. 2003. 'Economic Development as Self-discovery'. *Journal of Development Economics*, 72(2), 603–33.

Henrekson, M. and Jakobsson, U. 2003. 'The Swedish Model of Corporate Ownership and Control in Transition'. In H. Huizinga and L. Jonung (eds.), *Who Will Own Europe? The Internationalisation of Asset Ownership in Europe*. Cambridge: Cambridge University Press, 207–46.

Henrekson, M. and Rosenberg, N. 2001. 'Designing Efficient Institutions for Science-Based Entrepreneurship: Lessons from the US and Sweden'. *Journal of Technology Transfer*, 26: 207–31.

Hudson, R. 2010. 'Resilient Regions in an Uncertain World: Wishful Thinking or a Practical Reality?' *Cambridge Journal of Regions, Economy and Society*, 3(1): 11–25.

Hughes, A. 2012. 'Choosing Races and Placing Bets: UK National Innovation Policy and the Globalisation of Innovation Systems'. In D. Greenway (ed.), *The UK in a Global World, How can the UK Focus on Steps in Global Value Chains that Really Add Value?* BIS e-book, CEPR and Department for Business, Innovation and Skills.

IVCA. 2007. 'The Economic Impact of Venture Capital in Ireland—2007', Dublin, Ireland.

Jeng, L. and Wells, P. 2000. 'The Determinants of Venture Capital Funding: Evidence Across Countries'. *Journal of Corporate Finance*, 6: 241–89.

Lerner, J. 1999. 'Venture Capital and the Commercialization of Academic Research'. In L. M. Branscomb, F. Kodama, and R. Florida (eds), *Industrializing Knowledge*. Cambridge, MA: MIT, 385–409.

Lerner, J. and Tag, J. 2013. 'Institutions and Venture Capital'. *Industrial and Corporate Change*, 22(1): 153–82.

McCann, P. and Ortega-Argiles, R. 2013. 'Modern Regional Innovation Policy'. *Cambridge Journal of Regions, Economy, and Society*, 6: 187–216.

Martin, R. and Sunley, P. 2011. 'Conceptualizing Cluster Evolution: Beyond the Life Cycle Model?' *Regional Studies*, 45(10): 1299–318.

Mason, C. M. and Harrison, R. A. 2003. 'Auditioning for Money: What Do Technology Investors Look for at the Initial Screening Stage?' *Journal of Private Equity*, 6(2): 29–42.

Mason, C., Botelho, T., and Harrison, R. 2013. 'The Transformation of the Business Angel Market: Evidence from Scotland'. Working Paper, December, University of Glasgow and University of Edinburgh. Available at: <http://www.gla.ac.uk/media/media_302219_en.pdf> (last accessed 10 September 2015).

Mastroeni, M. 2011. 'Finance for High Tech Sectors: State-Led Support for Start-Ups and Spin-Offs'. *International Journal of Entrepreneurship and Innovating Management*, 14(2/3): 176–89.

Mastroeni, M. 2012. 'Engaging the Evolution of Varieties of Capitalism: A Two-tier Approach to Examining Institutional Change'. *Business and Politics*, 14(4): 1–30.

Mastroeni, M., Tait, J., and Rosiello, A. 2013. 'Regional Innovation Policies in a Globally Connected Environment'. *Science and Public Policy*, 40(1): 1–9.

Menon Publication. 2010. Nordic Venture Capital: Cross Border Investments. Menon publication number 20/2010. Available at: <http://www.svca.se/wp-content/uploads/2014/03/Report_Nordic_cross-border_venture_investments.pdf> (last accessed 10 September 2015).

Menzel, M. P. and Fornahl, D. 2009. 'Cluster Life Cycles—Dimensions and Rationales of Cluster Evolution'. *Industrial and Corporate Change*, 19(1): 205–38.

North, D., Baldock, R., and Ullah, F. 2013. 'Funding the Growth of UK Technology-Based Small Firms Since the Financial Crash: Are There Breakages in the Finance Escalator?' *Venture Capital: An International Journal of Entrepreneurial Finance*, 15(3): 237–60.

OECD. 2011. 'Regions and Innovation Policy'. *OECD Reviews of Regional Innovation*. Paris: OECD.

OECD. 2012. 'Draft Synthesis Report on Innovation Driven Growth in Region: The Role of Smart Specialisation', December, Paris.

O'Riain, S. 2004. 'The Flexible Developmental State: Globalization, Information Technology, and the Celtic Tiger'. *Politics and Society*, 28(2): 157–93.

Pfirrmann, O., Wupperfeld, U., and Lerner, J. 1997. *Venture Capital and New Technology Based Firms*. Heidelberg: Physica-Verlag.

Pierrakis, Y. 2010. *Venture Capital Now and After the Dotcom Crash*. London: NESTA.

Reiter, J. 2003. 'Changing the Microfoundations of Corporatism: The Impact of Financial Globalization on Swedish Corporate Ownership'. *New Political Economy*, 8(1): 103–25.

Rosiello, A., Avnimelech, G., and Teubal, M. 2011. 'Towards a Systemic and Evolutionary Framework for Venture Capital Policy'. *Journal of Evolutionary Economics*, 21: 167–89.

Rosiello, A. and Parris, S. 2009. 'The Patterns of Venture Capital Investment in the UK Bio-Healthcare Sector: The Role of Proximity, Cumulative Learning and Specialisation'. *Venture Capital*, 11(3): 185–211.

Sjogren, H. and Zackrisson, M. 2005. 'The Search for Competent Capital: Financing of High Technology Small Firms in Sweden and USA'. *Venture Capital*,7(1): 75–97.

Solvell, O., Zander, I., and Porter, M. 1993. *Advantage Sweden*. London: MacMillan.

Sunday Tribune. 2010. 'State Enterprise Agency Wants VC Fund Managers to Pull Their Weight'. 26 September. Available at: <http://www.ivca.ie/wp-content/uploads/2011/02/SundayTribune26September2010.pdf> (last accessed 10 September 2015).

Tillvaxtanalys. 2013. 'Venture Capital Market in Sweden 2013'. Available at <http://www.tillvaxtanalys.se/en/home/publications/statistics/statistics/2014-11-28-venture-capital-statistics-2013—investments-in-swedish-portfolio-companies.html> (last accessed 23 September 2013).

Uyarra, E. 2010. 'What Is Evolutionary About Regional Systems of Innovation? Implications for Regional Policy'. *Journal of Evolutionary Economics*, 20: 115–37.

von Burg, U. and Kenney, M. 2000. 'There at the Beginning: Venture Capital and the Creation of the Local Area Networking Industry.' *Research Policy*, 29(9): 1135–55.

Young Company Finance. 2012. 'The Risk Capital Market in Scotland 2009–2011', Edinburgh.

10

Public Policy Working

Catalyst for Olympic Success

Sue Konzelmann and Marc Fovargue-Davies

10.1 Introduction

Following the 2008 financial crisis, and with confidence in the financial sector severely shaken, policymakers have been seeking new sources of growth and employment; and 'there has been a "renaissance" of interest in industrial policy' (Warwick 2013: 47). Even in the UK, where manufacturing has been largely neglected since the end of the 1970s—and nothing in the way of a forward looking strategy had been seen for many years prior to that—things are starting to change. In a speech to the chairmen of Local Enterprise Partnerships in 2011, Prime Minister David Cameron acknowledged that radical change in the UK economy's composition was necessary:

> What we need to do in this country is a massive rebalancing of our economy. We have been too reliant on government spending, on housing and finance...We have got to be more reliant on manufacturing and investment (BBC 2011).

Whilst this sounds, in part, like a justification for austerity, rebalancing the economy towards manufacturing will require some kind of industrial strategy. The question—particularly given the UK's poor track record in this respect—is 'what kind?'

Countries such as Germany, which have historically taken an active approach to industrial policy, have proven much more resilient than those that have not. But whilst general lessons can be learned from abroad, merely attempting to transplant policy from a completely different culture and institutional structure—as well as starting point—is unlikely to be any more effective now than in the past (Rodrik 2008, 2011). More promising strategies are likely to be those that have already delivered success within a British context, since they share common historical, cultural and institutional roots. The UK elite sport strategy provides an obvious example: at the London 2012 Games, Team GB won sixty-five medals and a world ranking of third—a stark contrast to its dismal performance in Atlanta 1996, where it ranked thirty-sixth. But, in itself, London 2012 is merely the latest in a series of progressively better results—that began almost immediately after the new strategy was implemented.

Whilst there are different views about industrial policy, much of the recent literature suggests that there may be similarities of approach with the system underpinning the sustained competitive improvement of UK elite sport. This chapter explores the extent to which this might be the case. Analysing the strategies, systems, and institutional reforms underpinning the rapid and sustained competitive turnaround in elite sport, we assess how they might inform construction of a system for building competitiveness in UK industry. This includes the team's approach to selecting both the sports and athletes with the greatest potential, and supporting their development into world class competitors. Predictable financing has been important; but equally so has been strategic leadership and vision, a culture of winning and an institutional structure to coordinate the process of competitive improvement. These are also likely to be components of a strategy for competitiveness in business.

Section 10.2 traces the UK's evolving approach to industrial policy and its— so far at least—hesitant acceptance of a role for the state in addressing the challenges resulting from the 2008 financial crisis. What emerges is the central role that financialization has played, both in restructuring British manufacturing capability (particularly during the 1960s and 1970s) and the way that this, in turn, accelerated the process of financialization and the financial sector's rise to dominance. Section 10.3 examines the case of UK elite sport, focusing on its strategy for developing international competitiveness and Team GB's resulting competitive improvement since the Atlanta 1996. Section 10.4 identifies aspects of this approach that might have application in UK industry. Section 10.5 concludes.

10.2 Evolution of Industrial Policy in Britain

The history of industrial policy can be traced to the Industrial Revolution, which according to Robinson (2009: 4) was the result of the 'mother of all industrial policies . . . a vector of policies which probably constitutes one of the world's most successful and most consequential industrial policies'. Thus, contrary to the view of eighteenth-century British economists—of Britain as a free trade, free market economy—it was, in fact, the first to employ policies specifically designed for successful industrialization. Between the end of the Napoleonic Wars in 1815 and the beginning of the First World War in 1914, the rest of the developed countries also industrialized, using targeted policies of their own (Chang 2003; Reinert 1995).

The modern debate about industrial policy has its origins in the 1970s, with the rise of Japan, the first country to use the term 'industrial policy' (sangyo seisaku) to describe selective interventions (Chang 2010). However, even earlier, there had been an evolution in the rationale behind industrial intervention (Sharp 2001; Naude 2010; Owen 2012; Pryce 2012; Warwick 2013). The rebuilding of war-torn Europe brought acceptance of a role for the state in managing the economy, and Western governments prioritized *reind*ustrialization, through production subsidies, tax incentives, and other state aids. They also 'picked winners' through nationalization and promotion of 'national champions'.

Because of the perceived benefits from dynamic economies of scale from linkages between industry and the economy (and the central role of manufacturing in this context)—and inspired by the American mass production model—growth was encouraged through mergers and acquisitions (M and As). But instead of developing new industries and technologies, in response to well-connected special interest groups, UK industrial policy tended to take the form of shoring-up ailing industries and helping old ones to survive (Vickers and Yarrow 1988; Greenway and Milner 1994; Wren 1996; BIS 2010). It was therefore largely unsuccessful as a strategy for long-term industrial rejuvenation; and by the late 1960s, the service sector—especially financial services–was rapidly displacing manufacturing as a driver of growth.

During the 'stagflationary' crisis of the 1960s and 1970s, there was a retreat from active industrial policy.[1] Confidence in markets to select sectors and firms and to allocate resources efficiently meant that the state's role was restricted to correcting 'market failures' and supplying necessary public goods; it was also responsible for ensuring market freedom and a 'business friendly' environment through product, labour, and capital market regulation and policies aimed at macroeconomic and financial market stability. Industrial policy thus took the form of limited, sector specific (often piecemeal)

---

[1] 'Stagflation' describes the co-incidence of economic stagnation and inflation.

intervention; and the policy debate revolved around the relative costs of 'government failure' as compared with market failure.

This was also a period of growing confidence in financial markets—the stock market in particular—as drivers of economic growth, and a mechanism for restructuring industry.[2] The rationale was based on the 'efficient markets hypothesis': that a firm's share price is an accurate reflection of the value of the underlying productive enterprise. Using this logic, the stock market was theorized to be an efficient 'market for corporate control' and the 'discipline mechanism' by which underperforming management teams could be replaced by more effective ones through the hostile takeover (Schleifer and Vishny 1997).

However, the leverage used to finance these takeovers meant that the targets needed to be cash and asset rich, the selling off of which could be used to repay the debt (Lazonick and O'Sullivan 2000). Corporate raiders and investors made enormous profits, fuelling a stock market boom that only lent strength to the theory, since the boom was interpreted as evidence of improved industrial performance. The reality, however, was that asset stripping to repay the debt used to finance hostile takeovers dismantled vast segments of British industry. The resulting industrial unrest was met with fierce government opposition, which only served to exacerbate the problem, and in the end, manufacturing capability was severely weakened. But rather than evolve strategy for addressing this, the view was that the economy had reached a 'post-industrial' service based stage of capitalism (Gibson 1993; Dunham-Jones 2000).

During the 1990s, the 'market failure' debate about industrial policy ultimately evolved a role for the state in promoting 'competitiveness, resulting in a shift towards horizontal policies supporting a wider range of (primarily small) firms and sectors (Wren 2001). Mirroring similar initiatives by the Organisation for Economic Co-operation and Development (OECD 1992) and the European Union (CEC 1994), successive UK governments produced *Competitiveness White Papers* that set out their vision for 'active' industrial policy,[3] aimed at correcting market failures and building competitiveness in regions and firms by encouraging technological and productive development. This took the form of state support for investments in research and development (R&D), technology, education, and training, as well as selective policies aimed at high tech, advanced manufacturing and knowledge intensive businesses (Wren 2001; Andreoni 2011).

---

[2] British industry was particularly vulnerable, since it had historically been reliant on the stock market, instead of banks, for financing that could not be generated internally.
[3] DTI 1994, 1995, 1996, 1998.

During the decades preceding the 2008 financial crisis, the UK did not explicitly embrace the idea of industrial policy. This is despite calls from prominent captains of industry for leadership and support. In the 2007 Gabor Lecture, entitled 'Why Manufacturing Matters', Sir John Rose, chief executive of Rolls-Royce, expressed the view that since the mid-1960s, the UK's increasing reliance on services, particularly financial services, created growing risks for the economy as a whole. Advocating support for 'high value' manufacturing to act as a counterbalance to high value services, he called for the creation of a more diversified economy, and he urged the government to provide a clearer sense of direction for UK industry, high-lighting the need to articulate both its objectives with regard to the kind of manufacturing industry it would like to see develop and a strategy for achieving them. 'We need', Rose said, 'a framework, or a business route map, to create context, drive focus and help prioritise public and private sector investment' (Rose 2007, quoted in Owen 2012: 43). However, he acknowledged the political obstacles to making progress in these areas. Although New Labour had been in government for over a decade, the non-interventionist stance inherited from the Thatcher government remained in place and 'the fear of returning to anything that remotely resembles central-ized industrial planning has resulted in even the discussion of such a frame-work being off limits' (Rose 2007, quoted in Owen 2012: 43).

In February 2008, at a meeting of the House of Commons Business, Enter-prise and Regulatory Reform Committee, Rose responded to questions about the future of manufacturing in the UK. When asked what a manufacturing strategy should look like, he replied:

> In general, the government should do more to set priorities...It should have a better view about the technologies that the UK needs in the future...If you ask me about a lack of technology vision and sufficient amounts of funding, then both need to be improved (*Financial Times* 2008).

Shortly afterward, with the recession deepening and unemployment continu-ing to mount, New Labour took its first hesitant steps towards accepting a possible role for industrial policy. The UK Business Secretary Peter Mandelson, believing that the UK had become overly reliant on the financial services sector, saw the need to rebalance the economy and sought advice from Rose and other British industrialists. The result was a 2009 white paper, entitled *New Industry, New Jobs: Building Britain's Future* (BERR 2009), calling for a 'new activism' on the part of government to assist businesses in exploiting new, advanced technologies by means of 'targeted intervention'. To strengthen the economy's capacity for innovation, growth and job creation, a Strategic Investment Fund (SIF) was established, supporting a range of investments across the UK economy.

However, progress stalled when the new Conservative-Liberal Democrat Coalition government came to office in 2010; and the SIF was discontinued. In a speech at the Cass Business School, the new Secretary for Business, Innovation and Skills, Vince Cable, told the audience that '[w]hat we *shouldn't* be doing is trying to micromanage the economy at the level of individual companies or so-called national champions: trying to supersede the judgement of markets' (emphasis added) (Cable 2010).

However, in 2011, the government set out its vision for the economy's recovery in *The Plan for Growth* (BIS and HM Treasury 2011), advocating horizontal industrial policy measures and identifying key sectors where barriers to growth would be addressed. In his 2011 Budget Statement, George Osborne (2011), Chancellor of the Exchequer, talked about the need for a 'march of the makers'. And in a speech at the Policy Exchange, Cable (2011) called for a 'New Industrial Policy' aimed at supporting innovation and technological leadership, developing skills (centred on apprenticeships), re-building supply chains and implementing supply side reforms as a means of building and maintaining business confidence.

10.3 Building International Competitiveness in Elite Sport—A Real UK Success Story?

In September 2012, with the London Olympic Games still alive in the public imagination, Cable set out his expanded vision for a long-term UK industrial strategy—making direct reference to the strategy that had contributed to Britain's Olympic success:

> The Olympics provided a unique opportunity to celebrate the things the UK does well. . . . Our athletes achieved what they did because of their years of commitment and planning. I was initially a sceptic; I could see the costs but not the benefits. But the games proved to be a success. Years of planning and investment in pursuit of a clear and ambitious vision were realised. . . . I think there is a read-across to the way we approach our economic future.

He went on:

> We need to take the same approach: a clear, ambitious vision; the courage to take decisions that bear fruit over a long period; openness to new opportunities as they develop; focus on the things we do best; and an enduring commitment far beyond a five year parliament or spending review period (Cable 2012).

Thus, whilst much of the discussion about 'Olympic Legacy' following London 2012 focused on sport related issues, policymakers, and politicians from across the political spectrum are also looking for parallels between the

145

approach that so successfully turned around the competitiveness of UK elite sport and the evolution of an industrial strategy to address the challenges facing the UK economy.

10.3.1 *Creating Global Competitiveness UK Elite Sport: The Role of Strategy*

The UK elite sports system has much in common with the current systems based approach to industrial policy, in which the government assumes a 'market enhancing' role.[4] In fact, prior to the strategic changes following the 1996 Atlanta Games, the British Olympic Team was in a not dissimilar position to that faced by many UK medium sized businesses today.[5] The institutional structures underpinning sport—the National Sport Governing Bodies (NSGBs)—whilst present and functional to a degree, were largely under resourced and operating independently of each other, with little or no strategic leadership.

The disjointed nature of sport policy was recognized by the Sports Council in 1993, with the admission that 'the UK's sporting achievements have too often been secured in spite of the disparate goals having been set by our sporting community' (quoted in Houlihan and Lindsey 2013: 39). In any given year, only a small number of athletes managed to fight their way to Olympic or Paralympic success, where they competed largely as individuals, with little or no access to the resources of a team within which to develop their competitive capabilities, learn from each others' experience and build upon it for future events.

Peter Keen, a former cycling world champion and coach—and Performance Director of UK Sport from 2004 to 2012—summed the problem up:

> My career in sport...was that of a classic Alpinist. We were trying to climb this thing, but we weren't leaving any maps or ropes for anyone else. If anything, quite the reverse. That switch from one-off success to an approach that is a quite different set of values is probably the single biggest difference....The challenge was to convert those highly motivated, highly talented individuals into a system (quoted in Slater 2012).

---

[4] The 'market enhancing' view of government is informed by Aoki, Kim, and Okuno-Fujiwara 1997.

[5] According to the Confederation of British Industry's (CBI) 'Future Champion's' research, there are approximately 25,000 medium-sized British companies, with an annual turnover of £10 to £100 million. These enterprises account for approximately 1 per cent of British businesses but 25 per cent of revenues and 16 per cent of the UK workforce. They thus have the potential to significantly impact both employment and growth.

However, British elite sport suffered not only from poorly informed intervention, lack of stable funding and limited support services. It was also up against competitors that had none of these disadvantages.

The concept of elite sport *strategy* is hardly new. Long ago, the various nations of the former Soviet bloc laid the foundations of a system for talent identification, coaching, and medical support, and they provided promising elite athletes the best possible resources. The rewards were obvious as the USSR consistently accounted for a majority of Olympic medals won. However, following bloc's breakup in 1991, and with fewer resources available, the stream of medals quickly dried up.

The effects of a clear and coherent elite sport strategy, however, had a profound influence on the approaches subsequently developed by others. Australia was among the first, following its own Olympic nadir at the 1976 Montreal Games, when they won no gold medals at all. The new Australian elite sport system took much of its inspiration from East Germany (at the time, still part of the USSR). However, it was no mere copy. Building upon local conditions and existing institutional structures, the Australian interpretation took account of its large geographical spaces between population centres and the resulting challenges of accessing sporting resources. It thus created sports academies as centres of excellence for a restricted number of disciplines (not all of them Olympic), offering unwavering focus and state of the art resources and facilities. The result was a rapid reversal in the performance of Australian elite sport.

It is against this backdrop of increasing international competition that British elite sport performance in the run-up to Atlanta 1996 must be viewed. Whilst the breakup of the USSR five years earlier might have been expected to make life easier for competitors from outside the former bloc, the adoption of similar strategies by other countries had merely shifted the locus of competition, and an effective elite sports system was rapidly becoming a necessity rather than a luxury. Not having a strategy was increasingly a recipe for failure.

10.3.2 *From Indifference to Support: Politics and UK Sport*

An important problem then facing UK elite sport—that is an obstacle for British industry at present—was a lack of political will to get involved, let alone consider how best to intervene. As with industrial policy, Conservative governments of the 1980s took the view that, as far as possible, the state should *not* get involved in private sector activities. A similar approach applied to sport, where the Sports Councils (for England, Scotland, Wales, and Northern Ireland) maintained a generalist role in sport promotion, under the 'Sport for All' credo.

However, when Margaret Thatcher was succeeded by John Major, a decade of political indifference to sport came to an end. Unlike Thatcher, who saw no benefit in sport, Major was a lifelong cricket supporter, and he understood the political relevance of sport. Major's strong personal support would prove instrumental in the strategic changes upon which the Olympic team's competitive revival was based (Houlihan and Lindsey 2013: 40). Political support manifested itself in a number of ways. As well as structural change, the legal framework also required adjustment—which as something only the state could achieve. A step change in attitude was also necessary.

A significant obstacle to competitiveness—also the case for industry—was lack of access to predictable and competitive funding. Whilst it was clear that lack of political interest had resulted in the chronic underfunding of elite sport, both in absolute terms and by comparison to other countries, it was less obvious how this could be addressed. During the early 1990s, the UK was in recession, and Sterling's humiliating exit from the European Exchange Rate Mechanism (ERM) in 1992 had already damaged the government's reputation for financial prudence.

An alternative to exchequer funding lay in the possibility of a National Lottery, an idea that many countries in Europe had already successfully adopted. Thatcher had opposed it on the basis that some people would 'get something for nothing', whilst others had objected to the government promoting gambling. But the way was open for change, and in 1993, the UK's National Lottery was set up, with around 30 per cent of the proceeds earmarked for good causes—one of which was sport. The first draw was made in November 1994, some eighteen months prior to the 1996 Atlanta games. It is worth noting that the UK lottery was not a straightforward copy of the European model. Whereas most European lotteries are state operated, the UK lottery is privately operated, on a state-franchised basis.

Lottery funding, however, was not in itself sufficient. The absence of leadership, structure, and processes for identifying and developing competitive capabilities also needed to be addressed. Since the problems afflicting elite sport performance were no great secret, it was possible for an interested government to work with existing sporting institutions to make the necessary changes. This would also make it easier for the system to operate, once it was set up. The provision of funding was thus the first of only four—albeit highly significant—changes in the government's relationship with elite sport. In addition to significantly increased funding, the Major government also initiated the primary institutional change affecting elite sport. In July 1994, the Sports Minister Iain Sproat outlined proposals (1) to replace the UK Sports Council with UK Sport, a quango that would focus on elite sport only, with much closer links to the British Olympic Association;[6] and (2) to shift the

---

[6] A 'quango' is a quasi-autonomous non-governmental organization.

focus of the Home Country Sports Councils to mass participation sports. In January 1997, UK Sport was set up; and it was granted a licence to distribute Lottery funding to elite sport shortly afterwards.

This separation of elite from mass participation sport involved much more than a change of name and focus. Firstly, although a public sector institution, UK Sport is run at 'arm's length' from government; and it works in *partnership* with the UK's NSGBs to *lead* elite sport to world class success. This makes UK Sport an integral part of the system, rather than a top-down instrument of government policy, making it much more pragmatic and adaptive. UK Sport has also, so far, avoided capture by other parts of the institutional structure— both political and sporting. Secondly, UK Sport is not staffed by politicians or civil servants, but by people from the world of sport. This provides a far better understanding of—and relationship with—those whose purpose it is to support; and it focuses attention and effort on winning, rather than politics.

These changes also brought an entirely new attitude and vision. The politically motivated 'Sport for All' credo had resulted in the funding (such as it was) of over 110 sports, regardless of medal prospects. The new focus on winning targeted only those sports able to demonstrate a realistic chance of medal success, resulting in a dramatic reduction to around thirty funded sports. This meant that existing resources could be far more efficiently allocated.

Tony Blair's New Labour government also brought developments impacting elite sport, the first of which was a fundamental change in the uses to which lottery funding could be put. Instead of limiting funding to facilities only, money could now be allocated to individual athletes. This meant that athletes no longer had to juggle employment with training and competition; it also meant that coaches and other specialists could be funded. This introduced an important change in the way the system worked: Instead of the government dictating what the teams could spend money on, the teams were free to spend it on what was *actually* needed, *when* it was needed. Discipline was provided by the hard-nosed rule that funding was contingent upon competitive success.

Government involvement via UK Sport soon proved successful, both in terms of driving change and improving results. However, if proof of the effectiveness of this approach (as opposed to direct, political intervention by government) was required, it soon was—by the 2005 Athletics World Championships debacle.

London's successful bid to host the 2005 Championships had followed two unsuccessful bids by UK cities to host the Olympics. The International Olympic Committee had listed various reasons for rejecting the Birmingham bid, including lack of support from the Thatcher government; however Manchester's bid for the 2000 Games did no better, despite strong support from the Major government. It was therefore felt that only London had the clout to bring the Olympics to the UK; and having won the right to host the 2005 Championships, London could now show the world its sporting and organizational credentials. However, uninformed, direct political intervention would soon compromise the UK's ability to attract major future international sporting events.

In 2001, the then Sports Minister Richard Caborn and Culture Secretary Tessa Jowell decided that the cost of a new stadium for the Athletics World Championships in London would be too high; and they suggested, instead, that the Championships be hosted at existing facilities in Sheffield. This was rejected, on the basis that having London as the host city had been a key reason for accepting the bid. London was therefore forced to withdraw, and the Championships went to Helsinki—the first time that any developed nation had withdrawn an offer to host a major international sporting event (BBC 2001).

However, perhaps surprisingly, it did not undermine London's 2007 bid to host the 2012 Olympic Games, reinforcing a very high profile medium term commitment to elite sport. The bid had also demonstrated closer cooperation between government and sporting institutions than had been the case with the 2005 Championships affair. The successful delivery of the event would be crucial, with any underperformance by either organizers or the team being both highly public and politically unhelpful. But by the time 2012 arrived, New Labour had been unseated by the Lib–Dem Coalition government, the UK was once again in recession and the cost of hosting a major international sporting event was being questioned. In the end, political support for London 2012 was based on the expected positive effect that the Games would have on Britain's construction and tourism industries.

The contrast between state involvement via UK Sport and top-down ad hoc political intervention is striking. What is clear from the discussion above is the importance of government involvement in the development and articulation of a vision for the future, in facilitating the implementation of a strategy for achieving international competitiveness and in removing obstacles as they become apparent. However, equally important is the *way* that the state is involved. Short-term political ends do not usually contribute positively to the stable longer-term development and effective operation of the system. This is also true of industrial strategy. As discussed above, Britain's recent experience has been characterized by interventions based on short-term political motives instead of being part of an overall approach aimed at strengthening the international competitiveness of the British economy—and this has hampered progress.

10.3.3 *The British Olympic Team's Competitive Turnaround*

Table 10.1 shows the medals won by the British Olympic team and its Summer Games world rankings since 1996, illustrating the speed of the Team's

Table 10.1. British Olympic Team's Performance in the Summer Olympic Games (1996–2012)

Summer Games	Number of Medals	Number of Gold Medals	World Ranking
Atlanta 1996	15	1	36th
Sydney 2000	28	11	10th
Athens 2004	30	9	10th
Beijing 2008	47	19	4th
London 2012	65	29	3rd

competitive turnaround as well as its steady improvement ever since. Here, it is worth noting that the progression in competitiveness in many ways reflects the cumulative effect of successive changes in the institutional structure underpinning elite sport development.

The inevitable conclusion is that whilst both increased funding and intelligent state involvement have certainly helped, they are far from the whole story; equally important are the institutions making up the bulk of the system, the way they work together, and their relationship with the state.

10.3.4 *UK Elite Sport Institutions—and Their Relationship with the State*

Much of the credit for the improvement in British elite sport performance has been given to the increased funding by the National Lottery, which has certainly played its part. According to Liz Nicholl, a former international netball player and now Chief Executive of UK Sport, 'we were investing in the outcome of medal success' (Slater 2012). Since Olympic medalists attract additional funding from commercial sponsorship, UK Sport's investment of public funds set into motion a virtuous cycle in which public investment is augmented by private sector funding. This enables UK Sport to oversee a well-resourced system for identifying and developing the Olympic medal winning capabilities of British athletes and sports.

However, finance is not the only critical success factor. Working with the UK's NSGBs, UK Sport's mission is to *lead* elite sport to success. According to Baroness Sue Campbell, also a former international netball player and current Chair of UK Sport, in addition to predictable funding and a new culture focused on winning 'the other big deciding factor was *leadership*. Someone had to articulate the mission and the vision' (Gibson 2012; emphasis added). In this, the individuals responsible include UK Sport's Performance Director and the Performance Directors of the NSGBs. Baron Sebastian Coe, a former double gold medalist and Chair of the London 2012 Organising Committee, in summing up the requirements for competitive success in high performance sport, also expressed the view that money is not, in itself, enough:

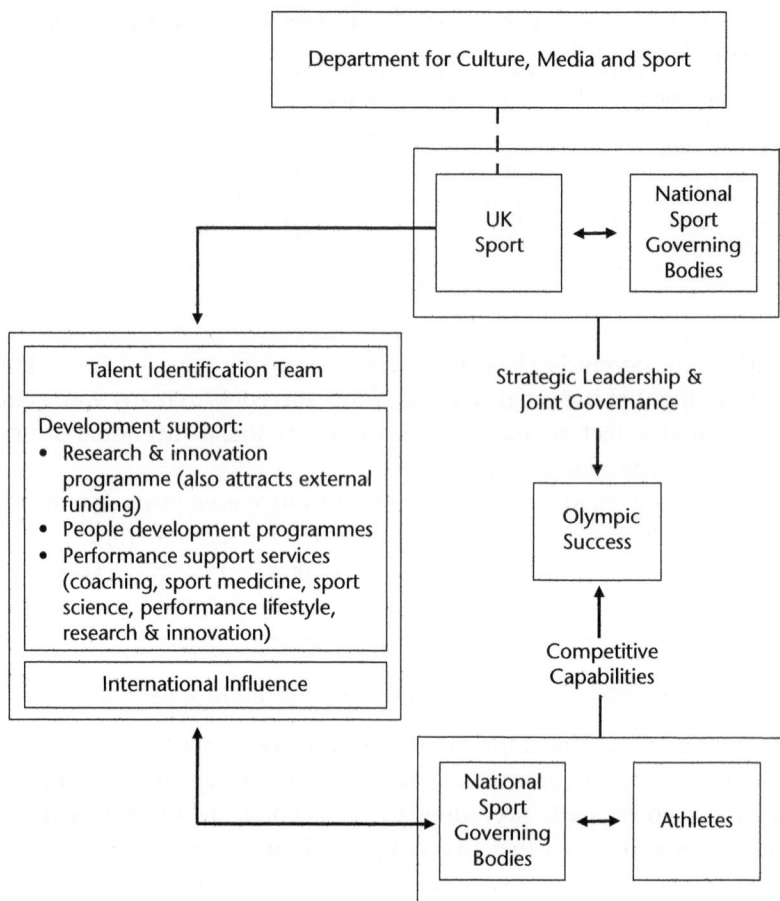

Figure 10.1 The UK Elite Sport Competitiveness Development System

there are four things you need. You need them all. Smart governing bodies, world class coaches, talented athletes with the good sense to pick their parents carefully, then you need predictable levels of funding (Gibson, 2012).

Figure 10.1 illustrates the structure of the UK elite sport competitiveness development system, which clearly shows the limited, but highly necessary role that the state plays in the integrated system. UK Sport is an executive non-departmental public body of—and accountable to—the Department for Culture, Media and Sport (DCMS).[7] It sits between DCMS and the rest of the system and is unusual in many respects. As discussed above, UK Sport is run largely by former sporting world champions, instead of politicians and civil

---

[7] See agencies and public bodies that DCMS works with at: <https://www.gov.uk/government/organisations#department-for-culture-media-sport> (last accessed 19 September 2015).

servants. This contributes to the quality of its relationship and communication with the rest of the system and its ability to put a clear case to government for funding and other needs of elite sport.

The bulk of the rest of system is made up of institutions whose daily business it is to develop athletes. The result is an 'expert driven' system, with access to state resources, rather than the other way round. By distributing resources to the most successful athletes and teams, UK Sport enhances the 'market' within which British elite sport operates, ensures that it is highly competitive—and that the focus is on winning.

The environment within which UK elite sport operates is thus no longer comparable to that of a 'free' market system—but due to UK Sport's 'market enhancing' role, it is a highly 'competitive' one. There is competition for team places as well as for funding, both within sports and between them. Competition takes place within a transparent framework designed to maximize performance, learn from failures, and, where possible, turn them into successes. This requires a very active role for UK Sport and the NSGBs; and it demands the formulation of both short- and long-term objectives within a system designed to produce a continuous stream of winners. Thus, since 1997, Britain's Olympic performance has not been entrusted to the random interplay of 'free' market forces.

As evident in Figure 10.1, at the highest institutional level within the elite sport development system, there is strategic collaboration between UK Sport and the NSGBs that together share responsibility for creating and maintaining a system that supports the Olympic team's international competitiveness. The state's involvement is thus neither direct nor 'top down'. Instead, the relationship between the state and elite sport is a largely horizontal and integrated one, which relies upon open communication to function effectively. UK Sport is the strategic lead body and facilitator of the processes required, with the NSGBs having input into what those processes include and how they are carried out. Because recognizing talent within particular disciplines resides at the level of the individual sports, the sharing of information between the NSGBs and UK Sport is essential.

By facilitating the sharing of information *among* the NSGBs, individual sports can also learn from each other. Although development programmes within particular disciplines vary, by facilitating information flows between UK Sport and the NSGBs and between the individual sport disciplines—and by continually mapping the international sporting landscape—the overall competitiveness development system is able to evolve to meet changing requirements, exploit opportunities, and remove obstacles as they appear. UK Sport's responsibilities are thus:

> essentially...to underpin and unlock the nation's Olympic and Paralympic performance potential by: investing a significant majority of its income into the

World Class Performance Programme, and working closely with the national governing bodies of sport to ensure they operate as effectively as possible; working with partners to develop the people and systems that support our leading athletes, principally in the areas of coaching, talent identification and sports science and medicine practitioners and Performance Lifestyle, to ensure a continuing legacy for our investment; [and] seeking cutting edge research and innovative solutions to performance challenges' (UK Sport 2013).

10.3.5 *Potential Challenges Ahead*

It is significant that UK Sport is an arm's length public sector body, responsible for the investment of public funds. Not only has it delivered international competitive success, it has also (so far) managed to protect itself from political decisions that might compromise delivery of its strategic objectives. At the same time it has also avoided 'capture' by elite sport. In many respects, Team GB's success provides evidence that UK Sport represents a significant public sector success story.

However, vulnerability to political decisions should not be underestimated. Even during the London 2012 Games, UK Sport's certainty about exchequer funding went only as far as the first part of 2015—the period covered by the last Comprehensive Spending Review (CSR), but only halfway through the run-up to the 2016 Games in Rio. But under heavy pressure from the British media and public, the government made an exception and provided financial certainty to plan for the next Olympic Games. In a more promising motion— that would further reduce financial uncertainty over the longer term and reduce Team GB's vulnerability to the vicissitudes of politics—Labour Leader Ed Miliband has proposed a cross-party review of the elite sport funding system: 'My proposal to David Cameron has been to put together a 10 year plan across all parties. Let's not make it political, let's get all the sporting bodies involved and look at how we do it' (UK Sport 2013).

10.4 UK Olympic Legacy for Business?

Clearly, sport is a different business from other industries, with its own structure, culture, and criteria for success. The approach adopted by UK elite sport should, however, be seen for what it is: a strategy designed to build and maintain international competitiveness, instead of merely being a 'strategy for sport'. Seen from this perspective, the elite sport case may reveal more poten- tially transferable insights for industry. Since many of the approaches to elite sport competitiveness development are *non*-sport specific, our analysis avoids delving into the minutiae specific to winning a gold medal in a particular sporting discipline. Instead, we consider the case of UK elite sport from the perspective of the systems based, expert driven approach, in which the government assumes a 'market enhancing' role. This allows us to identify the most significant *strategic* components that might inform the design of institutions and systems aimed at strengthening the international competitiveness of select sectors of UK industry.

The objective of industrial strategy is to improve the international (market) competitiveness of a country's firms and industrial sectors by not only countering 'market failures' but also improving on market outcomes. It includes horizontal policies designed to improve broad segments of the economy's supply side, vertical policies aimed at particular sectors, firms, or activities, and public-private strategic collaborations to improve the institutional environment within which firms and industries operate. Because markets are embedded in broader social and institutional structures, the effectiveness of industrial strategy depends to a large extent upon local circumstances and capabilities as well as institutions in which information can be shared and learning can take place.

Three broad areas stand out as key contributors to the success of UK elite sport. These include: (1) an enabling competitive environment in which access to a reliable source of finance forms a part; (2) an institutional structure to provide strategic leadership, identify talent, and support the development of internationally competitive athletes and teams—insulated from interference by short-term political (or elite sport) interests; and (3) an institutional system that encourages the dynamic processes underpinning learning, innovation and responsiveness to opportunities and constraints. Taken together, these areas—if available to medium sized British businesses and industrial sectors—would be likely to facilitate improvement in the UK's international industrial performance.

10.4.1 *Enabling Competitive Environment*

Peter Keen's reference to his early 'Alpinist' experience highlights the value of an environment in which athletes and teams can focus on developing their competitive capabilities, rather than being distracted by other considerations, and he cites the development of the system as being at least as important as finance. It is important to recognize that finance is not, in itself, sufficient: it merely allows the system to exist and to function—neither part can work effectively without the other.

This is also true of the environment within which many British businesses operate, except that step changes in finance and support have yet to come. The UK is one of very few developed countries without a system for directly supplying finance and other resources to growing businesses. The German government, for example, underwrites bank loans to businesses to spread the risks of lending to start-ups. Like lottery funding for UK sport, this also reduces reliance on exchequer funding. This 'low maintenance' finance, on competitive terms, is thus comparable to the system of sport funding, where it allows a similarly sharp focus on what the organization is there to do, rather than how it is to be funded. Other resources, such as legal services, are also provided to German businesses, allowing smaller firms to focus on their core business. As elite sport used to, UK businesses are currently competing against those with the clear advantage of support systems. Many of the changes in the sporting system were aimed at addressing obstacles of this nature.

The absence of longer term, stable bank finance for smaller UK businesses has its roots in the history of British industry. Unlike many nations that industrialized later, British firms have traditionally been reliant on the stock market for finance. This meant that growth at some point required selling a significant stake to shareholders. Widely dispersed shareholder ownership—particularly where investors collectively own the majority of the shares—has been recognized as a constraint on the ability of senior managers to focus on the productive purpose of the business (Konzelmann et al. 2010). This is due to the need to prioritize the short-term interests of shareholders and avoid the risk of hostile action.

Since investment in production precedes the realization of returns—often over a medium or long-term—facilitating access to cost effective finance for new or existing businesses (particularly during a recession) would make a credible contribution to economic recovery. However, whilst some attempts to channel more credit to smaller businesses have been made, they have so far lacked both the scale and clarity that characterizes funding for sport—and they have not changed the game. Efforts to encourage banks to lend to businesses, such as Project Merlin, launched in February 2011 to deliver £190bn to businesses, have been largely ineffective.

This is in no small part the result of government not being integrated into the industrial system—and as a result, failing to identify the problem correctly. This approach owes more to politically driven 'ad hoc' intervention than it does to the forward looking, problem centred approach of UK Sport—which is likely a significant contributor to its failure.

A possible step in the right direction has more recently been made, partly in response to the findings of Tim Breedon's report on long-term structural problems in the supply of finance to UK businesses. In September 2012, UK Business Secretary Vince Cable announced plans to create a UK Business Bank that would be independent of existing banks and financed by the wholesale money markets (BIS 2012). Like UK Sport, which distributes funding to organizations and individuals in elite sport, the UK Business Bank would be set up and operated at arm's length from government. Whether it would also play any kind of coordinating role, comparable to that of UK Sport, is at present unclear—as is whether or not it will be able to provide a similar step change for industry.

As well as finance, UK industry also lacks an institutional structure that provides support for building competitive capabilities. In industry, although competitive success is realized in markets, since these rely on supporting non-market institutions and policies to function properly, the provision of a supporting framework would enable firms and sectors to realize their competitive potential. These might include support for learning and innovation. Institutions, such as universities, research centres, and technical institutes are important supports for technological progress, knowledge generation, and commercialization. Due to the dynamic nature of economic progress, institutions supporting the recognition of—and responses to—changes in the economic environment (i.e., exploiting opportunities, removing obstacles, avoiding lock-in to outmoded activities and facilitating innovation) are essential to competitive advancement.

10.4.2 Institutional Structure—Supporting Competitive Improvement

The strategic partnership between UK Sport and the NSGBs is one of 'joint governance' of the system within which international competitiveness is developed. Through leadership, support, predictable funding, articulating the conditions for access to support, and monitoring performance, success is rewarded and underperformance sanctioned. However, the coordination and effort that goes into actually delivering medals takes place at the grassroots level, within the NSGBs, where talent is identified and the processes supporting the competitive development of UK elite athletes and sporting teams takes place.

The few political decisions since the early 1990s that have been made have radically changed the environment within which elite sport operates; and in the process, they demonstrate the value of this joint governance approach to strategic decision making. Since the NSGBs are the experts on the circumstances their sports face, they are best placed to participate in high level decisions that affect them. The relative infrequency of random political interventions thus lends stability to the system.

Continued effectiveness of this strategic collaboration—and its delivery of sustained competitive improvement—is dependent upon its core components remaining in balance, with no part being captured by another. Loss of this balance can be extremely counterproductive: Excessive state influence can result in the interference of political ideology and inflexibility. Conversely, capture of the state by private non-state institutions within the system risks chaos—like that which produced the 2008 financial crisis.

Joint governance has clear implications for medium sized businesses in competitive market places. Firstly, the fewer the changes required to build an institutional framework capable of strengthening industrial competitiveness, the easier and quicker it will be to implement. Thus, the degree to which industrial strategy can build upon existing institutions, including governmental agencies, trade and industry bodies, universities, and technical institutes, the more effective it is likely to be in delivering results quickly. Secondly, whilst sport has a regular schedule, with easily identified criteria for success, this is less clearly the case in industry.

For industrial strategy to deliver against its objectives, speed of input from actors in industries and firms is even more important than in sport—particularly when identifying areas both in need of support and where support is no longer justified. Similarly, whilst one of the most obvious indicators of business success is export sales, other factors might also be identified such as revenue growth, innovation, commercialization, and so on. It is important to develop institutions capable of communicating with cutting edge organizations, who are most able to identify emerging technologies and competitive situations. The design of industrial strategy is therefore reliant on information flows between the government and industrial sectors as well as between these and local institutions involved in innovation and knowledge generation and transfer. There is thus a premium on the quality of communication and relationships as well as a shared vision. An effective strategy is also one that fosters competition within, strengthening the capabilities of athletes, sectors, and firms alike. All of these are evident in the UK elite sports system.

10.4.3 Systems That Learn and Develop

Not all of the ideas contributing to the evolution of British elite sport were learned from scratch; many were adapted from other teams or best practice. However, they were not simply transplanted; they inspired change—in a UK context. When Australia studied the East German elite sports programme, for example, they concluded that whilst many ideas were transferable, others were inconsistent with Australian values. Similarly, when the UK later learned from the Australian system, some elements were considered applicable and adapted to fit the British context, whilst others were not. An equivalent to Australia's sports academies, for example, was discussed, but it was not adopted due to geographical considerations and difficulties in fundamentally altering the institutional structure of British sport.

Similarly, industrial strategy for the UK might well draw upon ideas from elsewhere. But it should take local culture, institutional context, and conditions into account. This requires fully understanding the ideas behind the changes that might be made, the context in which they proved effective, and how they might be adapted.

Another source of learning is from failures—even relative ones—as well as successes. The expectation of UK Sport is one of winning; this was evident in the profuse apologies from London 2012 athletes for not winning gold, even when they won silver or bronze—a far cry from the British culture of old. However, the response to underachievement is constructive: Preparation and performance are carefully reviewed, to identify causes, and develop remedial strategies; less successful athletes and teams that still have medal potential are helped to compete more effectively—sometimes by more successful teams. When British Swimming failed to meet its medal target in London, for example, a post-games review was quickly underway. According to Michael Scott, British Swimming's Performance Director:

> Everything is on the table. We cannot close our mind to any ideas or suggestion . . . We have made approaches and not necessarily to people within the sport of swimming. You have to look at Team GB as a whole and say there is expertise in this country that could be used to sharpen our focus (White 2012).

Team GB also continues to learn from best practice and other countries' teams. So there is potential for the bar to be continuously raised, through a virtuous cycle of competitive development and improvement, nationally and internationally.

The same can be said about the possibilities for cumulative learning in medium sized businesses. With an effective industrial strategy and appropriate institutional structures, they would be better equipped to adapt and implement the strategies through which competitiveness could be developed; they would be able to learn from others, such as the successful export driven manufacturing sectors of Germany's 'Mittelstand', Northern Italy's industrial districts and successful industrial networks and clusters of other countries.

10.5 Conclusions

The contemporary debate about industrial strategy in the UK has largely revolved around the question of *whether* the state should be involved as an economic actor rather than *how* it should be involved. However, whilst Britain has had a supposedly 'free market' culture, for at least the past three decades, the reality is that governments from across the political spectrum have routinely intervened, usually for short-term political purposes.

The justification for non-intervention in the economy has been based on a number of flawed assumptions. The first is the idea that 'free market' is synonymous with 'competitive market'. In the case of the progressively deregulated financial sector, failure to address the underlying cause of the resulting succession of increasingly more serious crises associated with the bursting of asset bubbles serves as an illustrative example of the effect of capture of the state by a single powerful industry. Equally damaging is the lingering view that manufacturing is inefficient and strike ridden—and that those employed in it are likely to hold the economy to ransom. This view was initially responsible for a string of ill-advised industrial interventions during the 1960s and 1970s that illustrated the equally detrimental effects associated with the capture of industry by the state—and has served as a sort of 'aversion therapy' for any form of industrial policy ever since. These two polar examples stand in stark contrast to the elite sport case—of an expert-driven integrated system, involving the state and other resources in an intelligent way, realizing a shared vision—and avoiding capture from either direction. The results have been remarkable—and swift.

By contrast, in the case of British industry, politically driven interventions have had a detrimental effect on industrial development. But compounded by the process of financialization, the privatizing of large segments of the economy, and encouragement of an increasingly debt-funded consumer-oriented society, it has been arguably far worse. One of the early stages of this process took the form of highly leveraged hostile takeovers, starting in the 1960s, the financing of which dismantled large parts of asset rich 'shareholder-owned' businesses. This not only reduced the productive capacity of the UK (and indeed America); it also marked the separation of the interests of the financial industry from those of the 'real' economy as symbiosis gave way to a far more predatory relationship.

London's 1986 'Big Bang' stock market deregulation brought an end to the long-term relationships that had characterized the merchant banks, and it ushered in the American style 'deal based' model of investment banking. The quick gains to be made from M and As, consumer loans and, later, complex derivative products, meant that even if the vast amounts of credit flowing into the international financial markets were not used to actively attack productive businesses, these companies—particularly those with business models dependent upon a long-term planning horizon—were hardly the banks' preferred clients. The failure of successive governments to address this problem of access to patient capital on appropriate terms has had dire effects on British business—especially manufacturing.

Funding had been a major problem for elite sport as well. However, the political will was there to come up with an innovative solution—in this case, Lottery funding—which provided money without taxing the exchequer. A similar approach is entirely possible in the case of industry; whilst recent years have seen a rise in such things as funding circles and crowd funding, there are also signs of possible change from a strategic, state-driven perspective. The creation of the British Business Bank is a possible step in the right direction. The extent of the communication between it and the sectors it will serve, in terms of design and functionality is so far unclear. But like UK Sport, although it is accountable to the Department of Business, Innovation and Skills (BIS), it is intended to operate at arm's length from government. In terms of inspiration from elsewhere, the German approach, in which the state underwrites a percentage of a business loan in order to spread the risk, might also provide food for thought.

It is worthy of note that in spite of the industrial equivalent to Peter Keen's 'Classic Alpinist' environment, manufacturing in the UK has done surprisingly well. This however, merely serves to highlight the scale of the missed opportunity: three decades of enhanced industrial growth and a far more balanced economy.

In terms of making such a change possible, elite sport had the advantage of a relatively low political profile. Prior to the strategic changes since the 1990s, whilst it was not covering itself in glory, nor was it attracting media headlines for social unrest. Margaret Thatcher largely ignored it, and many British sports fans became accustomed to failure—with the occasional success to keep hope alive. This made elite sport's underperformance much easier to address since, at first glance, it appeared to operate outside of the 'free' market system and was therefore less subject to political idealism (although in fact, it was one of the most 'free' markets in existence—with no regulation, very few rules, structure, resources, support, or overall vision).

John Major's personal interest—and the political capital to be garnered from much of the British population's love affair with sport—provided the motivation to address the problem. This stands in sharp relief against the politicized view (of the electorate, interest groups and politicians) of British manufacturing and industry. Even thirty years later, the scars of the turbulent 1970s remain; and the nation's view of manufacturing is one of dirt, strikes, low quality goods and services and uninspiring pay—rather than hi tech design, state of the art manufactures, world leading products and solid rewards. Because the popular view is that 'nothing is made in the UK any more', programmes of study like Media Studies are a more popular choice than Engineering. So long as this attitude persists, change will be more difficult to accomplish.

This helps to explain why leadership in international competitiveness has come from elite sport instead of industry. Whereas the hands-off approach that characterized elite sport until the late 1990s was clearly holding back competitiveness. The new approach focuses on competition and team work—with both sports and individual athletes doing the competing and the state providing strategic leadership and support. What makes the system work is the quality of relationships and communication among the various institutions involved and the clarity of the overall vision. Instead of interventions based on political force majeure, the state is making informed, timely, and problem centred interventions on the basis of good information. This is partly why so few have been required and their overall effect has been positive—in spite of three changes of government. It is also important to note that with one exception—the creation of a more elite sport focused institution to replace the Sports Council—all of the changes were in the legal environment, so only the state could have made them. This clearly demonstrates that the state *must* be involved.

Informed, intelligent, and timely intervention requires the government to be an insider, with a clear understanding of its role and the sector it is supporting, a good relationship with the agents involved and the institutions it interacts with and a well developed system of communication. This is clearly demonstrated by its part in the success of elite sport. The approach to elite sport has also succeeded in radically changing attitudes, both within the sector and in the general public. It is no longer sufficient to put up a creditable performance—there is now a 'win at all costs' mentality and vastly heightened expectations. This has contributed to success in traditionally strong areas, but also a number of more surprising ones—cycling and gymnastics being two of the latest. There are clear implications for industry in both of these areas.

We initially posed the question: 'Can British industry learn anything from UK elite sport?' The academic literature on the systems based approach to industrial strategy and the 'market enhancing' role of government centres around the process of rapidly developing international competitiveness in industrial production, in which the government plays a central role in addressing problems in the legal environment, fostering institutions (market and non-market), and interacting with them to improve the international competitive capabilities of firms, industrial sectors, and hence the economy of which they form a part. Although this resonates with the experience of British elite sport, we have no evidence that this literature had any influence on developments in elite sport. However, it is significant that the approaches it champions have been effective in both elite sport and industry—especially in East Asia.

The motivation for the spread of elite sport development systems—from the former Soviet bloc, to Australia and most other developed countries—is clear: They were seen to work. In fact, it is now difficult to compete without one. The same can be said of industry. Politicians have expressed the wish for the UK industrial sector to perform as well as its Olympic team. There is a significant academic literature on the nature of industrial systems that have many similarities to that which has proven effective in elite sport, and such systems adapt to suit their cultural and institutional contexts. There is thus clearly a potential read-across to British industry.

In short, Britain clearly possesses the entrepreneurial, production, and innovation capabilities required to successfully compete in global markets. In a wide range of industries—from sparkling wine to audio equipment and sports cars—British producers regularly win international awards. However, in many ways, these are the 'Classic Alpinists' of industry, often succeeding against the odds, instead of being part of a team. The absence of a coherent institutional framework within which they, along with future businesses, can develop the competitive capabilities required for success, is limiting the numbers of successful businesses, and thus the performance of the broader economy.

The UK strategy for elite sport illustrates how to build an institutional framework for developing the capabilities required for world class competitive success in industry. The time has come for the political rhetoric about industrial policy to finally give way to active progress towards articulating a vision for the future of British industry and a strategy for achieving it.

References

Andreoni, A. 2011. 'Productive Capabilities Indicators for Industrial Policy Design'. Development Policy, Statistics and Research Branch Working Paper 17/2011, UN Industrial Development Organization, Vienna. Available at: <http://www.unido.org/fileadmin/user_media/Publications/Research_and_statistics/Branch_publications/Research_and_Policy/Files/Working_Papers/2011/WP172011%20Productive%20Capabilities%20Indicators%20for%20Industrial%20Policy%20Design.pdf> (last accessed 19 September 2015).

Aoki, M., Kim, H.-K., and Okuno-Fujiwara, M. 1997. *The Role of Government in East Asian Economic Development: Comparative Institutional Analysis*. Alderley: Clarendon Press.

BBC. 2001. 'Picketts Lock Bid Scrapped'. 4 October. Available at: <http://news.bbc.co.uk/sport1/hi/athletics/1577797.stm> (last accessed 19 September 2015).

BBC. 2011. 'Cameron Urges Economy "Rebalance" to Restore Growth'. 7 March. Available at: <http://www.bbc.co.uk/news/uk-politics-12665344> (last accessed 19 September 2015).

BERR. 2009. 'New Industry, New Jobs'. London: Department of Business, Enterprise and Regulatory Reform. Available at: <http://www.berr.gov.uk/files/file51023.pdf> (last accessed 19 September 2015).

BIS (Department for Business Innovation and Skills). 2010. 'Learning from Some of Britain's Successful Sectors: An Historical Analysis of the Role of Government'. Economic Paper No. 6. Available at: <http://www.bis.gov.uk/assets/BISCore/economics-and-statistics/docs/10-781-bis-economics-paper-06.pdf> (last accessed 19 September 2015).

BIS (Department for Business Innovation and Skills). 2012. 'Business Secretary Vince Cable Announces First steps in a Government Funded Bank to Help Small and Medium Sized Businesses'. *Announcement: New Business Bank to Boost Lending*.

24 September. Available at: <https://www.gov.uk/government/news/new-business-bank-to-boost-lending> (last accessed 19 September 2015).

BIS (Department for Business Innovation and Skills) and HM Treasury. 2011. 'The Plan for Growth'. London: Department for Business, Innovation and Skills and HM Treasury.

Cable, V. 2010. Speech at Cass Business School. Department for Business, Innovation and Skills, 3 June. Available at: <https://www.gov.uk/government/news/vince-cable-speech-cass-business-school-june-3-2010> (last accessed 19 September 2015).

Cable, V. 2011. 'Business Secretary Speech on Industrial Policy at Policy Exchange'. Department for Business, Innovation and Skills and UK Export Finance, 26 October. Available at: <https://www.gov.uk/government/speeches/business-secretary-speech-on-industrial-strategy-at-policy-exchange> (last accessed 19 September 2015).

Cable, V. 2012. 'Strategy: Cable Outlines Vision for Future of British Industry'. Department for Business, Innovation and Skills and UK Export Finance, 11 September. Available at: <https://www.gov.uk/government/speeches/industrial-strategy-cable-outlines-vision-for-future-of-british-industry> (last accessed 19 September 2015).

Chang, H.-J. 2003. *Kicking Away the Ladder: Development Strategy in Historical Perspective*. London: Anthem Press.

Chang, H.-J. 2010. 'Industrial Policy: Can We Go Beyond an Unproductive Confrontation?' Annual World Bank Conference on Development Economics, pp. 83–109. Available at: <http://www.rrojasdatabank.info/wbdevecon10-9.pdf> (last accessed 19 September 2015).

Cimoli, M., Dosi, G., Nelson, R., and Stiglitz, J. 2006. 'Institutions and Policies Shaping Industrial Development: An Introductory Note'. LEM (Laboratory of Economics and Management) Working Paper, January. Available at: <http://www.lem.sssup.it/WPLem/files/2006-02.pdf> (last accessed 19 September 2015).

Commission of the European Communities (CEC). 1994. *Growth*, 'Competitiveness, Employment: The Challenges and Ways Forward into the 21st Century'. CEC: Brussels.

DTI (Department of Trade and Industry). 1994. 'Competitiveness: Helping Business to Win, Cm 2563'. London: The Stationery Office.

DTI (Department of Trade and Industry). 1995. 'Competitiveness: Forging Ahead, Cm 2867'. London: The Stationery Office.

DTI (Department of Trade and Industry). 1996. 'Competitiveness: Creating the Enterprise Centre of Europe, Cm 330'. London: The Stationery Office.

DTI (Department of Trade and Industry). 1998. 'Our Competitive Future: Building the Knowledge Driven Economy, Cm 4176'. London: The Stationery Office.

Dunham-Jones, E. 2000. 'New Urbanism as a Counter-Project to Post-Industrialism [The Promise of New Urbanism]'. *Places*, 13(2): 26–31.

Financial Times. 2008. 'Transcript: Sir John Rose, CEO of Rolls-Royce'. 21 February. Available at: <http://www.ft.com/cms/s/0/987f1a72-e097-11dc-b0d7-0000779fd2ac.html#axzz2Q4BvwaPk> (last accessed 19 September 2015).

Gibson, D. 1993. 'Post-Industrialism: Prosperity or Decline?' *Sociological Focus*, 26(2): 147–63.

Gibson, O. 2012. 'London 2012: How Team GB's Fortunes Turned Around After Disaster in Atlanta'. *The Guardian*, 24 July. Available at: <http://www.guardian.co.uk/sport/2012/jul/24/london-2012-team-gb-atlanta> (last accessed 19 September 2015).

Greenaway, D. and Milner, C. 1994. 'Determinants of the Inter-Industry Structure of Protection in the UK'. *Oxford Bulletin of Economics and Statistics*, 56: 399–419.

Griffiths, A. and Zammuto, R. 2005. 'Institutional Governance Systems and Variations in National Competitive Advantage: An Integrated Framework'. *Academy of Management Review*, 30(4): 823–42.

Houlihan, B. and Lindsey, I. 2013. *Sport Policy in Britain*. Oxford: Routledge.

Konzelmann, S., Wilkinson, F., Fovargue-Davies, M., and Sankey, D. 2010. 'Governance, Regulation and Financial Market Instability: The Implications for Policy'. *Cambridge Journal of Economics*, 34(5): 929–54.

Lazonick, W. and O'Sullivan, M. 2000. 'Maximizing Shareholder Value: A New Ideology for Corporate Governance'. *Economy and Society*, 29(1): 13–35.

Naude, W. 2010. 'Industrial Policy: Old and New Issues.' United Nations University World Institute for Development Economics Research Working Paper Number 2010/106. Available at: <http://www.wider.unu.edu/publications/working-papers/2010/en_GB/wp2010-106/_files/84251275913199632/default/wp2010-106-revised.pdf> (last accessed 19 September 2015).

OECD (Organisation for Economic Co-operation and Development). 1992. *Technology and the Economy: The Key Relationships*. Paris: OECD.

Osborne, G. 2011. 'Budget Statement by the Chancellor of the Exchequer, the Rt Hon George Osborne MP'. London: HM Treasury, 23 March. Available at: <http://webarchive.nationalarchives.gov.uk/20130129110402/http://www.hm-treasury.gov.uk/2011budget_speech.htm> (last accessed 19 September 2015).

Owen, G. 2012. 'Industrial Policy in Europe Since the Second World War: What Has Been Learnt?' ECIPE (European Centre for International Political Economy) Occasional Paper No 1/2012. Available at: <http://www.ecipe.org/media/publication_pdfs/OCC12012-revised.pdf> (last accessed 19 September 2015).

Pryce, V. 2012. 'Britain Needs a Fourth Generation Industrial Policy'. London: Centre Forum. Available at: <http://www.centreforum.org/assets/pubs/4gip.pdf> (last accessed 19 September 2015).

Reinert, E. 1995. 'Competitiveness and Its Predecessors—A 500 year Cross-National Perspective'. *Structural Change and Economic Dynamics*, 6:23–42.

Robinson, J. 2009. 'Industrial Policy and Development: A Political Economy Perspective'. Paper presented at the 2009 World Bank ABCDE Conference, 22–24 June Seoul. Available at: <http://scholar.harvard.edu/files/jrobinson/files/jr_wb_industry_policy20-20Robinson.pdf> (last accessed 19 September 2015).

Rodrik, D. 2008. 'Normalizing Industrial Policy'. Commission on Growth and Development, Working Paper No. 3. Available at: <http://dev.wcfia.harvard.edu/sites/default/files/Rodrick_Normalizing.pdf> (last accessed 19 September 2015).

Rodrik, D. 2011. *The Globalization Paradox: Why Global Markets, States and Democracy Can't Coexist*. Oxford: Oxford University Press.

Rose, J. 2007. 'Why Manufacturing Matters'. Gabor Lecture. Video and podcast. Available at: <http://www3.imperial.ac.uk/events/dennisgaborlecture> (last accessed 19 September 2015).

Schleifer, A. and Vishny, R. 1997. 'A Survey of Corporate Governance'. *Journal of Finance* LII(2): 737–83.

Sharp, M. 2001. 'Industrial Policy and European Integration: Lessons from Experience in Western Europe over the Last 25 Years'. Centre for the Study of Economic and Social Change in Europe Working Paper No. 30, University College, London. Available at: <http://discovery.ucl.ac.uk/17546/1/17546.pdf> (last accessed 19 September 2015).

Slater, M. 2012. 'How GB Cycling Went from Tragic to Magic'. *BBC News*. Available at: <http://news.bbc.co.uk/sport1/hi/olympics/cycling/7534073.stm> (last accessed 19 September 2015).

UK Sport. 2013. 'What We Do'. Available at: <http://www.uksport.gov.uk/pages/what-we-do/> (last accessed 19 September 2015).

Vickers, J. and Yarrow, G. 1988. *Privatization: An Economic Analysis*. Cambridge, MA: MIT Press.

Warwick, K. 2013. 'Beyond Industrial Policy—Emerging Issues and New Trends'. OECD Science, Technology and Industrial Policy Papers No. 2, OECD Publishing. Available at: <http://www.enterprise-development.org/download.ashx?id=2159> (last accessed 19 September 2015).

White, D. 2012. 'London 2012 Olympics: Team GB's Failures in the Swimming Pool Mean There Are Stormy Waters Ahead'. *The Telegraph*. 11 August. Available at: <http://www.telegraph.co.uk/sport/olympics/swimming/9469790/London-2012-Olympics-Team-GBs-failures-in-the-swimming-pool-mean-there-are-stormy-waters-ahead.html> (last accessed 19 September 2015).

Wren, C. 2001. 'The Industrial Policy of Competitiveness: A Review of Recent Developments in the UK'. *Regional Studies*, 35(9): 847–60.

11

Finance and Investment in the Eurozone

Giovanni Cozzi

11.1 Introduction

The systemic crisis and economic downturn, which are affecting the Eurozone, have their roots in the neoliberal shift that took place in the late 1970s. During this period, Eurozone countries, as many other countries around the world, were urged to change their priorities from a commitment to full employment and towards fighting price inflation and increasing labour markets flexibility. Since the early 1980s, Keynesian policies and a strong role of the state in the economy were seen as impediments to economic growth and development, while laissez-faire economic liberalism was seen as the solution (Petit 2012). Thus, in the name of inflation controls countries were urged to check and reduce government expenditure, by means of welfare reductions and fully fledged privatizations, so that budget deficits would not fuel inflation.

In parallel to these developments, there were also policy concerns that 'financially repressed' systems, as they were then called, were inefficient (Gurley and Shaw 1955; McKinnon 1973). Government regulations and restrictions on the financial system, such as, for example, interest rate ceilings that could be charged on loans, were seen as impediments to financial development, and could thereby hinder economic development (Sawyer 2014). Thus, since the early 1980s, several countries removed ceilings on interest rates and abandoned credit allocation policies. This was believed to increase the quantity and the quality of investment through a more efficient allocation of credit (McKinnon 1973). From a theoretical perspective, the idea that 'financial markets are efficient' encouraged financial liberalization, with light or no regulation (Cozzi and Griffith-Jones 2014).

This shift in economic priorities was followed by frequent and costly systemic financial and economic crises which culminated in the recent North Atlantic financial crisis and the ongoing economic stagnation in the Eurozone and other parts of the world. In other words, reforms of the financial system aimed at removing the alleged government induced distortions have brought several economies into various precarious economic conditions that can be synthetized with the words of Diaz Alejandro (1985): 'Good-bye financial repression, hello financial crash!'

Indeed, contrary to mainstream theoretical predictions, empirical evidence shows that the change in economic priorities has brought many economies into precarious conditions and has led to a secular decline in investment and slowdown in economic growth. For instance, in the Eurozone, the main focus of this chapter, it is evident that three decades of economic liberalism have increase economic and financial instability and have significantly slowed down economic growth, not least because investment has steadily fallen in most countries. It is thus clear that a serious reconsideration of economic policies is needed to create a new economic paradigm in Europe where sustainable growth and job creation take centre stage.

In view of this background, this chapter reviews some of the core constraints that have developed in the Eurozone on investment and growth as a result of the shift towards economic liberalism and advances some alternative policies for promoting growth and investment. Section 11.2 discusses the impact of financial liberalization on investment and growth in the Eurozone. Section 11.3 reviews the impact of the Eurozone fiscal policy stance on investment and growth. Section 11.4 puts forward some progressive economic policies for growth and investment in the Eurozone. Section 11.5 presents some concluding remarks.

11.2 Financial Liberalization and Investment in the Eurozone

During the period of financial liberalization and deregulation the world economy grew more slowly compared with the 1970s. Table 11.1 highlights the five years average gross domestic product (GDP) growth rate for selected world blocs and the total for the world since 1975. The picture that emerges is one of higher growth rates for several parts of the world during the mid-1970s. European countries currently forming the Eurozone recorded higher growth rates in the 1970s and experienced a significant decline in GDP growth from the early 1990s to present day both in absolute and relative terms vis-à-vis other world blocs.

There are several reasons for the poor growth performance of Eurozone countries since the early 1990s. One of the key reasons for the slowdown in

Table 11.1. Five Years Average GDP Growth Rate

	1975	1980	1985	1990	1995	2000	2005	2010	2015*
Core Eurozone, surplus countries	2.97	2.93	1.26	3.56	2.21	2.25	0.75	1.10	1.21
Eurozone Periphery	3.67	3.60	1.61	4.00	1.45	3.09	2.06	0.04	−0.47
France (Core Eurozone, Deficit)	4.07	3.09	1.47	3.38	1.27	2.69	1.42	0.61	0.95
North Europe, non-Eurozone	2.64	2.18	2.32	2.14	1.24	3.44	1.90	1.31	1.74
East Europe, non-Eurozone	6.21	4.52	1.20	−0.27	−4.90	3.30	4.10	3.16	1.13
United Kingdom	1.62	2.50	2.02	3.06	2.29	3.99	2.94	0.09	1.78
United States	2.60	3.38	3.38	3.26	2.64	4.43	2.41	0.64	2.42
Japan	4.32	3.90	4.60	5.04	1.47	0.75	0.80	−0.14	1.25
Brazil	9.94	7.40	1.29	1.33	3.31	1.60	2.73	5.30	2.45
Russia, CIS	2.46	4.35	5.37	−5.12	3.11	3.11	6.68	4.25	4.36
India	2.47	2.96	5.84	6.26	5.68	5.71	6.58	8.64	4.95
China	6.00	6.61	10.59	8.00	12.78	7.59	10.11	11.15	6.30
South Africa	5.59	4.30	0.62	1.40	0.58	2.63	4.20	4.20	2.80
East Asia High Income	9.30	10.10	8.50	11.70	7.30	3.60	2.70	2.70	3.40
East Asia Low income	7.20	8.80	4.10	6.00	7.20	2.80	4.50	4.70	5.70
North Africa and West Asia	11.01	9.28	3.22	−0.44	2.79	6.10	7.50	5.40	4.13
Africa Low Income	4.78	2.80	−0.53	0.90	0.70	4.68	7.16	6.94	5.76
World, Total	**3.96**	**4.25**	**2.94**	**3.55**	**2.57**	**3.73**	**3.66**	**3.44**	**3.30**

GDP growth is that private investment has fallen in most Eurozone countries and savings have not been sufficiently mobilized and intermediated into effective investment (Figure 11.1).

A well-functioning financial system needs to play an important role in achieving sustained growth. It needs to encourage and mobilize savings and ensure that these savings are channelled into efficient investment towards activities which promote innovation and structural change (Cozzi and Griffith-Jones 2014). In this respect, the banking system plays a fundamental role in supporting investment. Credit money created by the banking system is indispensable for financing investment expenditure; the investment expenditure then takes place, and through further expenditure and the generation of income, savings are made. The savings that have then been made have to be reallocated between the savers and investors (Sawyer 2013).

However, the financial system has not performed these functions effectively neither in Europe nor in other parts of the world. Instead, it has been extremely pro-cyclical and has had the tendency to over lend in boom times, and ration credit during periods of crisis and recession, thus limiting

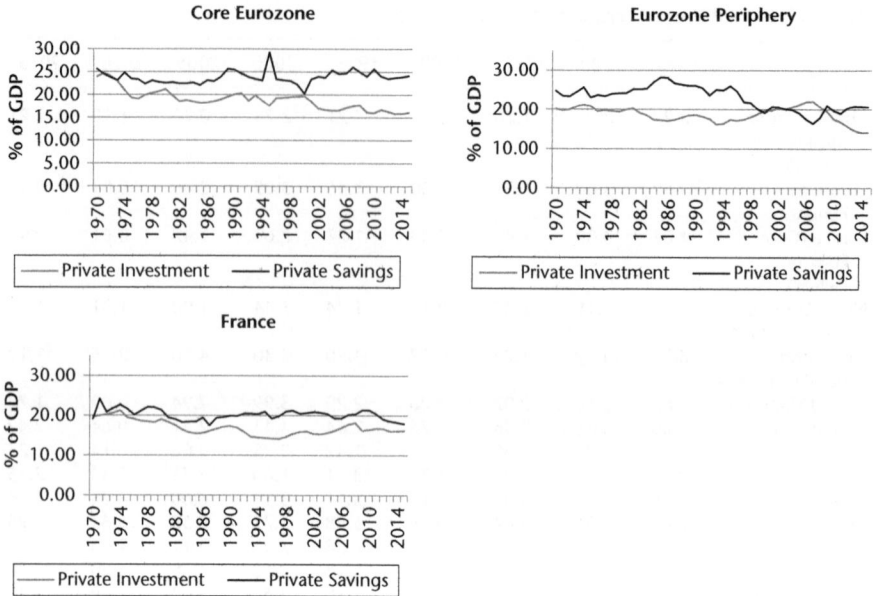

Figure 11.1 Private Savings and Investment as Per Cent of GDP

working capital and long-term finance for investment (Cozzi and Griffith-Jones 2014). The consequence of this malfunctioning for the Eurozone has been a secular decline in private investment (Figure 11.1), accompanied by a slowdown in economic growth.

For instance, in the core Eurozone (which comprises Germany, Austria, Belgium, Finland, The Netherlands, and Luxemburg) and in France, in the mid-2000s, private savings significantly exceeded investment. In 2005, investment in both the core Eurozone and in France stood at around 16 per cent of GDP whilst savings reached 25 per cent and 19 per cent of GDP respectively. On the other hand, in the Eurozone periphery (which comprises Italy, Greece, Spain, Portugal, and Ireland), by the mid-2000s, savings declined to 19 per cent of GDP whilst investment reached 21 per cent of GDP. The lower savings in the Eurozone periphery, combined with an increase in household debt in some peripheral countries (e.g., Spain) and with an inflow of capital from the rest of the world (the counterpart to the current account deficit), led to an increase in the budget deficits in the Eurozone periphery (from –1.8 per cent in 1999 to –2.5 per cent of GDP in 2005) prior to the crisis as an inevitable feature of the absorption of excessive savings of the core Eurozone and other parts of the world (Figure 11.2). After this period, investment in the Eurozone periphery sharply declined below 15% of GDP.

Thus, at the onset of the North Atlantic financial crisis, the lack of intermediation of savings into long-term investment in innovation and skills which

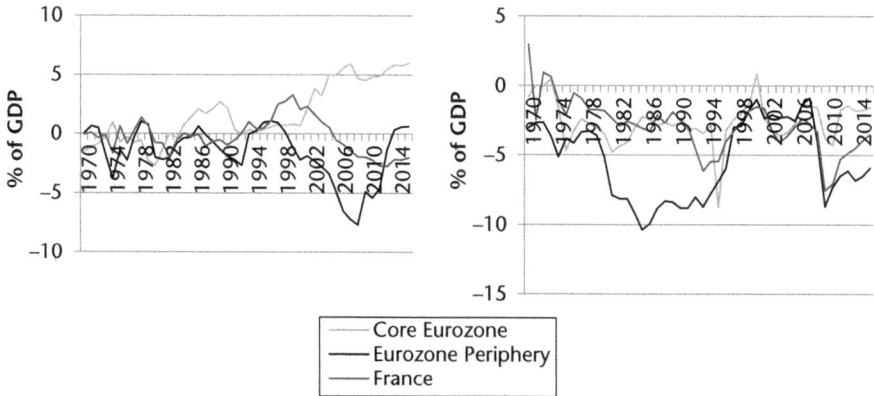

Figure 11.2 Current Account Balance and Government Sector Net Lending as Per Cent of GDP

businesses need to growth, meant that the Eurozone already presented significant imbalances and was already locked into a low-growth-low-investment scenario, which has been only aggravated by the events taking place since 2008.

Indeed, financial liberalization has led to a significant shift in the relationship between the financial sector and industry. Activities of the financial sector have become more concerned with transactions in 'existing pieces of financial papers' and with the profits generated from such transactions rather than with the funding of long-term investment (Sawyer 2013). Second, there has been an increased preference of liquidity among investors, as well as banks, which has been responsible for the limitation of the supply of credit in the economy (Kregel 1988; Wray 2009). Even when corporations have savings in excess of their investment, as in the case of the core Eurozone and France, rather than reallocating these savings into long-term investment, they have developed a preference to intermediate these savings towards the financing of consumer debt and the purchase of financial assets (Orhangazi 2011; Sawyer 2013).

What has come into dominance during the neoliberal period of slow growth and declining private investment is a form of capitalism that Minsky identified as 'money-manager capitalism' (Bellofiore 2013). This type of capitalism is the result of the evolution of financial practices towards more speculative activities and is also partly a product of institutional innovations that has dramatically altered the control of corporate equities and bonds. Central feature of this period is the presence of institutions that manage large portfolios of financial instruments (Whalen 1997). As a result, households' savings were channelled into private institutional funds and asset markets rather than into productive investment, which in turned fuelled 'capital-asset price inflation'. At the same time managers were assigned the mission of maximizing dividends and shares, and this was the sole criterion by which they were jugged (Whalen 1997; Bellofiore 2013). What followed was a significant change in corporate governance from a focus of maximizing productive investment towards innovation and structural change to the maximization of shareholders' value. Money-manager capitalism ultimately led to the creation of an environment where mergers, acquisitions, breakups, leverage buyout, and stock buybacks would take priority over long-term productive investment.

This change in preference by corporations was also induced by the secular stagnation in wages that has characterized Eurozone countries since the early 1980s (Stockhammer 2010). The general shift away from wages to profits meant that the one of the few options to boost aggregate demand was to increase borrowing opportunities of households. Indeed, as highlighted by Bellofiore (2013) indebtedness during this period emerged predominantly from financial businesses and households rather that from the physical investment of non-financial corporations. However, this approach, as demonstrated in recent years, has led to a severe over-indebtedness of the household sector in several Eurozone countries—one of the contributing causes of the North Atlantic financial crisis—and also to a significant slowdown in long-term investment in activities to promote innovation and structural change.

11.3 Fiscal Policies and Investment in the Eurozone

In the Eurozone, resources for investment have also been severely impaired by the fiscal policy stance adopted since the early 1990s. According to the dominant view in mainstream economics and policy circles, fiscal policy and budget deficits are seen as unimportant in affecting the level of economic activity. It is believed that the effects on aggregate demand of increased government expenditure or decreases in taxes would be exactly offset by changes in private demand. Thus, fiscal policy has been merely seen as a tool to encourage fiscal profligacy and public debt which would then lead to unsustainable public debt (Arestis and Sawyer 2010). A clear example of this is the intention of the Stability and Growth Pact for individual countries to have a budget position in balance or small surplus over the business cycle subject to a completely arbitrary 3 per cent of GDP limit in any year. It is also reflected in the 60 per cent ratio of debt to GDP imposed by the Stability and Growth Pact (Arestis and Sawyer 2010).

The Stability and Growth Pact, alongside the Maastricht Treaty, which set up the basic principles or a common currency, created four rules for economic policy in the Eurozone. The four rules are that the European Central Bank (ECB) was granted independence from political influence, the rule of non-bailout of national government deficits was introduced, the monetary financing of government deficits was prohibited, and member states must avoid excessive deficits. These rules were created in the belief that they would facilitate the ECB's primary task of price stability (Arestis, Mccauley, and Sawyer 2001). However, the imposition of these strict rules of behaviour paved the way for austerity policies as the only possible answer to any external change.

In addition, another institutional arrangement set up in the 1990s in the Eurozone is the complete separation between monetary authorities and the fiscal authorities (in the shape of national governments) and the absence of a European Treasury. Thus, there is not any significant fiscal policy operated at the European level. The size of the European budget is very small at around 1 per cent of combined EU member states' GDP and still dominated by the needs of the Common Agricultural Policy, which means that it cannot provide for a significant amount of resources for investment.

Further, the EU budget must be balanced, and the interaction between this and the limited size of the budget means that there is no scope for any active fiscal policy, and that the EU budget is too small to operate as an affective stabilizer. It cannot be used as a countercyclical instrument to provide financing for investment when required (Arestis, Mccauley, and Sawyer 2001). Apart from its small structural funds, the budget cannot provide for significant transfer from rich and poor nations of the Union (Irvin and Izurieta 2011). Arestis, Mccauley, and Sawyer (2001) calculate that the redistribution effects in the EU, in the form of structural and cohesion funds, is estimated to be around 0.5 per cent and 3 per cent of the difference between national GDP per capita and the EU average.

The EU has also imposed rules that specify a fixed limit on government borrowing. However, these rules fail to recognize that government borrowing serves as a mechanism for distributing over time the cost of adjustment to shocks and for smoothing tax burdens associated with public investment. In addition, constraints on government borrowing reduce the flexibility of national governments' fiscal policies and make fiscal consolidation very difficult (Arestis, Mccauley, and Sawyer 2001).

Thus, the monetary union, by way of its specific design, has removed three essential policy instruments from the domain of national policymaking: exchange rate management, monetary policy and fiscal policy. The latter became effectively dependent on the performance of the external sector and the financial behaviour of the private sector (Irvin and Izurieta 2011). Ultimately, this has significantly undermined the ability of the state to become a strong economic actor and has deprived it of any meaningful possibility to use deficit financing to promote growth, investment and innovation, with negative consequences for growth and jobs.

This fiscal stance has also characterized the policy responses to the North Atlantic financial crisis and the sovereign debt crisis in the Eurozone. Indeed, despite the significant deterioration in employment opportunities and growth in Europe as a result of the economic crisis, policy responses across Europe,

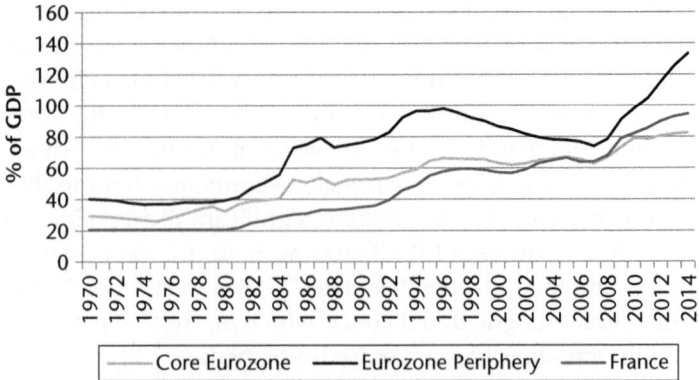

Figure 11.3 Government Debt as Per Cent of GDP

following temporary, piecemeal, and early attempts at fiscal stimulus, have focused on fiscal containment and debt reduction rather than promoting growth and job creation (Bettio et al. 2013: 120).

The preoccupation with fiscal deficits and government debts has led governments to implement harsh austerity policies in order to significantly reduce government expenditures, with negative repercussion on public investment, public sector employment and welfare. For instance, in the Eurozone periphery, government spending has decreased from 25 per cent of GDP in 2010 to 22.8 per cent in 2014. However, despite cuts in government spending net government lending has not significantly improved (this has declined from -7.3 per cent in 2010 to -6.5 per cent in 2014) and government debt at percentage of GDP has increased from 98 per cent to 133 per cent (Figure 11.3). Further, the harsh fiscal consolidation implemented across Europe has led stagnant economic growth, which in 2014 has barely reached 0.8 per cent in the Eurozone periphery, and 1.5 per cent in the Core Eurozone.[1] Overall, austerity policies have moved the Eurozone from a sovereign debt crisis into recession and stagnation.

11.4 Progressive Economic Policies for Growth and Investment

The crisis and recession that are afflicting the Eurozone once again demonstrate how the fiscal policy stance in the Eurozone, coupled with financial liberalization and money-manager capitalism have had detrimental effects on growth and investment. Six years since the start of the North Atlantic financial crisis and the Eurozone sovereign debt crisis, investment levels are at a record

---

[1] Data source: UN Data, aggregation Cambridge Alphametrics Model (CAM).

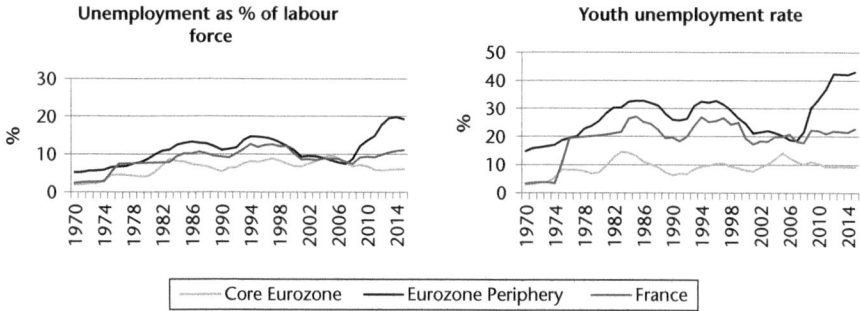

Figure 11.4 Unemployment and Youth Unemployment Rate

low, growth performance remains dismal across the Eurozone, and unemployment, especially among the young, has surged dramatically, particularly in the Eurozone periphery (Figure 11.4).

The response of several economists and policymakers to the current negative trends in employment, investment and growth across Europe has been to emphasize that an appropriate pace of fiscal consolidation (austerity) should go hand in hand with growth enhancing policies (Buti and Padoan 2012). To this end, a series of initiatives to mobilize additional public and private investment in the real economy, such as the European Commission's 315-billion-euro Investment Plan for Europe proposal,[2] have been put forward as a way to finance new, sustainable, and job creating projects.

Although these policy proposals might represent a positive first step to increase investment, they are not sufficient to build the institutional foundations of a European system that is more developmental and that has at its core an employment and investment focused recovery. Indeed, the majority of policy proposals in the Eurozone currently discussed or implemented have been merely preventive and reactive rather than representing a break from the laissez-faire policies that have characterized the past three decades and building the institutional foundations of a more sustainable economic system.

In particular, the dominant policy debate on enhancing growth and recovery in Europe is still based on the idea that policies aimed at stimulating investment have to go hand in hand with continued fiscal consolidation. However, the danger of such a policy stance, is that any positive effect of a pan-European investment plan might end up to be neutralized by continued

---

[2] The Investment Plan for Europe institutes a European Fund for Strategic Investment (EFSI) which aims at supporting investment in infrastructure, such as broadband and energy networks, as well as transport infrastructure, particularly in industrial centers, education, research and innovation, and renewable energy (European Commission 2014).

reduction of national government expenditure and public investment, both in surplus and deficit European countries.

Instead, it is essential move away from this policy stance and to start seeing fiscal policies as having the fundamental function of ensuring high levels of aggregate demand and of supporting economic growth. This implies that until investment has strongly recovered from its long-term decline and households are able to spend without incurring high levels of debt, expansionary fiscal policies, both at EU and national level, are a necessary tool to stimulate growth and investment. In other words, national budget deficits in the Eurozone will have to continue until the economy has fully recovered.

Further, at European level, it is also essential to seriously reconsider the role and size of the European budget, as this could play a fundamental role in stimulating European investment. The EU budget should be significantly increased in order to provide incentives for promoting investment and economic growth, to act as a countercyclical mechanism, and to redistribute funds from rich to poor nations in Europe. Indeed, already in 1977, the MacDougall Report on the Role of Public Finance in European Integration highlighted the importance of having a federal budget of at least 5–7 per cent of GDP of members' states in order for the monetary union to be viable. In a recent study Cozzi and Michell (2013) highlight how a gradual increase in the EU budget by an additional 3 per cent of members' countries GDP, combined with a complete reversal of austerity policies, could lead to a major boost in investment, higher GDP growth, and to an additional 15 million jobs by 2030.

This also implies that the Stability and Growth pact is in need of modification. The arbitrary 3 per cent fiscal deficit to GDP rule prevents the effective operation of automatic stabilizers and the use of fiscal policies for countercyclical operation, let alone stimulating aggregate demand (Laski and Podkaminer 2012). In this context, Arestis, Mccauley, and Sawyer (2001) argue for the need of a Full Employment Stability and Growth Pact where fiscal policy should be an active ingredient in achieving high levels of economic activity. In other words, fiscal policies should no longer be seen as a tool for balancing government budgets.

Furthermore, there is also a need to engage in a serious debate on the possibility of restructuring and consolidating government debt, especially in the Eurozone periphery where it is significantly undermining future growth perspectives. As highlighted in the previous section, attempts to reduce government debt by cutting government expenditure have failed as these cuts have ultimately halted economic growth in Europe. A range of proposals on how to reduce government debt has been put forward, with most centred on joint issuance of guarantees of debt. Several economists have also suggested the creation of a European Redemption Fund as a way to address the debt overhang faced by many Eurozone countries (e.g., Bofinger et al. 2012;

Buchheit et al. 2013; Cozzi and Michell 2013). These initiatives entail that part of the government debt is pooled in a common EU debt fund. It is assumed that debt repayment remains the obligation of the country of issue, but that through joint issuance, the yield demanded by holders of this debt can be reduced below the rates that otherwise would be demanded. This would then free up additional resources that could be used for investment in viable and innovative projects. However, although these studies have demonstrated the economic viability of such initiatives, there is currently no political will at European and national level to mutualize debt and thus freeing up resources for investment.

It is also essential to reconsider the role that the financial system plays in promoting investment, industrial development and innovation. In the past three decades the financial system has fallen short in providing enough credit towards productive activities. Instead, it has moved quite freely to take positions in speculative instruments and offshore markets (Dymski and Kaltenbrunner 2014).

Policymakers at the European level have been focusing their attention on the importance of adopting new financial regulations, such as the proposal of instituting a banking union and implementing a financial transaction tax, in order to reduce speculative activities. Although these policy initiatives represent a step forward in the direction of reducing speculative behaviour, they do not fully address the scope of possible risk. Indeed, these proposals fall short in addressing issues such as reducing the activities and the size of too big to fail mega banks, or increase regulatory control of shadow banking and offshore financial centres tax heavens (Dymski and Kaltenbrunner 2014).

Further, a mere focus on financial regulation misses out how finance is related to the rest of the economy (Orhangazi 2011). It is important that changes in financial markets and the adoption of stronger financial regulation is also accompanied by a reconsideration of the role that the financial sector should play in financing and supporting productive investment in feasible and innovative projects. In this context, the role of public development banks in supporting investment becomes of extreme importance and should be significantly reconsidered.

Given the procyclical nature of private capital, public development banks could play a fundamental role in providing both short-term countercyclical and long-term finance for investment in innovation and technological development. Indeed, development banks, such as the European Investment Bank (EIB) and national development banks as the German KfW, could be extremely important partners for financing and co-financing investment in new sectors or the deepening of existing sectors, such as, for instance, green and renewable energy, where private investors on their own would not invest as uncertainty is too high.

These banks have already provided significant amounts of funds in innovative projects across Europe, such as the creation of a smart intra-European electricity grid, to facilitate the transmission of renewable energy (Cozzi and Griffith-Jones 2014). However, in order to increase their capacity it is important not only to review and strengthen their functions but also to equip them with additional capital to co-finance projects. Indeed, an increase in the capital of the EIB could create significant leverage effects, which would then lead to a substantial increase in the lending that these type of banks can put towards productive investment (Cozzi and Griffith-Jones 2014).

11.5 Conclusion

The Eurozone is in its deepest crisis since its inception. A financial sector and sovereign debt crisis coupled with a real economy crisis has led to stagnating economies and rising unemployment in the Eurozone. Several commentators have described this crisis as a temporary and unpredictable phenomenon that requires extraordinary measures to then return to normal once the crisis has subdued. As a result, in the Eurozone, the majority of policy proposals have been preventive and reactive rather than building the institutional foundations of a European economic and financial system that is, on the whole, more developmental and equitable.

However, this chapter has highlighted that the crisis and the recession that followed have their roots in the transformation that took place in the economy and the financial sectors in Europe, as in other parts of the world, since the beginning of the 1980s, and as such, precarious economic conditions are systemic rather than temporary.

Since the 1980s the overwhelming majority of economists and policy-makers believed that financial liberalization and deregulation, combined with policies to promote price stability, would create the necessary conditions to spearhead aggregate demand, increase investment, and as a result, economic growth and employment. However, empirical evidence demonstrates that during this period the economy of the Eurozone grew more slowly, not least because of the secular decline in private investment. Indeed, financial liberalization, coupled with fiscal austerity, which is intrinsically built in the various European treaties and pacts, has created the condition for bringing Europe in a dangerous low-growth-low-investment scenario.

It follows that a serious reconsideration of the role that the financial sector and fiscal policies play in the Eurozone in promoting investment and growth has to be undertaken. Fiscal policy should no longer be seen as a tool for promoting fiscal profligacy but as an instrument for stimulating aggregated demand and investment. Further, financial sector reforms should go beyond the introduction of preventive and reactive regulation. It is thus essential to reconsider the role that the financial and banking sector play in financing and supporting productive investment in feasible and innovative projects in Europe. Only with these significant changes the Eurozone will be able to embark on a new economic trajectory where sustainable growth and jobs take centre stage.

References

Arestis, P., Mccauley, K., and Sawyer, M. 2001. 'An Alternative Stability Pact for the European Union'. *Cambridge Journal of Economics*, 25: 112–30.

Arestis, P. and Sawyer, M. 2010. 'The Return of Fiscal Policy'. *Journal of Post Keynesian Economics*, 32: 327–46.

Bellofiore, R. 2013. 'Two or Three Things I Know About Her': Europe in the Global Crisis and Heterodox Economics'. *Cambridge Journal of Economics*, 37: 497–512.

Bettio, F., Corsi, M., D'Ippoliti, C., Lyberaki, A., Samek Lodovici, M., and Verashcha-gina, A. 2013. 'The Impact of the Economic Crisis on the Situation of Women and Men and on Gender Equality Policies'. Luxembourg: European Union.

Bofinger, P., Buch, C. M., Feld, L. P., Franz, W., and Schmidt, C. M. 2012. 'A Redemption Pact for Europe: Time to Act Now'. Vox Research-Based Policy Analysis and Commentary from Leading Economists Available at: <http://www.voxeu.org/article/redemption-pact-europe-time-act-now> (last accessed 22 February 2014).

Buchheit, L. C., Gelpern, A., Gulati, M., Panizza, U., di Mauro, B. W., and Zettelmeyer, J. 2013. 'Revisiting Sovereign Bankruptcy'. Committee on International Economic Policy and Reform, Brookings Institution.

Buti, M. and Padoan, P. 2012. 'From a Vicious to a Virtuous Circle in the Eurozone—the Time Is Ripe'. Vox Research-Based Policy Analysis and Commentary from Leading Economists. Available at: <http://www.voxeu.org/article/vicious-virtuous-circle-eurozone> (accessed 10 September 2015).

Cozzi, G. and Griffith-Jones, S. 2014. 'Investment-Led Growth: A Solution to the European Crisis'. *FEPS Studies*.

Cozzi, G. and Michell, J. 2013. 'Employment Focused Recovery for Europe: An Alternative to Austerity'. *FEPS Studies*.

Diaz-Alejandro, C. 1985. 'Goodbye Financial Repression, Hello Financial Crash'. *Journal of Development Economics*, 19: 1–24.

Dymski, G. and Kaltenbrunner, A. 2014. 'Beyond Europe's Financial Bifurcation Point: Policy Proposals for a More Stable and Equitable Financial System'. FEPS Policy Brief No.4.

European Commission. 2014. 'An Investment Plan for Europe'. Communication from the Commission to the European Parliament, the Council, the European Central Bank, the European Economic and Social Committee, the Committee of the Regions and the European Parliament, COM(2014) 903 Final.

Gurley, J. G. and Shaw, E. S. 1955. 'Financial Aspects of Economic Development'. *The American Economic Review*, 45: 515–38.

Irvin, G. and Izurieta, A. 2011. 'Fundamental Flaws in the European Project'. *Economic and Political Weekly*, 6 (August): 4–16.

Kregel, J. A. 1988. 'The Multiplier and Liquidity Preference: Two Sides of the Theory of Efficient Demand'. In A. Barriere (ed.), *The Foundations of Keynesian Analysis*. London: Macmillan, 231–50.

Laski, K. and Podkaminer, L. 2012. 'The Basic Paradigms of EU Economic Policy-Making Need to Be Changed'. *Cambridge Journal of Economics*, 36: 253–70.

McKinnon, R. I. 1973. *Money and Capital in Economic Development*. Washington, D.C.: Brookings Institution Press.

Orhangazi, O. 2011. '"Financial" vs. "Real". An Overview of the Contradictory Role of Finance'. Working Paper Series, No. 274, PERI, University of Massachusetts, Amherst.

Petit, P. 2012. 'Building Faith in a Common Currency: Can the Eurozone Get Beyond the Common Market Logic?' *Cambridge Journal of Economics*, 36: 271–81.

Sawyer, M. 2013. 'Financial Development, Financialization and Economic Growth'. Working Paper Series, No. 21, FESSUD Project.

Sawyer, M. 2014. 'Finance and Industrial Strategy'. Working Paper Series, No. 31, FESSUD Project.

Stockhammer, E. 2010. 'Financialization and the Global Economy'. Working Paper Series, No. 240, PERI, University of Massachusetts, Amherst.

Whalen, C. J. 1997. 'Money-Manager Capitalism and the End of Shared Prosperity'. *Journal of Economic Issues*, 31: 517–25.

Wray, L. R. 2009. 'An Alternative View of Finance, Savings, Deficit and Liquidity'. Working paper No. 580, Levy Economics Institute of Brad College.

12

Industrial Policy as a Contribution to Overcome the Crisis in Europe

Matthias Kollatz-Ahnen, Stephany Griffith-Jones, and Udo Bullmann

12.1 Introduction

Industrial policies are back on centre stage—somehow industrial policies can be understood as part of the positive response to the prevailing austerity policies in Europe. The austerity packages assumed that after decisive cuts in public spending, a self-sustainable growth would take place in the following year—as evidenced by the Economic Forecasts of the EU Commission (DG ECFIN—Directorate General for Economic and Financial Affairs) in 2011, 2012, and 2013. Two years of a shrinking EU economy as a whole in 2012 and 2013 and for 2014 a growth that was much too late and much too weak proves that the prevailing theory and practice of austerity delivered poor results, based on a poor economic foundation and incorrect models.

Industrial policies on the contrary deal with different growth paths and assume that packages including the right incentives, the right legal and budgetary decisions and the right cooperation with the private sector can move a country or the EU to another trajectory of higher growth. From this point of view some growth may come without changing anything (or much), but higher growth paths require interventions favouring certain new industries or supporting the revival of existing ones that have adapted to new challenges. The intervention has to target rather the real economy than the financial sector.

This chapter deals with the following topics:

– Some of the proposals for reindustrialization want to shape it as a small improvement of continued austerity policy; it will be shown that this will not deliver reindustrialization and in the best case may merely grant slower deindustrialization;

- Describe the main areas of increased investment for an industrial policy; with investment in infrastructure alone, sufficient growth and a new growth path cannot be achieved;
- Describe the orientation for the real economy;
- Warn that each year of prolonged crisis in countries, deepening the lack of growth in the productive sectors will result in a much longer catch-up phase, which has to be measured in decades.

12.2 Relevant Industrial Policies for Growth Do Not Exist

The EU Commission calls for reindustrialization, but the policy mix of the Commission leads to fast deindustrialization.

During the crisis, the EU Commission (and the Council) called for reindustrialization of the EU in 2012. The Commission defined the objective of 20 per cent of gross domestic product (GDP) in 2020 created by industrial production. Achieving this objective would require a turnaround of existing developments and existing policies.

The development follows a trend of deindustrialization, significantly accelerated by the crisis. During the year 2013 the industrial share in GDP fell from 15 per cent to 14 per cent at the EU level. One of the industrial champions in Europe, Germany (the others being Poland, Netherlands, Austria) showed in 2013 a share of industry of 25.5 per cent and an additional 4.7 per cent of construction, as sometimes the construction sector is included in the figure of industry. This is down from 30.2 per cent and 6.1 per cent respectively in 1991, the first year of common statistics after German reunification and shows a trend of –0.2 per cent per annum (see Statistisches Bundesamt 2014). Continuing the EU trend would imply 12 per cent of GDP and not 20 per cent for industry in 2020. To reverse such a trend, powerful action will be needed.

Existing EU policies have explicitly and implicitly favoured the transition from the industrial sector to the service sector, so with policies remaining basically unchanged, not even a slowdown of deindustrialization can be expected.

Therefore it is always important to look at the measures taken and planned with the objective at EU level. The measures communicated together with the objective of 20 per cent industrial share of GDP were not wrong, but not new, and as a matter of fact were basically existing ones (e.g., the SME (small and medium sized enterprise) initiative had already started before the crisis). Thus they will not even change the trend and the so-called EU industrial policy has to be considered rather a declaration than a policy with substance.

A slowing down of deindustrialization could result only from an EU policy moving EU funds in a very relevant volume to energy efficiency investments and moving EU funds in industry towards investment related to development and innovation. The scale of measures envisaged for such investment in the financial perspective 2014–2020 as it stands is completely insufficient for such a turnaround. With the volume envisaged there in ESIF (European Structural and Investment Funds) and Horizon 2020 a significant impact on an increase in the size of the industrial sector will not be achieved.

12.3 The Handling of the Crisis since 2008 has Accelerated Deindustrialization

The first anti-crisis package at EU level with the slightly too ambitious name 'European Recovery Programme' aiming at speeding up investments and facilitating deployment of EU funds for investment was pro-production and pro-industry. Several measures of the Member States such as car-scrapping premiums or support schemes for energy efficiency aimed at revitalizing production and industries.

However, the later handling of the crisis was different. The financial crisis moved the 'Euro crisis' into a new stage—with some countries achieving a safe harbour status paying significantly lower interest rates for government debt and some other countries facing much higher interest rates and finally losing in practical terms access to the capital markets.

The European Central Bank (ECB) (mainly), the EU Commission, and the EU Member States successfully defended the euro. The Central Bank was the first and most prominent actor, the Member States created a sequence of new instruments for intervention and protection and a new set of rules, the main being the fiscal compound.

Repairing the budget was set as the first and only priority. In the long term, it is right that budget consolidation or a credible path to reduce the overall share of public indebtedness to GDP is necessary to retain or regain access to the capital markets. However, the existence of growth is very important and should be a key policy target. In a shrinking economy, even without new public indebtedness the ratio of debt to GDP will increase. And in the positive scenario, if the growth rate is positive (and higher than new debt) the ratio of debt to GDP will be reduced.

To express this in policy terms, the mistake of the Maastricht Treaty was repeated once again: the Maastricht-mistake took low indebtedness of the national budget as an indicator of the overall soundness of the economy. This turned out to be wrong; the best in class according to Maastricht were Ireland and Spain, countries moving in the Euro crisis soon into a dangerous zone, due to recession, high unemployment and high cost of rescuing the financial sector. Now again the budget consolidation was understood as a

Industrial Production

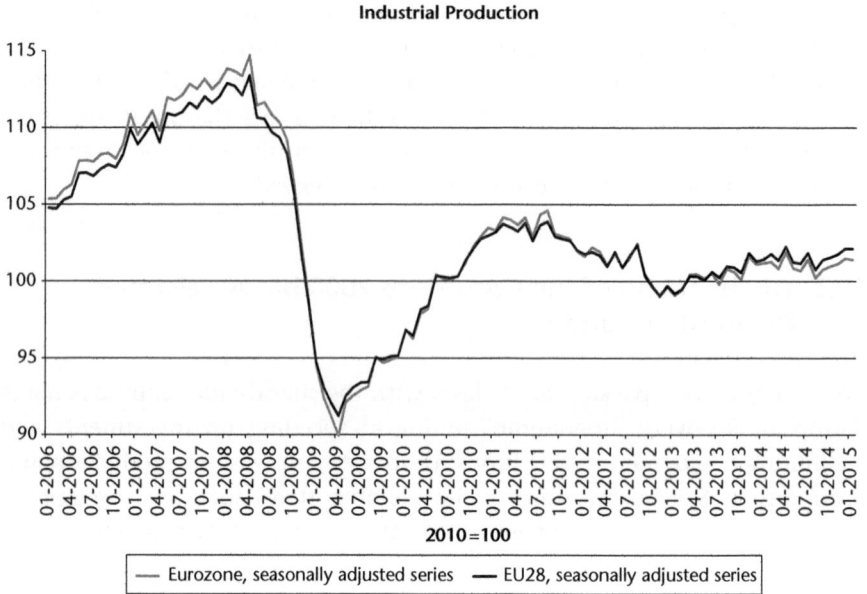

Figure 12.1 Industrial Production According to Eurostat in the EU and the Eurozone (Year 2010 Equals 100 Per Cent) (Eurostat 2014)

sufficient condition for 'spontaneous' growth. However, this growth did not come soon and the sharp downturn included the decline of industrial production, industrial capacities, and—perhaps most importantly—investment for industrial development and new industrial products.

Looking at budgets only in fact contributed to a downward spiral. Looking at budgets and growth with an equal footing is necessary.

According to Eurostat (see Eurostat 2014) the production index for industrial production in Portugal at the end of 2013 stands at 94.8 per cent compared to 2010, in Spain at 90.9 per cent, in Italy at 91.4 per cent, in Ireland at 98.6 per cent, in Cyprus at 71.0 per cent and in Greece at 89.4 per cent.

Industrial production in the EU as a whole has not reached the pre-crisis level and the trend is rather flat at more than 10 per cent below pre-crisis level. As the overall GDP of the EU in 2013 was 4.2 per cent higher than 2008 before the crisis and 5.8 per cent higher than 2010, one can conclude (i) that the crisis hit industry especially heavily, (ii) industry did not recover fully, and (iii) as industrial production is not growing at all the share of industrial production of GDP is falling (Figure 12.1).

Budget cuts do not automatically create growth, and growth does not automatically create more industrial production.

12.3.1 *Overall Investment is Too Low*

There are four main targets of investment, (i) investment in infrastructure, (ii) investment in (private) housing and in other investment goods, (iii) investment in corporates' infrastructure, and (iv) investment in creating, maintaining and modernizing industrial capacities.

It is self-explanatory that in a world with growing globalization and growing competition a higher share of industry can only come with higher investment. Firstly, competition and thus modernization requires a constant flow of investments. Secondly, industrial production requires investment in machines, production tools, production plants and pre-production. Even if the investments needed to launch services are not negligible, for example services of the banking sector requiring investments in IT and buildings, it seems convincing that industrial value chains require significantly more investment. Thirdly, industry requires infrastructure for example energy, transport, communication, waste handling and water.

In view of this key issue of investments in Europe, the finding since the crisis is clear. An investment ratio of 19–21 per cent of GDP can be considered as normal for a mature country with some industrial strength (see discussion in Klär 2014). The investment even in countries doing rather well like Germany is much too low by comparison with this benchmark. The year 2013 shows an all-time low of 16.9 per cent of GDP, for Germany (again down by 0.3 per cent in comparison with the previous year; see Statistisches Bundesamt, 2014).

The overall trend of the investment in Europe shows also no positive trend in the recent five years from 2009 to 2013.

Investment in countries catching-up after the crisis and/or convergence countries with a GDP per capita less than 75 per cent of the EU average should show a significant higher investment activity: without well-structured higher investment, catch-up will not take place. As a matter of fact the share of investment was above 20 per cent pre-crisis in countries such as Spain, Greece, Ireland, and Portugal. There was some misallocation and some overinvestment during a boom (creating one or more bubbles), but the order of magnitude of investment was right. In all these four countries the investments fell during the crisis, declining by 2013 to less than 15 per cent of GDP (see Klär 2014). Figures around 15 per cent go hand in hand with a rather fast deindustrialization, as existing stock is depreciated and no replacement or new formation of capital stock takes place.

Eurostat figures show the deindustrialization clearly. Just to name two big countries like Italy and Spain, the industrial production is down by 25 per cent compared to the pre-crisis level.

Boosting industrial production to 20 per cent from the current 14 per cent of GDP, with a need to reverse the trend to further deindustrialization until

2020, means an increase of industrial production and capacities by 40 per cent until 2020 (if the GDP grows at least slightly). This is an unprecedented and extremely ambitious turnaround, as it cannot be achieved with business as usual. Even the full utilization of existing capacities, the enlargement of existing production systems or the further trend in the development of industrial clusters will not be enough to make a turnaround of deindustrialization. New industries are needed, new infrastructure, new production capacities, and new clients to absorb and buy the new goods—or a significant replacement of other goods so far produced by non-European producers sold in EU markets.

It is obvious that such an ambitious turnaround will not work without some well-designed public intervention. The aircraft industry (Airbus) was developed with some public support, Renewable Energies are developed with some public support (as Nuclear Energy is and was as well), and ICT industry was and is supported by the public including infrastructure development (e.g., broadband grids). Other leading industries in Europe such as the Automotive sector, the Chemical, the Pharmaceuticals, and the Railway industry develop with a high share of innovation borne by the private sector, but specific projects, for example electric cars, will not move ahead without project sponsoring by public entities and budgets.

The intervention capacity of the EU budget to drive such a turnaround is not there. Today's budget on innovation is below 0.1 per cent of GDP per annum. Compared to the previous budget from 2006–2013, it has been increased by 0.02 per cent of GDP only. To put a halt to the deindustrialization trend and to revive industrialization again by 2020, additional spending for R&D&I (research, development, and innovation) from public and private sources needs to increase by about 1.0 per cent of GDP.

12.4 'They Never Come Back': Eastern Germany and the Long-Lasting Effects of Deindustrialization

Deindustrialization is very dangerous as it is extremely difficult to turn the trend back to industrial growth and may need decades to do so.

The German experience after reunification showed a very 'long tail' of deindustrialization, once it has taken place. One should always be careful with comparisons and the deindustrialization in the crisis countries of today will hopefully be less deep, and less structural, than in Eastern Germany. However the findings are quite clear. Until now, twenty-five years after the fall of the wall, (i) productivity in Eastern Germany has reached only 70 per cent of Western Germany, (ii) unemployment remained significantly higher than in former West Germany, and (iii) the migration from East to West Germany did not stop. Industry structure is still very different and (iv) much less resilient against crisis, there are (v) much fewer large corporations, (vi) much fewer headquarters of companies, and (vii) much less private spending on research, development and innovation in Eastern Germany (less than half of the spending in Western Germany, where it is 2.04 per cent of the GDP in 2010 and only 0.97 per cent in Eastern Germany (IWH 2013)).

Spending on research and development is mentioned here, because it is (i) considered by the EU Commission as a major source for renewed growth and (ii) the industry is the dominant player for the private sector, contributing 65 per cent in Europe (Sahl 2014).

The investment pattern in R&D&I in the other New Member States is not very different from Eastern Germany; private sector spending is reported at 0.96 per cent of GDP in the Czech Republic, 0.7 per cent in Hungary, and only 0.2 per cent in Poland (IWH 2013).

'Normal efforts' in the framework of the European Union Cohesion policy and a strong domestic transfer from West to East Germany adding up to meanwhile some 2000 billion euro were not able to rebuild an industrial sector in Eastern Germany of the same strength as that of Western Germany.

One could argue that the objective for Eastern Germany was the wrong one. A reindustrialization could have been planned in an alternative approach as a kind of distribution of headquarters and research centres in one country and production and/or pre-production in another country. It has however to be emphasized that in a competitive environment industry as a whole requires significant R&D&I spending and significant investment. Thus, in the current context, Europe (or the EU or the Eurozone) as a whole needs it. However, it would be possible to concentrate the R&D&I spending in some countries and the production and investment in some other countries—even if such a model would not fit into the cohesion and convergence policies of the Union.

Such an alternative approach is connected with a phase model of industrial development. The idea is that earlier stages of development in a country come with a pattern of first less complex production, medium stages come with complex production (but production only) and mature stages finally come with the full set activities including research and development, but with a shift in respect to production, which is partly moved to other countries. One expects to see research, development, innovation, but less production in the final phase, because it might be partly outsourced to less costly production sites. But no reindustrialization or even a stop of the deindustrialization will take place in Europe as a whole without keeping and enlarging the more upstream components of the innovation cycle of industry and the production as a whole. Unfortunately there is simply no sign of an increased industrial investment in Europe and no sign of an overall focus of upstream investments in selected countries at a level sufficient for the whole continent.

12.5 A Reminder: The Financial Sector Will Not Become a New Industry

Resizing the financial sector is one of the objectives and results of a stronger regulation after the crisis. The more the regulation includes all financial actors as originally emphasized by the G20 after the outbreak of the crisis—interestingly, at the initiative of the then British government—the better the result of a downsizing will be achieved (see for more detail Kollatz-Ahnen 2012, 2013). The pertinent discussion of the 'too big to fail' problem shows the two main oversizing concerns, the size of the sector and the size of the big players in the sector as well. Thus the financial sector will not compensate for missing growth in the real economy, but may act in the future to undermine it (see Easterly, Islam, and Stiglitz 2000). On the contrary, a smaller and more robust system can better serve the needs of the rest of the economy. In the US a year before the crisis a share of 40 per cent of corporate profits was acquired by the financial sector, thus contributing to leaving the rest of the economy without sufficient opportunities for investment in production and R&D&I.

Why a more robust financial sector? At the end a trade-off might exist on one hand between faster growth in a deregulated financial system, as claimed by the actors of the financial sector before the crisis along the line 'regulation stops innovation', and on the other hand lower growth in a more regulated financial system. As financial crises are prone to quickly develop into cross-sectorial crises as financial tools and financing are used in all sectors of the economy, the evidence shows that there is not enough gain before the crisis to justify the deregulation for the future (see, for example, Arcand, Berkes, and Panissa 2012; Cecchetti and Kharroubi 2012, on this subject). The data after the big financial crisis emerged in 2007/2008 are clear: the shrinking of the economy is leading to a 'lost decade' for growth in the Eurozone; furthermore, because of the austerity policies many countries in the EU will suffer from the 'long tail' of deindustrialization, possibly for a further decade. Thus the 'higher growth' from non-regulation or deregulation before the crisis does not pay off and the final growth is both, (i) less and (ii) connected with high volatility and the related societal costs of this volatility.

The so-called Anglo-Saxon model, that is to boost the financial sector as an alternative to keeping the industrial sector or reinventing the industrial base of countries can serve no longer as a model for any of the larger countries in the EU. Parallel to a successful recovery and growth hopefully achieved with such a recovery, the demand for financial products and financial services will grow as well. But the relative size of the financial sector will at least in large countries no longer grow at the expense of the rest of the economy without major conflict and damage.

12.6 What a Combination of Anti-Crisis and Industrial Policy Can Do at EU level

A new EU Parliament and a new EU Commission offer an opportunity to review the existing set of policies with (i) unrealistic promises (industrial share 20 per cent of GDP in 2020) and (ii) activities with impressive volumes but no intention to really put them into practice. When the fiscal compact was adopted, investment activities to balance the budget cuts in a kind of second pillar were announced. The only new investment capacity created was the capital injection to the European Investment Bank (EIB) (as proposed in Griffith-Jones et al. 2012). The necessary new EU budgetary elements were not implemented at all and the reshuffle of the then existing EU budget was only half-hearted and very much secondary to the announcements.

The discussions by the Parliament and the Commission, after the European Parliamentary elections of May 2014, brought an agreement between the main political forces on strengthening investment and to launch a new comprehensive package to bring anti-crisis and growth policy together. The main danger now is to see again at the EU level a package where the components are either too small or too much a restructuring of the EU budget, which is already very much focused on investment and innovation, but which is from its outset too small.

Commission President Juncker has proposed a European public and private investment package totalling a target of euro 315 billion over three years, which is meant to increase financing across the board: infrastructure in transport, energy and broadband, education, investment and R&D, and projects to reduce youth unemployment beyond the Youth Guarantee. He emphasized that the package has to be additional. The main components of the programme were announced in November 2014.

Interestingly the debate in 2014 was opened by the Minister of Finance of Poland Mateusz Szczurek. He called for an EU wide public investment programme of 5.5 per cent of GDP to overcome the constraints behind Europe's 'secular stagnation' (Szczurek 2014). He calculates that euro 700 billion of capital expenditures could close the output gap in the short-term while increasing long-term productivity growth. Funded by EU members and private leverage and invested over five years it could operate as a special purpose vehicle under the EIB. The alternative in his view is a 'lost decade' becoming a baseline scenario for the future (see also Griffith-Jones and Cozzi 2016, for modelling of such a baseline scenario, that would imply continued stagnation, and increased debt to GDP ratios, especially in the South Eurozone). There is currently a danger of a triple-dip crisis looming, a third hit of the crisis as a combination of a weak recovery and international slowdown. The Polish Finance Minister warned that the EU habit of window dressing and reselling of already approved budgets or to only count on the EIB will not completely solve the problem, as additional volumes and additional efforts are needed to enter a new path of growth.

A combination of pro-investment and pro-consumption macroeconomic policy is needed to overcome the stagnation. The core element should be an industrial policy for a new path of higher and sustainable growth. It has to be (i) additional, cannot be achieved with reframing existing rather small budgets, it needs to have (ii) an appropriate size, where the euro 300 billion (if really additional) could bring a significant push in the right direction, but where the euro 700 billion are closer to the real needs for a new higher growth path.

In the following sections we describe a pragmatic way how to achieve with a minimum on additional budget expenditure additional investments of euro 700 billion in the years 2015–2020. Some of the ideas presented are new, some of the ideas use proven instruments, all measures are classified either as already part of an existing scheme, and insofar not additional, or as additional. It is the intention of this article to stimulate further discussion. If the objective of additional investments for a new higher growth path could be achieved with other measures the authors welcome such proposals.

Our proposal shows how to achieve the euro 700 billion. However, we know that implementation in stages could be considered. Euro 300 billion on additional investment in three years could be a very important first step to achieve euro 700 billion of additional investments in six years. It is encouraging that the Juncker proposal leaves the door open for further measures to the initial package in future.

We see the following actions at EU level and the following elements:

– A shock-absorbing capacity for asymmetric shocks (e.g., an Unemployment Benefit Scheme) and/or a budget capacity for the Eurozone serving the purpose to act against asymmetric shocks, where neither one nor the other finds for the time being sufficient support. A higher budget for the EU was proposed by the EU Parliament, but not accepted by the member states in the decisions of the Council—therefore in a pragmatic way we focus on the following two elements;

– A push for investment in competitiveness, where the EIB can play a role in financing projects for competitiveness in companies through Europe;

– A push for investment in infrastructure, where the budget has to play a major role as most of infrastructure does not create sufficient revenue (if any) to pay for investment, operation, and maintenance; only the rather small segment of viable (i.e., profitable) infrastructure, for example toll roads, can be driven by private actors (and again there the EIB can play a valuable role).

12.7 Insurance Solutions Can Contribute in More Than One Way

Basically the European Stability Mechanism (ESM) and a potential new Unemployment Benefit Scheme (UBS) are insurance systems. The main purpose of insurance is protection against damages, when they occur (hopefully never). The second purpose of insurance is to invest the premiums paid in by the insured parties for treasury and custody purposes in a (i) prudent, (ii) viable, and (iii) liquid way.

In former times most of the insurance companies, and other institutional investors, like pension funds, in Europe were heavily invested in the real economy, for example in Germany in housing. But the situation has changed. Insurance companies today hold first and foremost government bonds and only a tiny share of their capital is invested in the real economy. The portfolio of German insurance at the end of 2013 includes 80.8 per cent state bonds, 10.1 per cent shares of companies such as subsidiaries, 3.5 per cent shares from the stock exchange, 3.3 per cent real estate, 2.3 per cent others, altogether about 9 per cent in the real economy.

If the ESM at the EU level were allowed to invest for treasury and custody purposes in the real economy in a very prudent way, the returns would be higher than the ones created with the treasury investments in AAA public bonds, where for example Germany in 2014 shows a yield of 1 per cent or less for a 10 years bond. But the liquidity requirement has to be fulfilled as well. Liquidity could be achieved in two ways, first investing in goods which could generate revenue in a midterm perspective, and second investing in a way so that in a difficult phase the loans could be immediately used by a bank trustee of the ESM with access to the financing facilities of the Central Bank to receive liquidity. To achieve this access to ECB liquidity certain requirements have to be fulfilled; this could be done by bank trustees out of the family of the promotional banks in the Eurozone. The loans for the described treasury and custody purposes have to be set up according to the criteria defined by the ECB and hold by a trustee with access to the ECB liquidity facilities.

The ESM has paid-in capital of euro 80 billion. If 20 per cent only of it were invested in the real economy, implying in this way a kind of diversification of the treasury investment portfolio into the real economy, additional private investments could be mobilized in the same order of magnitude (assuming a leverage 2). Euro 32 billion investments could be unleashed in the Eurozone. If in the future a UBS was set up, after a ramp up period, a further significant volume could be treated in a similar way to strengthen the investment volume.

12.8 What the EIB Can Do Within Its Existing Mandate

Before the crisis the annual lending of the EIB was about euro 50 billion per annum The so-called gearing ratio steered the lending capacity of the EIB as was the case for most other multilateral development banks (MDBs) or international financial institutions (IFIs). The gearing ratio was not fully exploited and therefore the EIB engaged in activities under the line 'take more risk for more value added' and put euro 1 billion of profits aside for risk cushions of innovation loans (RSSF) and other new activities. In addition to such special activities the EIB strongly supported the private economy mainly with corporate loans during the first phase of the crisis and the delivery of high volumes up to euro 79 billion in 2009 (EIB 2014a). The high volumes used most of the room for manoeuvre under the gearing ratio.

In addition the analyses of the rating agencies changed after the crisis began, and gave more weight to the leverage ratio. A leverage ratio of 9 turned out to be the maximum acceptable by the rating agencies. Since 2012 the international discussion on the requirements of own funds (Tier I capital) evolved further, so today a leverage of 8 seems to be a reasonable 'soft ceiling'. The capital injection of paid-in capital decided in 2012 and paid in 2013–2015 gave a signal to the EIB to keep a high activity level in a situation of a continuing lack of growth and insufficient credit, and a double-dip in many countries. With the euro 10 billion the EIB is able to generate euro 80 billion on new loans (leverage 8, for detailed discussion, see Griffith-Jones et al. 2012).

According to the recent Fitch rating report the average maturity of the outstanding EIB loans is 7.2 years (see Fitch Ratings 2014). Looking at Figure 12.2 the large programmes since 2008 will move significantly into repayment from 2016. The strong repayments should allow the EIB to continue with a high level of activity of euro 65–70 billion per annum with the given activity mix.

What is described here and in Section 12.7 could serve the purpose of a necessary push for more competitiveness and innovation. The leitmotif of these two sections shows the minimization of budget expenditure for the additional investment. If the new idea in respect to the ESM could be used, no additional budget will be needed.

12.9 What the EIB Can Do in Addition to Push
for Sustainable Growth

The EIB Group including the subsidiary EIF (European Investment Fund) could take more risks. The strategy to take more risks already started several

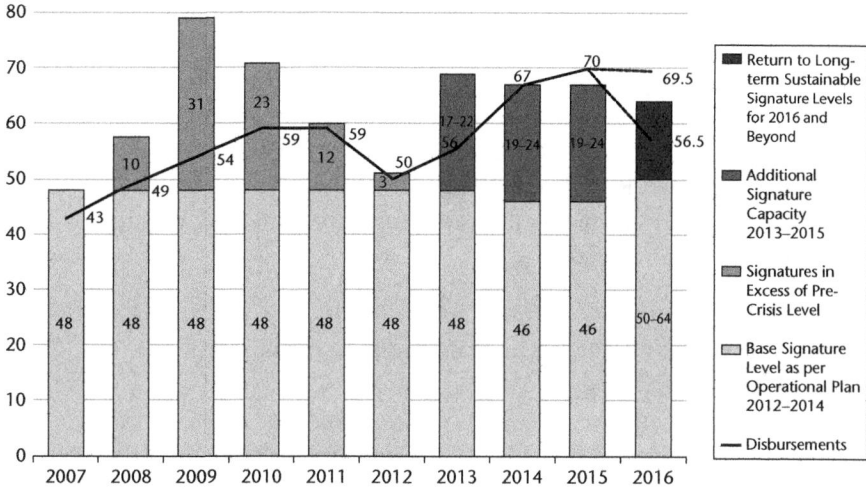

Figure 12.2 Lending Volumes of the European Investment Bank (EIB 2014a)

years before the crisis and should be considered as an enrichment and enlargement of the EIB business model. In the beginning of its existence the EIB mainly refinanced sovereigns in respect to infrastructure projects. The money was channelled through the budgets. In the future this channel will still also be an important means to finance infrastructure and other public investments, but it is evident that the approach will be much more limited. The fiscal compact and the national legislation (e.g., in Germany 'Schuldenbremse') have limited the possible use of budgets for investment—and will continue in the years to come to limit or to bring the budgetary space to zero, unless these rules are changed. In theory, with existing budget rules, the Member States could keep the investment high and cut other expenditure, but the reality shows that investment is cut first and has a long-lasting detrimental and counterproductive impact on future growth.

If the EIB finances projects directly without a state guarantee, it targets such projects which are either (i) fully viable or (ii) to a large extent commercially viable that they pass the breakeven point with a relatively small budget contribution of the member state (or the EU funds) will be doable.

One can give a rough estimate of what the EIB can do on its own; the profits are in the range of euro 2.5 billion per annum (In 2011 2.3 billion, in 2012 2.7 billion, in 2013 2.5 billion, in 2014 in the first half of the year 1.3 billion; see EIB 2014b). As shown in the last section the profits are not used to keep the high volume programmes running with the given risk profile. If the 2.5 billion are brought to an investment vehicle oriented on higher risk taking up to a close to equity risk the EIB could take direct project risk in a very junior loan position to a higher extent. One could imagine a leverage ratio of 2.5, due to the higher risk taken (instead of 8). With this approach project finance could be delivered by the EIB in a volume of additional euro 6.3 billion per annum, summing up in the years 2015–2020 to 37.5 billion. Private investors could be attracted with this form of higher risk—taking by the EIB, contributing with a higher leverage of 3–4, as they will take less risk, so contributing up to euro 150 billion to the overall investment package.

The leitmotif of minimizing budget expenditure holds here again, no additional budget will be needed.

12.10 What a Well-Structured Budgetary Initiative Can Contribute

But even with this large effort—which is beyond the mainstream of the 'political Brussels' as it is, one will not reach the euro 700 billion target proposed by Mateusz Szczurek.

That is why the Polish Minister of Finance proposed setting up the main vehicle for the investment programme as a subsidiary of the EIB (to avoid the long and arduous process in setting up a new international institution) and to exempt the contributions of the Member States to the investment vehicle from the fiscal compact rules (as was done with the contributions to the ESM as well, which are not counted for the deficit calculation, and has been done for additional voluntary national contributions to the announced Juncker investment package).

Euro 700 billion matched to an additional investment of close to 1 per cent of GDP until 2020. This 700 billion should be realized in such a way that any additional burden on the budgets is minimized. For this reason, we demonstrate how to combine the investment vehicle with existing sources and activities to arrive at the slightly more modest euro 600 billion, without any need to inject this sum in total.

- EIB: Using profits and dividends of EIB activity brings euro 150 billion to the overall package (see explanations under 9).
- ESM: Making use of small part of the capabilities of the ESM and leveraging this money could bring an additional euro 32 billion (investing euro 16 billion of the paid-in capital of euro 80 billion in the real economy according to ECB rules to have liquidity when needed, with a leverage of 2).
- European Investment Instrument (EII): Member states would pay in euro 100 billion into the EII over six years. Borrowing additional money on the capital market or co-financing with private partners might contribute another euro 300 billion, assuming a leverage of 4 as described above. Together with the paid-in capital of euro 100 billion this sums up to euro 400 billion.

- A capital increase for the EIB to allow for another euro 118 billion lending for viable projects in infrastructure and for lending to SMEs. A capital increase of euro 7.5 billion and the mobilization of the loans by EIB and private financiers would ensure additional lending capacity.

But there is one important issue that makes things more complicated. The first two components of the additional package we have already mentioned (investment of some ESM resources and utilization of EIB profits) and the large programmes of the EIB (not additional) target viable projects. Looking at the main three pillars of investment with policy support, (i) the financing of SME and their investments, (ii) the financing of infrastructure, and (iii) the financing of innovation and green economy, the first pillar, SME finance, is fully oriented on viable projects. But only smaller parts of infrastructure and innovation investment form short-term commercially viable projects. Many of them need heavy subsidies for construction, and many of them during operation as well (e.g., public transport). Thus it is possible that there will be not enough viable infrastructure and innovation projects to absorb another euro 400 billion.

To unleash investment potential of private sources as well it is therefore necessary to go beyond viable projects only and to identify a zone close to viability where rather small contributions in a form of a grant-loan combination can make the difference. The obvious sector for such investments is the sector of energy efficiency. The second to be developed could be investment in industrial innovation.

A recent EU Council decided on Energy Efficiency targets for 2030, setting an indicative target of at least 27 per cent for improving energy efficiency in 2030 compared to projections of future energy consumption based on current criteria in a base scenario. 'This will be reviewed by 2020, having in mind an EU level of 30 per cent' (EU Council 2014). In a simulation study of the EU Commission the investment needed to achieve 30 per cent in 2030 in comparison with 27 per cent are euro 54 billion higher in the EU 28. But the overall costs of the energy system increase according to the study much less, that is about euro 20 billion only (see EU Commission 2014). Some 63 per cent of the costs are repaid by savings mainly on fossil energy bills already in 2030. The share of the investments covered by revenue generating (or saving) will increase further in the future but not reach full cost coverage after twenty years. One could allow the investment vehicle of the EIB to develop zero interest rate loans or grant-loan combination with a subsidy element of up to 10 per cent of the investment to make energy efficiency investments break-even or viable and to finance them through this investment vehicle.

Technically speaking a zero interest rate loan forms a subsidy element in a low-interest-rate environment of about 2 per cent subsidy in strong countries and up to 7 per cent subsidy in weaker countries. The advantage would be combined with an element of solidarity inside the EU.

This article describes an investment package for the next five years up to 2020. The additional euro 54 billion per annum needed for energy efficiency could be covered by the investment vehicle. The earlier the investment in energy efficiency is made, the better the effect for greening the economy in the future, and the stronger the push for a higher growth path. Euro 270 billion out of the envisaged 400 billion could be earmarked for energy efficiency.

A similar approach could hold for investments in industrial innovation addressing the grand societal challenges of the EU. The remaining euro 130 billion could be earmarked for such purposes.

What is described here, and in the previous section, will contribute significantly to the necessary push for more investment in infrastructure. A part of the activities of the investment vehicle will be driven by a policy goal for energy efficiency. The beneficial effect to the economic system will be not only on infrastructure development but rather on a more comprehensive concept, including strengthening industry and SMEs in general.

12.11 Some Final Words

Experience from the past shows that anti-crisis activities need to be effective and require an additional annual investment injection of 0.5–1.0 per cent of the GDP. Considering the way ahead until 2020 the size of a successful anti-crisis programme has to be between euro 390 and 780 billion. The proposed 300 billion falls a little bit short (and it is not sure this amount will be achieved through the Juncker Plan, and there is the risk that continued rapid fiscal consolidation will in part counteract the positive increase by cutting national public investment); the other proposal of the 700 billion is at the higher end and close to 1 per cent of GDP. Table 12.1 summarizes the proposed investment strategy.

The article shows a way for the EU to avoid window dressing and explains how to create additional investments in a mix of public and private contributions in the key sectors (i) SME financing, (ii) infrastructure financing, and (iii) financing of innovation and greening the economy. The leverage by the EIB comes with the range of 2 for the insurance facilities up to 8 for the EIB facilities in a lower risk area.

The article assumes a need for an additional investment push of around 1 per cent of GDP per annum until 2020. It aims at achieving it by minimizing the requirement of money injection from budgets. To avoid double-counting

Table 12.1. Summary of Proposed Investment Blocks

Tool	Description/Sector	Injection 2015–2020	Total Investment 2015–2020	Notes
EIB (annual normal activity at a high programme level of euro 65 billion p.a.)	60% Infrastructure	euro 234 billion	euro 468 billion	Existing, repayment of former programmes allows to continue
	40% SME, Services and Corporates	euro 156 billion	euro 312 billion	
Insurance system, with small use ESM (alternative approach could be capital increase of the EIB of euro 7.5 billion from the budgets of the Member States)	Infrastructure	euro 16 billion	euro 32 billion	New, but no new budget injection needed
EIB (annual profits, undisbursed dividends dedicated to riskier operations)	50% Innovation (Corporates)	euro 19 billion	euro 75 billion	New, but no new budget injection needed
	50% Infrastructure (e.g., Project Bonds)	euro 19 billion	euro 75 billion	
Investment Vehicle (IV) as subsidiary of EIB and budgetary injection of euro 100 billion by the Member States	Up to 10% intensity of subsidy, not fully viable projects; 60% of first injection will reflow for further lending			New, and new budget injection needed
	67% Energy Efficiency, not fully viable	euro 67 billion (2/3 of volume)	euro 270 billion (objective EE 30%)	
	33% Industrial Innovation, higher risk or not fully viable	euro 33 billion	euro 130 billion	
EIB capital increase	Following the actual split one could assume 60% infrastructure, 40% SME	euro 7.5 billion	euro 118 billion (71 infrastructure, 47 SME)	New, and new budget injection needed

Total investment euro 1480 billion, including 700 additional. Infrastructure euro 646 billion, Energy Efficiency 270 billion, corporates 564 billion. Budgetary injection euro 108.

or reselling of what is already available in the existing budget of the EU and the existing EIB capabilities should be fully exploited.

To come close to the 1 per cent of GDP on additional investment, euro 700 billion on investment push is required.

To sum up again how to arrive at euro 700 billion without the need to inject budget money in the same magnitude:

– Making use of the crisis insurance facility (ESM) for low risk lending and the retained profits of the EIB for high risk lending contributes euro 182 billion of investment.

– The new investment vehicle EII with its paid-in capital of euro 100 billion may unleash additional investment of euro 400 billion. It is responsible for direct project financing with a focus on quasi-equity and equity support, as well as projects close to viability e.g. in energy efficiency.

– A capital increase of euro 7.5 billion for the EIB pursuing additional 'normal lending' contributes the remaining euro billion 118.

This push of investments will grant sustainable growth and the switch to a higher growth path. This is the main prerequisite to stop deindustrialization and to create a much stronger productive sector in Europe.

References

Arcand, J. L., Berkes, E., and Panissa, U. 2012. 'Too Much Finance?' IMF Working Paper No. 12/161.

Cecchetti, S. G. and Kharroubi, E. 2012. 'Reassessing the Impact of Finance and Growth'. BIS Working Papers, No. 381, Monetary and Economic Department.

Easterly, W., Islam, R., and Stiglitz, J. 2000. 'Shaken and Stirred, Explaining Growth Volatility'. Annual Bank Conference on Development Economics, World Bank, Washington D.C.

EIB. 2014a. 'Corporate Operational Plan 2014–2016'. Available at: <http://www.eif.org/news_centre/publications/corporate-operational-plan-2014-2016.htm> (last accessed 14 May 2015).

EIB. 2014b. 'EIB Investor Presentation, September 2014'. Available at: <http://www.eib.org/attachments/fi/eib-investor-presentation.pdf> (last accessed 14 May 2015).

EU Council. 2014. 'Conclusions on 2030 Climate and Energy Policy Framework', 23 and 24 October 2014.

European Commission. 2014. 'Communication from the Commission to the EU Parliament and the Council on Energy Efficiency', COM (2014) 520 final.

Eurostat. 2014. 'Eurostat News Release Euro Indicators 152/2014', Brussels.

Fitch Ratings. 2014. 'European Investment Bank, Full Rating Report', 30 September 2014.

Griffith-Jones, S. (forthcoming). 'The Case for Prudent Financial Liberalization and Its Policy Implications'. In F. Bourginon and S. Klasen (eds), *Proceedings of Berlin Conference* AFD/BMZ/EUDN 2013 Finance and Development, Berlin.

Griffith-Jones, S. and Cozzi, G. 2016. 'Investment-led growth a solution to the European crisis' in Jackobs, M. and Mazzucato, M. (eds), *Rethinking Capitalism*: Economic Policies for Equitable and Sustainable Growth, London: Wiley-Blackwell.

Griffith-Jones, S., Kollatz-Ahnen, M., Andersen, L., and Hansen, S. 2012. 'Shifting Europe from Austerity to Growth: A Proposed Investment Programme for 2012–2015'. FEPS, IPD and ECLM Policy Brief, Brussels.

Institut für Wirtschaftsforschung Halle (IWH). 2013. *Deutsche Wirtschaft im Aufschwung*, Konjunktur Aktuell, No. 4. Halle: IWH.

Klär, E. 2014. 'Die Eurokrise im Spiegel der Potentialschätzungen'. WISO Diskurs, Friedrich Ebert Stiftung, Berlin.

Kollatz-Ahnen, M. 2012. 'Eine robustere internationale Finanzwirtschaft'. *Neue Gesellschaft*/Frankfurter Hefte 04/2012, Bonn.

Kollatz-Ahnen, M. 2013. 'The Euro Crisis—An Interim Report', *Journal of Social Democracy*, 01/2013. Available at: <http://www.frankfurter-hefte.de/upload/International_Edition/NGFH_International-Quarterly_2013-1.pdf> (last accessed 10 September 2015).

Sahl, D. 2014. 'Industriepolitik für Europa/Chancen für einen neuen Wachstumspfad', *ImpulseWirtschaft und Politik*, Friedrich Ebert Stiftung, Berlin.

Statistisches Bundesamt. 2014. 'Bruttoinlandsprodukt 2013 für Deutschland', Press Conference, 15 January, Berlin.

Szczurek, M. 2014. 'Investing in Europe's Future'. Speech in Brussels, delivered at the Annual Bruegel Dinner 2014. Available at: <http://www.voxeu.org/print/11132> (last accessed 10 September 2015).

Index